INTERNATIONAL RADIO STATIONS GUIDE

(Revised Edition)

OTHER TITLES OF INTEREST

INTERNATIONAL RADIO STATIONS GUIDE

(Revised Edition)

by

PETER SHORE

BERNARD BABANI (publishing) LTD
THE GRAMPIANS
SHEPHERDS BUSH ROAD
LONDON W6 7NF
ENGLAND

PLEASE NOTE

Although every care has been taken with the production of this book to ensure that any projects, information, designs, modifications and/or programs etc. contained herein, operate in a correct and safe manner and also that any components specified are normally available in Great Britain, the Publishers do not accept responsibility in any way for the failure, including fault in design, of any project, design, modification or program to work correctly or to cause damage to any other equipment that it may be connected to or used in conjunction with, or in respect of any other damage or injury that may be so caused, nor do the Publishers accept responsibility in any way for the failure to obtain specified components.

Notice is also given that if equipment that is still under warranty is modified in any way or used or connected with home-built equipment then that warranty may be void.

First Published – June 1988

New Revised Edition – July 1991

British Library Cataloguing in Publication Data:
Shore, Peter
International radio stations guide
1. Radio stations – Lists
I. Title
621.3841'6

ISBN 0 85934 200 X

Set from disk by Commercial Colour Press, London E7
Printed and bound in Great Britain by Cox & Wyman Ltd, Reading

CONTENTS

Acknowledgements

The publishers would like to acknowledge with great thanks the contributions made to previous editions of this book by the late Mr Bernard Babani and Mr Charles Molloy and also those made by Mr Maurice Jay and Mr James Chalmers.

Preface

The world of international broadcasting surrounds us all the time, with the air filled with tens of thousands of radio signals from every corner of our planet. With a short wave radio, it is possible to tune in to any of them – Moscow, Beijing, Washington, Delhi and so on.

This latest edition of the *International Radio Stations Guide* offers a useful map to the short wave radio spectrum, containing details of which station is where on the dial, a trip through the broadcasts in English of the main international radio broadcasters, and useful data including a world time chart and some handy translations for listeners to use when writing to foreign radio stations.

Listening to far off radio signals (or DXing, as it is known to many hobbyists worldwide) is a great pastime, whether you spend twenty minutes or twenty hours in front of your set this latest edition of the *International Radio Stations Guide* will prove an invaluable companion as you journey around the globe.

Good listening!

*Peter Shore**
July 1991

* Peter Shore is a pseudonym.

Translation Table

	Station Site	Country	Frequency (kHz or MHz)	Wavelength (metres)	Effective Radiated Power ERP (kW)	State	Call	Province
Français	Poste D'emetteur	Pays	Fréquence	Longeur D'onde	Puissance Effective Reyonement	Etat	Indicatif D'appel	Province
Deutsch	Standort der Sendestation	Land	Frequenz	Wellenlänge	Ausgangsleistung	Staat	Rufzeichen	Provinz
Nederlands	Lokatie van Zender	Land	Frequentie	Golfengte	Effectief Stralingvermogen	Staat	Oproepen	Gewest
Espanol	Sitio De Transmisor	Páis	Frecuencia	Longitud De Onda	Potencia Irradiada Efectiva	Estado	Indicativo De Llamada	Provincia
Portugues	Sitio De Transmissor	Pais	Frequencia	Comprimento De Onda	Potencia Irradiacao Efectivo	Estado	Sinal De Chamada	Provincia
Italiano	Sito De Transmettitore	Paese	Frequenza	Lunghezza D'onda	Potenza Radiazione Effettiva	Stato	Segnale Di Chiamata	Provincia
Dansk	Stationsbe-liggenhed	Land	Frekvens	Bølgelængde	Udstrålet Effekt	Stat	Kaldesingnal	Provins
Svenska	Stationsläga	Land	Frekvens	Våglängd	Utstrålad Effekt	Stat	Anropssignal	Provins
Norsk	Stasjons-plasering	Land	Frekvens	Bølgelengde	Utstrålad Effekt	Stat	Kaldesignal	Provins

Section 1

LISTENING TO SHORT WAVE RADIO

It is unlikely that many people in the developed world give a second thought to the world of short wave radio, and yet all around us, throughout the day and night, radio signals from all around the planet are sent from hundreds of radio stations in dozens of languages.

For people living in western Europe and North America, radio tends to be something which one has on in the background as one gets up in the morning and gets ready to leave for work, or as an accompaniment for driving. Research by broadcasters shows that radio audiences decline steadily from their early morning peak to a very low figure in the evening when television takes over providing entertainment. It has also been shown that radios mostly stay tuned to one station, with listeners reluctant to move the dial in case they caanot find their favourite radio station again. Broadcasts on VHF-FM are most popular, offering high quality stereo music with modern technology ensuring excellent reception in most areas.

But to leave a radio receiver tuned to one station is to miss out on so much. It is perhaps like limiting ones reading to a single author. Whilst we all expect news to be brought to us from around the world by our local radio and television stations, few people consider the possibility of tuning in to the radio stations of countries where the news is being made.

In some parts of the world, people listen to overseas radio broadcasts as a matter of course. In Africa, South America, China and the Soviet Union, national broadcasting uses short wave radio. This is because signals transmitted on medium wave and VHF-FM have only limited coverage, and to broadcast throughout the whole of a sparsely populated country the size of Zaire, for example, a more cost effective means of broadcasting is required. Short wave radio fills this need, since signals travel in a different way to those on VHF-FM or medium and long waves. Meanwhile, broadcasts from other countries offer a lifeline of news free from the censorship which affects domestic broadcasting in many countries.

If one turns on a short wave radio receiver and tunes along the broadcast bands, it is possible to hear broadcasts from every continent in a multiplicity of languages including for example English, Chinese, Spanish, Arabic, Farsi, Indonesian and Korean. There has been international broadcasting since the beginning of radio. But in the last few decades its popularity has waned in Europe and North America because of the explosion of home grown broadcasting, both sound and vision, and the improvement in quality which has resulted in stereo sound and the added enhancement through the transmission of music recorded on compact disc and R-DAT digital audio tape. In Britain, whilst youngsters may tune in to Radio Luxembourg which broadcasts in English during the evening, few will explore their radio dials further to discover that Radio Moscow, Radio Tirana, Belgium Radio and others are on offer.

How Radio Signals Travel

All radio waves travel at the speed of light, 300 million metres a second. Not all radio waves behave in the same way, however. Short wave, or high frequency, radio signals make use of a part of the earth's atmosphere which has been ionised by the ultra violet and soft X-rays emitted by the sun and is known as the ionosphere. A transmitted signal travels up to the ionosphere where it is effectively bounced back to earth. A short wave signal is able to travel many thousands of kilometres by bouncing off the earth and the ionosphere several times. Signals from Australia routinely reach northern Europe, and vice-versa.

But several factors affect how well short wave signals can travel. Higher short wave frequencies travel during the day, whilst during the night, lower frequencies work best. And the ionosphere changes in relation to the number of sun spots. The sun has a cycle, with periods of high solar activity, and therefore the greatest number of sun spots, occurring each 11 years. Currently we are benefitting from reasonably high sun spot numbers, and therefore higher short wave broadcast frequencies, such as those in the 25 MHz, or 13 metre band, can be used by broadcasters and will travel tremendous distances. At the times when sun spot numbers are low, higher frequencies are all but useless for radio broadcasting.

To ensure good reception in the area to which a broadcaster is transmitting, engineers use several frequencies in a number of parts of the short wave broadcast bands. Listeners are encouraged to try each frequency that is being transmitted to find which works best. And listeners should remember that unlike on medium wave or VHF-FM, one frequency will not work for all of the day!

What Is On The Air?

The choice for the listener is immense, with a multiplicity of programmes from many stations to choose from. The peak listening times are at local dawn and mid-evening when stations vie for your attention.

The principal players in international broadcasting are the BBC World Service, which has a twenty-four hour a day English service and highly respected news on the hour; Radio Australia, in English twenty-four hours a day with news on the hour and the Pacific as the main target area; Radio Moscow World Service, again on the air twenty-four hours, and with news on the hour (although of a different type to that of the BBC); Radio France International, with a French world service on twenty-four hours a day and English bulletins regularly through the day; and the Voice of America which is on the air for most of the day, but directed to specific regions.

There are many smaller stations which are on the air for much less time, but nonetheless have large followings – Radio Netherlands, Swiss Radio International, the Christian Science Monitor from the United States (a relative newcomer to international radio, but now operating twenty-four hours a day and with four transmitting sites in the United States and the Pacific) and Deutsche Welle from Germany.

Details of the English schedules of all of these stations are included in the *International Radio Stations Guide*.

Short wave radio offers a unique way of following international news stories. At the time of the crumbling of the eastern European frontiers, listening to the late (although perhaps not lamented) Radio Berlin International gave some indication of the situation within that country. When Kuwait was being invaded in August 1990, the short wave services from Kuwait City provided dramatic listening, whilst Radio Baghdad offered an insight in to the mind of President Saddam Hussein. Regional international stations in the Soviet Union have enabled listeners in the west to keep in touch with the pro-democracy movements even when Moscow was barring foreign journalists from Vilnius and the other Baltic state capitals.

And the BBC Monitoring service in England keeps a well tuned ear to the world's airwaves to report what domestic and international radio stations are broadcasting. From a mansion above the town of Reading, teams of language monitors have flashed news around the world within moments of its broadcast: the ending of Prague Spring, Chernobyl, the invasion of Kuwait, military clampdowns in the Soviet Asian republics – and all of which short wave listeners with a good radio receiver have been able to listen to as well.

There is much that can be written about international radio, but there is no substitute for tuning around the short wave bands and discovering for oneself what is there.

The Short Wave Broadcast Bands

Broadcasting is not the sole user of the short wave radio spectrum. There are many other forms of communication, including the military, maritime mobile, aviation, news agencies, radio amateurs and others. The short wave frequency range (3 to 30 MHz) has been divided by World Administrative Radio Conferences in order to meet the requirements of all users. The broadcast bands are the most crowded of the short wave spectrum, and although there are certain areas designated for radio broadcasting, many stations now operate on frequencies outside these official areas to avoid the overcrowding. In 1979, a World Administrative Radio Conference voted to increase the range of frequencies for broadcasting, but subsequent Conferences have not sanctioned their use pending some form of planning and effective regulation of broadcasting on short wave. However, the extensions are used almost as heavily as the official frequency ranges. A further World Administrative Radio Conference (or WARC) will take place in February 1992 and may well agree to further extensions, although when they will be released is another matter.

The table below indicates the currently sanctioned bands, and the extensions agreed in WARC 1979. Listeners will find that many stations, such as the BBC, Voice of America, Radio Beijing and so on operate outside these bands in order to ensure that their programmes can be heard by their audiences around the world.

Frequencies in kilohertz (kHz)	*Agreed extensions (at WARC 1979)*	*Metre Bands*
2 300– 2 495		120 metre band
3 200– 3 400		90 metre band
3 900– 4 000		75 metre band
4 750– 5 060		60 metre band
5 950– 6 200		49 metre band
7 100– 7 300		41 metre band
9 500– 9 775	9 780– 9 900	31 metre band
11 700–11 975	11 950–12 050	25 metre band
13 600–13 800		21 metre band
15 100–15 450	15 455–15 600	19 metre band
17 700–17 900	17 550–17 895	16 metre band
21 450–21 750	21 755–21 850	13 metre band
25 600–26 100	*25 670–26 100*	11 metre band

[WARC 1979 agreed that the 11 metre band should be reduced in range]

The 120, 90 and 60 metre bands are allocated to tropical domestic broadcasting where the effectiveness of medium wave broadcasting is severely impaired as a result of high atmospheric noise levels.

Section 2

CHOOSING A SHORT WAVE RADIO RECEIVER

There is a staggeringly wide range of radio equipment available in the developed world, but little of it offers short wave frequencies. In the most part, short wave radio is an unknown quantity for radio shop staff. Large retail chains may offer a limited selection of short wave receivers, but will not have much expertise in listening, or knowing what makes one set better than another.

It is essential to set a budget for a new receiver. Prices range from around £40 in the United Kingdom, through to well in excess of £2,000 for a top of the range communications receiver. The majority of short wave listeners are likely to look at sets costing up to, say, £200, and there is a good choice available from the main makers of short wave sets. It is better to buy a dedicated short wave set, rather than a multipurpose radio which may have a cassette player built in. Here are some suggestions for what to look for in a new short wave receiver:

Frequency coverage

Short wave frequencies range from 3 to 30 megahertz (3 000 to 30 000 kilohertz) and a good set will cover as many of those as possible. Many modern radios offer continuous coverage, and this is to be recommended to enable listeners to tune in to frequencies outside the official broadcast bands (detailed in Chapter One) which many stations use to escape the worst overcrowding. Some sets will offer a range of short wave frequency bands, which cover the main bands, with some frequencies either side. Check to see whether main BBC World Service frequencies such as 9 410 or 12 095 kHz are included in the range.

Frequency display

It is helpful for a set to give an accurate indication of the frequency it is tuned to. Analogue displays (where a needle moves along the frequencies printed on a dial) are most common, but are not always accurate. More sets are being provided with a digital display of the frequency, either in kilohertz or megahertz. This enables easy identification of a station using frequency lists in the *IRSG*.

Tuning

Radios are usually tuned by a rotary knob which causes the frequency to be moved up or down the bands. There may be a selector switch to enable a different short wave range to be chosen if the set has divided the short wave spectrum in to different bands. More common amongst radios with a digital display is a keypad which enables frequencies to be entered directly. Manual tuning in sets with a keypad is generally possible using a rotary tuning knob, or by arrow keys which increase or decrease the frequency in the same manner as a rotary knob.

Other facilities

Radio receivers which are digitally tuned (in other words with a keypad) usually offer a number of memories into which regularly used frequencies may be stored. This eliminates the need to remember a large number of separate frequencies, and allows almost instantaneous tuning.

Make sure that your set has a socket for the connection of headphones or an ear piece. It is often more comfortable to listen to short wave broadcasts through headsets since interference can make listening difficult through a loudspeaker.

Ensure that there is a connection for a tape recorder if you think that you might want to record programmes in the future.

An external aerial socket is highly useful.

Some sets offer single side band [ssb] reception. This is a form of transmission used by radio amateurs, and by broadcast stations for feeding relay stations. Few stations use ssb for mainstream broadcasts, but they may be required to by future World Administrative Radio Conferences.

Short Wave on the Move

Many of the short wave radio sets made today are designed for travelling, and so are small (around the size of a paperback book) and light weight. The benefit of frequency memories and digital tuning are obvious for frequent travellers. Bear in mind the size of the set you are looking at if you travel a great deal.

Short wave radio is available in the car, although the choice of receivers is limited. Three European manufacturers make car radio/ cassette players with short wave : Blaupunkt, Grundig and Philips.

Several of the DX programmes broadcast by international radio stations carry reviews of new equipment — details are included in this book. The main manufacturers of short wave radios are Grundig, Panasonic, Philips, Sangean and Sony. All offer a range of receivers with a wide variety of different features.

Improving Reception

The most important part of a radio is the aerial, and yet most people rely solely on the telescopic antenna provided with the set. The advice however is to use an outdoor aerial if at all possible. The most rudimentary aerial will generally improve reception greatly. Invest in a piece of copper wire (insulated if possible) and sling it between the house and a convenient tree in the garden, and connect it to the radio. Make sure that the copper wire does not touch any building or tree as this will cause the incoming signal to earth. Also ensure that it does not pass near any exposed electrical cables. More complicated aerials will help to overcome any particular local interference problems, or to pull in signals from a particular direction.

If you are not able to use an outdoor aerial, keep your set next to a window or an outside wall, and away from televisions or electrical motors which may cause very heavy electrical interference.

Section 3

HOW TO USE THE IRSG

This latest edition of the *International Radio Stations Guide* offers the casual listener and the professional radio monitor an essential reference work to enable him to steer around the changing face of the radio dial. The *IRSG* has been totally revised and rewritten, including a great deal of new information. It offers a comprehensive guide to international radio on short wave, as well as up-to-the-minute data on European and North American medium wave and long wave services.

The *International Radio Stations Guide* contains a complete listing of all the short wave spectrum, in the officially designated broadcast bands, and in the adjacent frequency ranges. The information contained in the main short wave section has been compiled from registrations lodged with the International Frequency Registration Board [IFRB] in Geneva, coupled with extensive monitoring research carried out in the United Kingdom and overseas.

For the first time this year's *IRSG* denotes whether a user has registered (denoted R) with the IFRB or has been observed (denoted O) as occupying a frequency.

For example :

7 110	POL	Warsaw	60	R Polonia	R

shows that Poland has registered a 60kW transmitter at Warsaw for Radio Polonia broadcasts, whilst

9 410	G	Daventry	100/300	BBC	O

shows that this frequency has been observed to carry BBC World Service from either a 100 or 300 kW transmitter at Daventry.

In some cases, registrations with the IFRB tally exactly with actual usage, but in others there is no use of the channel by the broadcaster shown according to monitoring. However, including both registrations actually used, and those not monitored, enables the *IRSG* to be as up-to-date as possible, as some registrations may be brought in to operation at a later date.

The table of English broadcasts in the *IRSG* shows times for winter, but some stations will alter their transmission times in the spring to take account of local clock changes. If the broadcast listed cannot be traced at the time shown, try an hour either side. Alterations to times and frequencies are generally given at the opening of transmissions.

The country shown is that where the transmitter is located, but if another country is shown following [eg HKG/G or CHN/E] this shows that a programme from another international broadcaster is being carried as part of a relay agreement – in the cases shown the BBC from its Hong Kong relay, and Radio Exterior de Espana from Chinese transmitters. An increasing number of relay arrangements have come in to operation during 1990, with agreement between Radios Moscow and Beijing to transmit from each other's territory.

Feeder channels have been included as they have been observed. Some broadcasters still use feeders despite the advent of satellite links, particularly when satellite services fail or no ground station is available. Frequencies change regularly.

The indications for usage of Soviet frequencies is generally shown as either domestic, external or domestic/external. The transmission network within the Soviet Union is extremely complex, and many frequencies switch between domestic programmes, such as the Mayak service, and external transmissions. Regional Soviet Republican services may also be heard.

The main Moscow radio services:

First which is a general programme covering the entire country with five time shifted versions;

Second or **Mayak** which is a musical entertainment network, similar to Britain's **BBC Radio Two** with news casts every thirty minutes;

Third which is an arts and music channel with five time shifted versions for national coverage.

In addition to the national networks, each Soviet Republic has its own **Republican First Programme** which alternates between the Moscow First programme, Russian language programmes and broadcasts in the Republic's own language. Some Republics have a second programme in the local language.

Identification of the service is usually straightforward, with an announcement of "Govorit Moscow" or the name of the city or republic from which it is being broadcast. "Radiostanza" is an alternative. More Republics seem to be introducing English language international services as the Soviet Union slides further towards break up. Those monitored at the time of compilation are included in the Broadcasts in English section of the *IRSG*.

It should be noted that the Soviet Union benefits from having three country codes (and therefore three votes on the International Telecommunication Union) – URS for the Soviet Union, UKR for the Ukraine and BLR for Byelorussia. The US state of Alaska is classified separately from the United States as ALS. A complete listing of country codes is included in the *IRSG*.

It is likely that there will be many changes to international short wave radio broadcasting during 1991. Radio Kuwait will probably return to the air following the cessation of hostilities in the Gulf, but Radio Budapest may be severely cut back during the summer. Radio Canada International's future is also uncertain, as a result of budgetary problems. More relay agreements are likely to be signed and new transmitters and sites will come in to use. These will be included in the next revision of the *International Radio Stations Guide* which will probably be published in 1992/1993.

Section 4

ABBREVIATIONS USED IN THIS BOOK

AFN	American Forces Network
AFRTS	American Forces Radio and TV Service
AIR	All India Radio
AWR	Adventist World Radio
BBC	British Broadcasting Corporation
BC	Broadcast, Broadcasting
BRT	Belgische Radio en Televisie, Brussels
BSKSA	Broadcasting System of the Kingdom of Saudi Arabia
CBS	Central Broadcasting System, Taiwan
CPBS	Central People's Broadcasting System, Peking
Dem	Democratic
DLF	Deutschlandfunk, Cologne
DW	Deutsche Welle, Cologne
dom	Domestic
ELWA	Cultural Missionary Broadcasting Service of Sudan Interior Mission
ERT	Elliniki Radiophonia Tileorassis, Athens
ext	External
FEBA	Far East Broadcasting Association
FEBC	Far East Broadcasting Company
FM	Frequency Modulation
HCJB	Hail Christ Jesus Blessings, Ecuador
Intl	International
ISB	Iceland State Broadcasting
kHz	kilohertz
kW	kilowatt
LW	long wave
MHz	megahertz
MW	medium wave
N, Nat	National
ORF	Osterreichischer Rundfunk, Vienna
ORT	Office de Radiodiffusion et Television
OAS	Organisation of American States
PBS	People's Broadcasting System, Peking
R	Radio
RAI	Radiotelevisione Italiana, Rome
RCI	Radio Canada International
RDP	Radiodifusao Portugesa, Lisbon
REE	Radio Exterior de Espana
Rev	Revolution
RFE	Radio Free Europe, Munich
RFI	Radio France International

RFO	Radiodiffusion Francaise d'Outre Mer
RIAS	Radio in the American Sector, Berlin
RL	Radio Liberty, Munich
RPD	Radio Pemerintah Daerah
RRI	Radio Republik Indonesia
RSA	Republic of South Africa
RTBF	Radio-Television Belge de la Communaute Francaise, Brussels
SBC	Singapore Broadcasting Corporation
SDR	Suddeutscher Rundfunk, Stuttgart
SFB	Sender Freies Berlin
SLBC	Sri Lanka Broadcasting Corporation
SRI	Swiss Radio International
SSB	Single Side Band
SWF	Sudwestfunk
TRT	Turkish Radio-Television Corporation, Ankara
TWR	Trans World Radio
UAE	United Arab Emirates
v	variable
V	Voice
VHF	Very High Frequency
Vo	Voice of
VoA	Voice of America
VoOAS	Voice of Organisation of American States
VoFC	Voice of Free China, Taiwan
VoIRI	Voice of the Islamic Republic of Iran
WCSN	Christian Science Monitor, Boston
WHRI	World Harvest Radio International, South Bend
WINB	World international Broadcasters Inc, Red Lion
WMLK	Assemblies of Yahweh, Bethel
WRNO	WRNO New Orleans
WYFR	Family Radio, Oakland

Section 5

COUNTRY CODES USED IN THIS BOOK

Listed in alphabetical order

AFG	Afghanistan
AFS	South Africa
AGL	Angola
ALB	Albania
ALG	Algeria
ALS	Alaska
AND	Andorra
ANG	Anguilla
ARG	Argentina
ARS	Saudi Arabia
ARU	Aruba
ASC	Ascension Island
ATG	Antigua
ATN	Netherlands Antilles
AUS	Australia
AUT	Austria
AZR	Azores
B	Brazil
BAH	Bahamas
BDI	Burundi
BEL	Belgium
BEN	Benin
BFA	Burkina Faso
BHR	Bahrain
BGD	Bangladesh
BLR	Byelorussia [part of USSR]
BLZ	Belize
BOL	Bolivia
BOT	Botswana
BRB	Barbados
BRM	Burma
BRU	Brunei
BUL	Bulgaria
CAF	Central African Republic
CAN	Canada
CBG	Cambodia
CHL	Chile
CHN	People's Republic of China
CHR	Christmas Island
CKH	Cook Islands
CLM	Colombia
CLN	Sri Lanka
CME	Cameroon
CNR	Canary Islands
COG	Congo
COM	Comoro Republic
CPV	Cape Verde
CTI	Ivory Coast
CTR	Costa Rica
CUB	Cuba
CVA	Vatican City
CYP	Cyprus
D	Germany
DJI	Djibouti
DNK	Denmark
DOM	Dominican Republic
E	Spain
EGY	Egypt
EQA	Ecuador
ETH	Ethiopia
F	France
FJI	Fiji
FLK	Falkland Islands
FNL	Finland
G	United Kingdom
GAB	Gabon
GDL	Guadeloupe
GHA	Ghana
GIB	Gibraltar
GMB	Gambia
GNB	Guinea Bissau
GNE	Equatorial Guinea
GRC	Greece
GRD	Grenada
GRL	Greenland
GTM	Guatemala
GUF	French Guiana
GUI	Guinea
GUM	Guam

GUY	Guyana
HKG	Hong Kong
HND	Honduras
HNG	Hungary
HOL	Netherlands
HTI	Haiti
HWA	Hawaii
I	Italy
CO	Cocos Island
IND	India
INS	Indonesia
IRL	Ireland
IRN	Iran
IRQ	Iraq
ISL	Iceland
ISR	Israel
J	Japan
JMC	Jamaica
JOR	Jordan
KEN	Kenya
KIR	Kiribati
KOR	South Korea
KRE	North Korea
KWT	Kuwait
LAO	Laos
LBN	Lebanon
LBR	Liberia
LBY	Libya
LSO	Lesotho
LUX	Luxembourg
MAC	Macau
MAU	Mauritius
MCO	Monaco
MDG	Madagascar
MDR	Madeira
MEX	Mexico
MLA	Malaysia
MLD	Maldives
MLI	Mali
MLT	Malta
MNG	Mongolia
MOZ	Mozambique
MRA	Northern Marianas
MRC	Morocco
MRT	Martinique
MSR	Montserrat
MTN	Mauritania
MWI	Malawi
MYT	Mayotte
NCG	Nicaragua
NCL	New Caledonia
NGR	Niger
NIG	Nigeria
NIU	Niue Island
NMB	Namibia
NOR	Norway
NPL	Nepal
NRU	Nauru
NZL	New Zealand
OCE	French Polynesia
OMA	Oman
PAK	Pakistan
PHL	Philippines
PNG	Papua New Guinea
PNR	Panama
POL	Poland
POR	Portugal
PRG	Paraguay
PRU	Peru
PTR	Puerto Rico
QAT	Qatar
REU	Reunion
ROU	Romania
RRW	Rwanda
S	Sweden
SDN	Sudan
SEN	Senegal
SEY	Seychelles
SHN	St Helena
SLM	Solomon Isles
SLV	El Salvador
SMA	American Samoa
SMO	Western Samoa
SNG	Singapore
SOM	Somalia
SRL	Sierra Leone
STP	Sao Tome et Principe
SUI	Switzerland
SUR	Surinam
SWZ	Swaziland
SYR	Syria
TCH	Chad

TCH	Czechoslovakia
TGO	Togo
THA	Thailand
TON	Tonga
TRD	Trinidad
TUN	Tunisia
TUR	Turkey
TUV	Tuvalu
TWN	Taiwan
TZA	Tanzania
UAE	United Arab Emirates
UGA	Uganda
UKR	Ukraine [part of USSR]
URG	Uruguay
URS	Soviet Union
USA	United States of America
VEN	Venezuela
VIR	American Virgin Isles
VTN	Vietnam
VUT	Vanuatu
WAL	Wallis Island
YEM	Yemen
YUG	Yugoslavia
ZAI	Zaire
ZMB	Zambia
ZWE	Zimbabwe

Section 6

WORLDWIDE SHORT WAVE RADIO STATIONS

Frequency [kHz]	Country	Station Site	Power [kW]	Programme/ Network	O or R
2 310	AUS	Alice Springs	50	ABC Alice Springs	O
	CHN	Kunming	15	PBS	O
2 325	AUS	Tennant Creek	50	ABC Tennant Creek	O
2 340	CHN	Fuzhou	10	PBS	O
2 350	INS	Yogyakarta	1	RRI Yogyakarta	O
2 360	GTM	Huehuetenango	0.5	R Maya de Barillas	O
2 380	B	Limeira	0.25	R Educadora	O
2 390	GTM	Santiago	1	La Voz de Atitlan	O
	MEX	Huayacocotla	0.5	R Huayacocotla	O
	INS	Cirebon	1	RRI Cirebon	O
2 410	B	Senr Guiomard	1	R Transamazonica	O
	PNG	Wabag	10	R Enga	O
2 415	CHN	Wenzhou	10	PBS Zhejiang	O
2 420	B	Sao Carlos	0.5	R Sao Carlos	O
2 432	INS	Sumatera	1	RRI Palembang	O
2 440	INS	Java	1	RRI Surakarta	O
2 445	CHN	Nanchang	10	PBS Jiangxi	O
2 475	CHN	Hangzhou	10	PBS Zhejiang	O
2 485	AUS	Katherine	50	ABC Katherine	O
2 490	B	Desxalvado	0.25	R 8 Setembro	O
2 560	CHN	Urumqui	15	CPBS	O
2 582	INS	Timur	0.3	RPD Tengah Selatan	O
2 618	INS	Kalimantan	0.25	RPD Sambas	O
2 695	INS	Flores	0.5	RPD Ende	O
2 850	KRE	Pyongyang	100	Korean Central BS	O
2 905	INS	Tenggara	0.5	RPD Ngada	O
2 963	INS	Flores	0.3	RPD Manggaraj	O
3 143	INS	Tanjung Pandan	0.3	RPD Belitung	O

Frequency [kHz]	Country	Station Site	Power [kW]	Programme/ Network	O or R
3 159	INS	Tembilahan	0.3	RRI	O
3 200	SWZ	Manzini	25	TWR	O
3 205	INS	Java	10	RRI Bandung	O
	B	Ribeirao Preto	1	R Ribeirao Preto	O
	B	Humaita	5	R Vale Rio Madeira	O
	PNG	Vanimo	10	R Sandaun	O
3 210	MOZ	Maputo	100	R Mozambique	O
3 215	INS	Sulawesi	10	RRI Manado	O
	AFS	Meyerton	100	R Oranje	O
3 220	CHN	Beijing	50	CPBS	O
	EQA	Quito	10	HCJB	O
	PNG	Lae	10	R Morobe	O
3 222	TGO	Lama Kara	10	R Lama Kara	O
3 223	IND	Simla	2.5	AIR	O
	INS	Lombok	5	RRI Mataram	O
3 230	LBR	Monrovia	10	ELWA	O
	NPL	Kathmandu	100	R Nepal	O
	PRU	Juliaca	0.5	R Sol de los Andes	O
3 232	MDG	Antananarivo	2	R Madagasdcar	O
3 235	IND	Gauhati	10	AIR	O
	PNG	Kimbe	2	R West New Britain	O
	B	Marilia	0.5	R Clube	O
3 240	SWZ	Manzini	25	TWR	O
3 240	EQA	Esmeraldas	1	R Antena Libre	O
3 242	INS	Maluku	1	RRI	O
3 245	B	Varginha	1	R XClube	O
	VEN	Caracas	1	R Libertador	O
	PNG	Kerema	10	R Gulf	O
3 250	KRE	Pyongyang	100	R Pyongyang	O
	INS	Kalin	10	RRI	O
	HND	Santa Barbara	0.8	R Luz y Vida	O
3 255	IND	Shillong	50	AIR	O
	LBR	Monrovia	50	Liberian BC	O
	LSO/G	Lancers	100	BBC O	
	B	Crato	1	R Educadora	O
3 260	NGR	Niamey	4	Voix de Sahel	O
	CHN	Guiyang	10	PBS	O

Frequency [kHz]	Country	Station Site	Power [kW]	Programme/ Network	O or R
3 260	EQA	Calceta	3	La Voz de Rio Carrizal	O
(cont'd)	PRU	Oxapampa	2.5	La Voz de Oxapampa	O
3 265	INS	Sulawesi	10	RRI	O
3 270	NMB	Windhoek	100	R Namibia	O
3 275	PNG	Mendi	2	R South Highlands	O
3 277	IND	Srinagar	50	R Kashmir	O
3 280	MOZ	Beira	100	R Beira	O
	PRU	Ayacucho	1	R Huari	O
3 285	HNB	Belmopan	1	R Belize	O
	B	Obidos	1	RTV Sentinela	O
	EQA	Cuenca	0.3	R Rio Tarqui	O
	INS	Madiun	10	RRI	O
3 290	NMB	Windhoek	100	R Namibia	O
	CHN	Beijing	10	CPBS	O
	PNG	Port Moresby	10	R Central	O
3 295	ISL	Reykjavik	10	IBS	O
	IND	Delhi	20	AIR	O
3 300	GTM	Guatemala	10	R Cultural	O
3 305	ZMB	Gweru	100	Zimbabwe BC	O
	IND	Ranchi	2	AIR	O
	PNG	Daru	10	R Western	O
	INS	Timur	10	RRI	O
3 310	CHN	Changchun	10	PBS Jilin	O
	PRU	Bagua	1	R Bagua	O
	PRU	Cusco	2	R Universal	O
	BOL	Riberalta	1	R San Miguel	O
3 315	IND	Bhopal	10	AIR	O
	EQA	Puya	2.5	R Pastaza	O
	PNG	Lorengau	2	R Manus	O
3 320	AFS	Meyerton	100	R Orion/R Suid Afrika	O
	KRE	Pyongyang	120	R Pyongyang	O
3 325	NIG	Lagos	50	R Nigeria	O
	B	Belem	5	R Liberal	O
	B	Guarulhos	2.5	R Universitaria	O
	GTM	Huehuetenango	1	R Maya de Barillas	O
	EQA	Quevedo	1.5	Ondas Quevedenas	O
3 330	RRW	Kigali	5	R Republic Rwandaise	O
	IND	Leh	10	R Kashmir	O
	COM	Moroni	4	R Comoro	O

Frequency [kHz]	Country	Station Site	Power [kW]	Programme/ Network	O or R
3 335	TWN	Taipei	10	Central BC System	O
	PNG	Wewak	10	R East Sepik	O
3 340	MOZ	Maputo	10	R Mozambique	O
	BOL	Viloco	1	R Viloco	O
3 345	ZMB	Lusaka	50	R Zambia	O
	INS	Maluku	10	RRI	O
	IND	Jammu	2	R Kashmir	O
	PNG	Popondetta	2	R Northern	O
3 350	GHA	Accra	10	Ghana BC Corp	O
	KRE	Pyongyang	120	R Pyongyang	O
3 355	BOT	Gabarone	50	R Botswana	O
	IND	Kureseong	20	AIR	O
	INS	Java	1	RRI	O
	PNG	Kundiawa	10	R Simbu	O
	NCL	Noumea	20	RFO New Caledonie	O
3 360	EQA	Sucua	10	R Federacion	O
	GTM	Nahuala	1	La Voz de Nahuala	O
3 365	GHA	Accra	50	Ghana BC Corp	O
	IND	Delhi	10	AIR	O
	PNG	Alotau	10	R Milne Bay	O
	B	Araraquara	1	R Cultura	O
	CUB	Havana	50	R Rebelde	O
3 370	MDG	Antananarivo	5	R Madagascar	O
	MOZ	Beira	10	R Beira	O
	GTM	Caban	5	R Tezulutlan	O
3 375	AGL	Luanda	10	R Nacional	O
	IND	Gauhati	50	AIR	O
	B	Guajara Mirim	5	R Educadora	O
	B	S Gabriel	5	R Nacional	O
	PNG	Mount Hagen	10	R Western Highland	O
	INS	Sumatera	7.5	RRI	O
3 378	AUT	Vienna	10	Austrian Army Training	O
3 380	MWI	Limbe	100	Malawi BC	O
	GTM	Jocotan	1	R Chortis	O
	BOL	Tazna	1	R Cumbre	O
	EQA	Quito	1	R Iris	O
	INS	Java	1	RRI	O
3 385	GUF	Cayenne	4	RFO Guyane	O
	B	Tefe	1	R Educacao Rural	O

Frequency [kHz]	Country	Station Site	Power [kW]	Programme/ Network	O or R
3 385	MLA	Miri	10	RTM Sarawak	O
(cont'd)	INS	Timur	10	RRI	O
	PNG	Rabaul	10	R East New Britain	O
3 390	ZAI	Bunia	1	R Candip	O
	BOL	Camargo	1	R Camargo	O
3 395	ZMB	Gweru	100	Zimbabwe BC Corp	O
	EQA	Santa Domingo	5	R Zaracay	O
	INS	Sum	10	RRI	O
	PNG	Goroka	2	R Eastern Highlands	O
3 400	B	Xapuri	2	R 6 de Agosto	O
3 422	INS	Rabu	0.2	RRI	O
3 447	INS	Kalimantan	1	RRI	O
3 450	PRU	Oyon	1	R Oyon	O
3 460	INS	Sumatera	1	RPD	O
3 475	BOL	Padilla	0.5	R Padilla	O
3 480	KRE	Pyongyan	100	Vo National Salvation	O
3 570	B	Brasilia	15	R 3 de Julho	O
3 645	INS	Irian Jaya	0.5	RRI Fak Fak	O
3 655	INS	Sulawesi	1	RRI	O
3 665	PAK	Muzaffarabad	1	Azad Kashmir R	O
3 775	INS	Sumbawa Besar	0.075	RRI	O
3 778	IRN	Tehran	100	VoIRI	O
3 815	CHN	Beijing	10	CPBS	O
3 875	INS	Sumatera	0.5	RRI	O
3 900	CHN	Hailar	2	PBS	O
3 905	IND	Delhi	100	AIR	O
	PNG	Kavieng	2	R New Ireland	O
	INS	Jaya	1	RRI	O
3 910	CHN	Kunming	10	CPBS	O
3 915	SNG/G	Kranji	100	BBC	O
3 920	KRE	Sinuiju	100	North Pyongyang PS	O
3 925	J	Tokyo Yamata	50	RCI	O
	J	Tokyo Nagara	50	R Tanpa	O

Frequency [kHz]	Country	Station Site	Power [kW]	Programme/ Network	O or R
3 925	IND	Delhi	20	AIR	O
(cont'd)	AFS	Umtata	20	Capital R	O
3 930	KOR	Seoul	5	Korean BC System	O
3 935	NZL	Levin	1	Print Disabled R	O
	INS	Java	5	RRI	O
3 940	CHN	Wuhan	1	PBS Hubei	O
	HKG	Kowloon	2	RTV Hong Kong	O
3 945	J	Tokyo Nagara	10	R Tanpa	O
	VUT	Efate Island	10	R Vanuatu	O
	INS	Bali	10	RRI	O
3 950	CHN	Xining	10	PBS Qinghai	O
3 955	G	Daventry	100	BBC	O
	G	Skelton	250	BBC	O
	PAK	Rawalpindi	10	R Pakistan	O
3 960	D	Lampertheim	100	RFE/RL	O
	MNG	Ulan Bator	12	R Ulan Bator/R Moscow	O
	CHN	Beijing	10	R Beijing	O
	CHN	Urumqi	50	PBS Xinjiang	O
	INS	Sulawesi	10	RRI	O
3 965	F	Allouis	4	RFI	O
	URS	Moscow	50	R Afghanistan	O
3 970	D/USA	Biblis	100	RFE/RL	O
	CME	Buea	4	Cameroon BC Corp	O
	J	Nagoya	0.3	NHK	O
	J	Sapporo	0.6	NHK	O
	CHN	Hohhot	100	PBS Monggol	O
3 975	G	Skelton	250	BBC	O
	INS	Java	10	RRI	O
3 980	D/USA	Ismaning	100	RFE/RL	O
	PAK	Islamabad	100	R Pakistan	O
	PRU	El Porvenir	0.5	R El Porvenir	O
3 985	SUI/ CHN	Lenk	250	R Beijing	O
	SUI	Beromunster	250	SRI	O
	D/USA	Biblis	100	RFE/RL	O
	INS	Irian Jaya	1	RRI	O
3 990	D/USA	Biblis	100	RFE/RL	O
	LBR	Careysburg	50	VoA	O

Frequency [kHz]	Country	Station Site	Power [kW]	Programme/ Network	O or R
3 990	CHN	Shanghai	10	PBS	O
(cont'd)	CHN	Urumqi	50	CPBS	O
3 995	D	Julich	100	DW	O
	URS	Khabarovsk	50	Domestic/External	O
4 000	CME	Bafoussam	20	Cameroon RTV Corp	O
4 002	INS	Sulawesi	5	RRI	O
4 010	URS	Frunze	50	R Frunze	O
4 020	CHN	Beijing	10	Domestic/External	O
4 025	URS	Vladivostock	250	Domestic/External	O
4 030	URS	Anadyr	15	Domestic/External	O
4 035	CHN	Lhasa	50	Domestic/External	O
4 040	URS	Yerevan	15	R Yerevan	O
	URS	Vladivostock	50	Domestic/External	O
	PRU	Tocache	1	R Marginal	O
4 045	URS	Moscow	120	Domestic/External	O
4 050	URS	Frunze	50	R Frunze	O
	URS	Sakhalinsk	15	Domestic/External	O
4 055	URS	Moscow	120	Domestic/External	O
4 060	URS	Kharkov	100	Domestic/External	O
4 080	MNG	Ulan Bator	50	R Ulan Bator/R Moscow	O
4 100	CHN	Tianjin	0.5	PBS Tianjin	O
4 120	B	Sena Madureira	0.25	R Difusora	O
4 130	CHN	Beijing	10	Domestic/External	O
	CHN/E	Beijing	10	REE	O
4 190	CHN	Beijing	50	Domestic/External	O
4 200	CHN	Beijing	10	Domestic/External	O
4 220	CHN	Urumqi	10	CPBS	O
4 250	CHN	Beijing	50	CPBS	O
4 270	EQA	Gonzanama	1	R Gonzanama	O
4 300	PRU	Celendin	0.25	R Moderna	O
4 330	CHN	Urumqi	50	CPBS	O

Frequency [kHz]	Country	Station Site	Power [kW]	Programme/ Network	O or R
4 395	URS	Yakutsk	2	Kazakh R	O
	URS	Yakutsk	100	R Moscow	O
4 420	BOL	Reyes	0.35	Radioemisora Reyes	O
	PRU	Bambamarca	0.85	Frecuencia Lider	O
4 455	KRE	Haeju	100	Vo National Salvation	O
4 460	CHN	Beijing	10	CPBS	O
4 465	D/USA	Holzkirchen	10	RFE/RL [feeder]	O
4 472	BOL	Santa Ana	0.25	R Movima	O
4 485	URS	Petropavlovsk	50	Domestic/External	O
	URS	Ufa	50	Domestic	O
4 500	CHN	Urumqi	50	PBS Xinjiang	O
4 510	URS	Fergana	15	Fergana R	O
4 520	URS	Khanty-Mansiysk	50	Domestic	O
4 525	CHN	Dongsheng	10	CPBS	O
4 545	URS	Alma Ata	50	Kazakh R	O
4 565	D/USA	Holzkirchen	10	RFE/RL [feeder]	O
4 588	ARG	Buenos Aires	2.5	R Continental [feeder]	O
4 590	URS	Moscow	120	Domestic/External	O
4 605	INS	Irian Jaya	0.5	RRI	O
4 610	URS	Khabarovsk	50	Domestic	O
4 620	CHN	Beijing	10	R Beijing	O
4 635	URS	Dushanbe	50	Tadzhik R	O
4 650	BOL	Santa Ana	1	R Santa Ana	O
4 680	EQA	Quito	5	R Nacional Espejo	O
	BOL	Guayaramerin	0.75	R Paititi	O
4 700	INS	Java	2	R K Informasi Pern	O
	PRU	Chota	1	R Waira	O
4 705	PRU	Rioja	0.25	R Alto Valle	O
4 720	INS	Ujung Padang	50	RRI	O
	BOL	Riberalta	0.5	R Abaroa	O
4 725	BRM	Yangon	50	Burma BC Service	O
4 735	CHN	Urumqi	50	CPBS	O

Frequency [kHz]	Country	Station Site	Power [kW]	Programme/ Network	O or R
4 740	URS	Ashkhabad	120	R Afghanistan	O
	BOL	Guayaramerin	0.5	R Mamore	O
4 747	BOL	Villa Tunari	0.25	La Voz del Tropico	O
	PRU	Huanta	0.5	R Huanta 2000	O
4 750	ZAI	Lubumbashi	10	La Voix du Zaire	O
	CME	Bertoua	20	Cameroon RTV Corp	O
	MNG	Ulan Bator	12	R Ulan Bator/R Moscow	O
	CHN	Lhasa	50	CPBS	O
4 755	B	Campo Grande	10	R Educacao Rural	O
	CLM	Bogota	5	Caracol Bogota	O
	HND	Puerto Lempira	10	Sani R	O
	INS	Ujung Pandang	50	RRI	O
4 760	LBR	Monrovia	10	ELWA	O
	SWZ	Manzini	25	TWR	O
	IND	Port Blair	10	AIR	O
	IND	Leh	10	AIR	O
	CHN	Kunming	50	CPBS	O
	EQA	Guayaquil	5	Emisora Atalaya	O
4 765	COG	Brazzaville	50	RTV Congolaise	O
	CUB	Havana	10	R Moscow	O
	B	Cruzeiro do Sul	10	R Integracao	O
	BOL	Huanay	1	R Huanay	O
4 770	NIG	Kaduna	50	R Nigeria	O
4 775	AFG	Kabul	100	R Afghanistan	O
	AFG	Kabul	100	R Iran Toilers	O
	IND	Gauhati	10	AIR	O
	B	Cuiaba	1	Portal da Amazonia	O
	B	Congonhas	1	R Congonhas	O
4 780	AGL	Menongue	5	EP Cuando-Cubango	O
	DJI	Djibouti	20	RTV de Djibouti	O
	PAK	Islamabad	100	R Pakistan	O
4 785	MLI	Bamako	18	RTV Malienne	O
	TZA	Dar es Salaam	50	R Tanzania	O
	URS	Baku	50	Azerbaijani R	O
	BOL	San Borja	0.5	R Ballivan	O
	B	Campinas	1	R Brasil	O
	B	Porto Velho	1	R Caiari	O
	CLM	Ibague	5	Ecos del Combeima	O
	PRU	Satipo	1	R Cooperativa	O
4 790	SWZ	Manzini	25	TWR	O
	IND	Shillong	50	AIR	O

Frequency [kHz]	Country	Station Site	Power [kW]	Programme/ Network	O or R
4 790	INS	Irian Jaya	1	RRI Fak Fak	O
(cont'd)	PRU	Iquitos	3	R Atlantida	O
4 795	URS	Ulan Ude	50	Domestic	O
	CME	Douala	100	Cameroon RTV Corp	O
	B	Aquidauana	1	R Aquidauana	O
	EQA	Bahia Caraquez	5	La Voz de los Caras	O
	BOL	La Paz	10	R Nueva America	O
4 800	LSO	Maseru	100	R Lesotho	O
	URS	Yakutsk	50	Yakut R	O
	IND	Hyderabad	10	AIR	O
	CHN	Urumqi	2/50	CPBS	O
	PRU	Puno	1.5	R Onda Azul	O
	EQA	Cuenca	5	R Popular	O
4 805	INS	Timor	0.3	RRI	O
	B	Manaus	5	Difusora Amazonas	O
4 810	URS	Yerevan	50	Armenian R	O
	AFS	Meyerton	100	R Orion/R Suid Afrika	O
	PRU	Tarapoto	3	R San Martin	O
	EQA	San Cristobal	5	La Voz de Galapagos	O
4 815	BFA	Ouagadougou	50	RTV Burkina	O
	CHN	Togtoh	10	R Beijing	O
	PAK	Karachi	10	R Pakistan	O
	BOL	La Paz	1	R Nacional	O
	B	Londrina	10	R Difusora	O
	PRU	Iquitos	1	R Amazonas	O
4 820	URS	Khanty-Mansiysk	50	Domestic	O
	AGL	Lubango	10	ER da Huila	O
	HND	Tegucigalpa	5	La Voz Evangelica	O
	PRU	Cajamarca	1	R Atahualpa	O
4 825	URS	Ashkhabad	50	Turkmen R	O
	GTM	Cabrican	1	Radio Mam	O
	B	Braganca	10	R Educadora	O
	PRU	Iquitos	10	La Voz de la Selva	O
4 830	BOT	Gabarone	50	R Botswana	O
	MNG	Altai	12	R Ulan Bator/R Moscow	O
	THA	Pathum Thani	10	R Thailand	O
	VEN	San Cristobal	10	R Tachira	O
	BOL	Santa Cruz	1	R Grigota	O
4 832	CTR	San Jose	3	R Reloj	O

Frequency [kHz]	Country	Station Site	Power [kW]	Programme/ Network	O or R
4 835	MLI	Bamako	18	RTV Malienne	O
	PRU	Jaen	1	R Maranon	O
	GTM	Coban	3	R Tezulutlan	O
	B	Corumba	5	R Atalaia	O
	MLA	Kuching-Stapol	10	RTM Sarawak	O
	AUS	Alice Springs	50	ABC	O
	PAK	Islamabad	100	R Pakistan	O
4 840	IND	Bombay	10	AIR	O
	CHN	Harbin	50	PBS Heilongjiang	O
	CHN	Fuzhou	10	Vo the Strait	O
	VEN	Valera	1	R Valera	O
	PRU	Andahuaylas	2	R Andahuaylas	O
	GTM	San Cristobal	5	R K'ekchi	O
4 845	MTN	Nouakchott	100	ORT de Mauritanie	O
	PRU	Loma Alta	0.5	R Bella Vista	O
	B	Ibitinga	1	R Meterologica	O
	B	Manaus	250	R Nacional Brasilia	O
	BOL	La Paz	5	R Fides	O
4 850	URS	Tashkent	50	Uzbek R	O
	CME	Yauonde	100	Cameroon RTV Corp	O
	IND	Kohima	50	AIR	O
	MNG	Ulan Bator	50	R Ulan Bator/R Moscow	O
	VEN	Caracas	1	R Capital	O
	EQA	Loja	5	R Luz y Vida	O
4 855	YMS	Sana	50	Yemen R	O
	MOZ	Maputo	20	R Mozambique	O
	BOL	Santa Cruz	1	R Centenario	O
	B	Barra da Garcas	1	R Aruana	O
	INS	Sumatera	10	RRI	O
4 860	URS	Tchita	15	Domestic	O
	URS	Serpukhov	100	Domestic	O
	AGL	Saurimo	5	Er do Lunda Sul	O
	IND	Delhi	50	AIR	O
	VEN	Maracaibo	10	R Maracaibo	O
4 865	MNG	Saynshang	12	R Ulan Bator/R Moscow	O
	MOZ	Maputo	20	R Mozambique	O
	CHN	Lanzhou	50	PBS Gansu	O
	CLM	Arauca	5	La Voz del Cinaruco	O
	B	Cruzeiro do Sul	5	R Verdes Florestas	O
4 870	BEN	Cotonou	30	ORT du Benin	O
	CLN	Ekala	10	SLBC	O
	EQA	Macuma	5	R Rio Amazonias	O

Frequency [kHz]	Country	Station Site	Power [kW]	Programme/ Network	O or R
4 875	URS	Tbilisi	2	Georgian R	O
	CHN	Nanjing	50	Vo Jinling	O
	B	Rio de Janeiro	10	R Jornal do Brasil	O
	INS	Irian Jaya	10	RRI	O
	CLM	Medellin	2	R Super	O
	BOL	La Paz	10	R la Cruz del Sur	O
4 880	AFS	Meyerton	100	R Five	O
	IND	Lucknow	10	AIR	O
	PAK	Quetta	10	R Pakistan	
	BGD	Dhaka	100	R Bangladesh	O
4 883	CHN	Hohhot	50	R Beijing	O
4 885	AGL	M'banza Congo	5	ER do Zaire	O
	KEN	Nairobi	10	Kenya BC Corp	O
	B	Belem	5	R Clube do Para	O
	CLM	Villavicencio	5	Ondas del Meta	O
4 890	GAB	Moyabi	250	RFI	O
	SEN	Dakar	100	ORT du Senegal	O
	PNG	Port Moresby	10	National BC of PNG	O
4 895	MNG	Murun	12	R Ulan Bator/R Moscow	O
	URS	Tyument	15	Tyumen R	O
4 900	GUI	Conakry	18	RTV Guineenne	O
	CHN	Fuzhou	50	Vo the Strait	O
	INS	Java	0.5	RRI	O
	CLN	Ekala	10	SLBC	O
4 905	CHN	Beijing	10	CPBS	O
	B	Rio de Janeiro	5	R Relogio Federal	O
	CBG	Phnom Penh	50	Vo the People	O
4 910	ZMB	Lusaka	50	R Zambia	O
	AUS	Tennant Creek	50	ABC	O
	PRU	Trujillo	1	R Libertad	O
4 915	URS	Moscow	120	R Afghanistan	O
	KEN	Nairobi	100	Kenya BC Corp	O
	GHA	Accra	50	Ghana BC Corp	O
	B	Goiania	10	R Anhanguera	O
4 920	URS	Yakutsk	50	Yakut R	O
	IND	Madras	10	AIR	O
	EQA	Quito	5	R Quito	O
	AUS	Brisbane	10	ABC	O
4 925	GNE	Bata	100	R Nacional	O
	MOZ	Maputo	7.5/10	R Mozambique	O

Frequency [kHz]	Country	Station Site	Power [kW]	Programme/ Network	O or R
4 925	CHN	Harbin	50	PBS Heilongjiang	O
(cont'd)	CLM	Arauca	2.5	Em Meridiano70	O
	B	Taubate	1	R Difusora	O
4 930	URS	Ashkabad	50	Domestic/External	O
	URS	Tbilisi	50	Domestic/External	O
	INS	Java	10	RRI	O
4 935	KEN	Nairobi	100	Kenya BC Corp	O
	B	Jatai	2.5	R Difusora	O
	BOL	Sucre	1	R Cordech	O
4 940	URS	Moscow	100	R Afghanistan	O
	UKR	Kiev	50	Ukrainian R	O
	CTI	Abidjan	100	RTV Ivoirienne	O
	CLN	Ekala	10	SLBC	O
	IND	Gauhati	50	AIR	O
4 945	CLM	Neiva	2.5	Caracol Neiva	O
	B	Port Velho	50	R Nacional	O
	B	Pocos de Caldas	1	R Difusora	O
4 950	CHN	Hohhot	10	PBS	O
	IND	Jammu	2	R Kashmir	O
	MLA	Kuching-Stapok	10	RTM Sarawak	O
	PAK	Islamabad	100	R Pakistan	O
	PRU	P. Maldonado	5	R Madre de Dios	O
4 955	B	Campos	2.5	R Cultura	O
	B	Belem	10	R Marajoara	O
4 957	URS	Baku	50	Azerbaijani R	O
4 960	IND	Delhi	10	AIR	O
	CHN	Kunming	50	R Beijing	O
	EQA	Sucua	5	R Federacion	O
4 965	B	Parintins	5	R Alvorada	O
	PRU	Cusco	5	R San Miguel	O
4 970	CHN	Urumqi	50	CPBS	O
	MLA	Kota Kinabalu	10	RTM Kota Kinabalu	O
	PRU	Tarapoto	1	R Imagen	O
	VEN	Caracas	10	R Rumbos	O
4 975	URS	Moscow	120	R Afghanistan	O
	CHN	Jianyang	10	PBS Fujinan	O
	B	Sao Paulo	1	R Tupi	O
	B	Osasco	1	R Iguatemi	O
	BOL	Montero	1	Maria Auxiliadora	O
4 976	UGA	Kampala	50	R Uganda	O

Frequency [kHz]	Country	Station Site	Power [kW]	Programme/ Network	O or R
4 980	SWZ	Sandlane	100	Swazi Comm R	O
	PAK	Islamabad	100	Azad Kashmir R	O
	CHN	Urumqi	50	CPBS	O
	VEN	San Cristobal	10	Ecos del Torbes	O
4 985	B	Goiania	10	R Brasil Central	O
4 990	URS	Yerevan	50	Yervan R	O
	NIG	Lagos	50	R Nigeria	O
	IRN	Tehran	100	VoIRI	O
	IND	Madras	100	AIR	O
	CHN	Changsha	10	PBS Hunan	O
	INS	Sulawesi	10	RRI	O
	BOL	Chocaya	1	R Animas	O
4 995	MNG	Choybalsan	12	R Ulan Bator/R Moscow	O
	PRU	Huancayo	1	R Andina	O
5 004	GNE	Bata	100	R Nacional	O
5 005	MLA	Sibu	10	RTM Sarawak	O
	NPL	Harriharpur	100	R Nepal	O
	BOL	La Paz	1	R Cristal	O
	SUR	Paramaribo	0.35	R Apintie	O
5 010	CME	Garoua	100	Cameroon RTV Corp	O
	MDG	Antananarivo	100	R Madagascar	O
	CHN	Nanning	10	PBS Guangxi	O
	SNG	Jurong	50	SBC	O
5 015	URS	Archangelesk	50	Archangelsk R	O
	URS	Vladivostock	50	Domestic/External	O
	B	Cuiaba	5	R Brasil Tropical	O
5 020	NGR	Niamey	20/100	La Voix du Sahel	O
	SLM	Honiara	10	Solomon Islands BC	O
	CLN	Ekala	10	SLBC	O
	CHN	Nanchang	10	PBS Jiangxi	O
	CLM	Quibdo	2	Ecos del Atrato	O
	VTN	Hanoi	10	Vo Vietnam	O
5 023	BHU	Thimbu	50	Bhutan BC Service	O
5 025	BEN	Parakou	20	ORT du Benin	O
	UGA	Kampala	50/250	R Uganda	O
	AUS	Katherine	50	ABC	O
	B	Altamira	5	R Transamazonica	O
	PRU	Quillabamba	5	R Quillabamba	O
	CUB	Havana	50	R Rebelde	O

Frequency [kHz]	Country	Station Site	Power [kW]	Programme/ Network	O or R
5 030	MLA	Kuching-Stapok	10	RTM Sarawak	O
	TON	Nukualofa	1	Tonga BC Commission	O
	CHN	Xian	10	CPBS	O
	EQA	Quito	9	R Catolica	O
	PRU	Huamachuco	1	R Los Andes	O
5 035	CAF	Bangui	100	RTV Centrafricaine	O
	AUT	Vienna	10	Austrian Army Training	O
	URS	Alma Ata	50	R Alma Ata	O
	PRU	Moyobamba	1	R Moyobamba	O
	B	Aparecida	10	R Aparecida	O
5 040	URS	Tbilisi	50	Georgian R	O
	AGL	Benguela	1	Er de Benguela	O
	CHN	Fuzhou	10	PBS Fujian	O
	EQA	Macas	10	La Voz del Upano	O
5 045	PAK	Islamabad	10	R Pakistan	O
	B	Belem	10	R Cultura do Para	O
	INS	Java	20	RRI	O
5 047	TGO	Lome	100	R Lome	O
5 050	BLR	Minsk	50	Domestic	O
	TZA	Dar es Salaam	10	R Tanzania	O
	IND	Aizawl	50	AIR	O
	CHN	Nanning	50	Domestic/External	O
	PRU	Cangallo	0.5	R Municipal	O
	CLM	Yopal	1	La Voz de Yopal	O
5 052	SNG	Jurong	50	SBC	O
5 055	GUF	Cayenne	10	RFO Guyane	O
	SWZ	Manzini	25	TWR	O
	B	Caceres	1	R Difusora	O
	INS	Irian Jaya	1		O
5 057	ALB	Gjirokaster	50	RTV Shqiptar	O
5 060	CHN	Changji	10	CPBS	O
	EQA	Loja	5	R Nac Progreso	O
5 065	URS	Tashkent	20	Kazakh R	O
	ZAI	Bunia	1	R Candip	O
5 075	CHN	Urumqi	50	CPBS	O
	CLM	Bogota	50	Caracol Bogota	O
5 080	PAK	Islamabad	100	R Pakistan	O
5 090	CHN	Xian	50	CPBS	O
	PAK	Islamabad	100	R Pakistan	O

Frequency [kHz]	Country	Station Site	Power [kW]	Programme/ Network	O or R
5 125	D/USA	Holzkirchen	10	RFE/RL [feeder]	O
	CHN	Beijing	10	CPBS	O
5 145	CHN	Beijing	120	Domestic/External	O
5 160	PRU	Cajamarca	1	R Nuevo Continente	O
5 163	CHN	Xian	50	CPBS	O
5 188	PRU	Bambamarca	0.25	R Onda Popular	O
5 220	CHN	Beijing	10	R Beijing/REE	O
5 250	CHN	Beijing	10	R Beijing/REE	O
5 256	INS	Sumatera	1	RRI	O
5 260	URS	Alma Ata	50	Kazakh R	O
	PRU	S R Huayabamba	0.5	R Nororiental	O
5 275	TWN	Taipei	50/250	WYFR	O
	PRU	Bambamarca	0.25	R Onda Popular	O
5 286	TCD	Moundou	5	R Moundou	O
5 290	URS	Krasnoyarsk	100	Krasnoyarsk R	O
	TCD	Moundou	2.5	Radiodif. N	O
5 295	D/USA	Holzkirchen	10	RFE/RL [feeder]	O
5 320	CHN	Beijing	15	CPBS	O
5 420	CHN	Beijing	10	CPBS	O
5 440	CHN	Urumqi	50	CPBS	O
5 510	CHN	Fuzhou	10	Vo the Strait	O
5 567	CLM	Tibu	0.2	R Nueva Vida	O
5 582	BOL	S J Chiquitos	0.5	R San Jose	O
5 645	PRU	Bambamarca	0.1	Bambamarca	O
5 660	VTN	Hoang Len Son	10	Vo Vietnam domestic	O
	PRU	Cutervo	0.7	La Voz de Cutervo	O
5 780	URS	Noginsk	15	Tass News	O
5 800	CHN	Urumqi	50	CPBS	O
	PRU	Cajamarca	0.25	R Nuevo Cajamarca	O
5 815	URS	Moscow	15	R Moscow [feeder]	O
5 835	URS	Moscow	120	Domestic/External	O
5 850	CHN	Beijing	120	R Beijing	O

Frequency [kHz]	Country	Station Site	Power [kW]	Programme/ Network	O or R
5 860	CHN	Shijiazhuang	50	CPBS	O
5 875	G	Rampisham	500	BBC	O
	ARS	Riyadh	50	BSKSA	O
5 880	CHN	Shijiazhuang	50	CPBS	O
5 895	PRU	Arequipa	0.08	R Hispana	O
5 900	ISR	Jerusalem	20	Kol Israel	O
	IND	Peshawar	10	V of Afghanistan	O
	URS	Kazan	100	Domestic/External	O
	CHN	Chengdu	15	CPBS	O
5 905	URS	Kiev	240	External	O
	URS	Riazan	100	External	O
	URS	Minsk	20	Domestic	O
5 910	BEL	Wavre	100/180	BRT	O
	URS	Tchita	100	Domestic/External	O
	URS	Moscow	50	Domestic/External	O
5 915	URS	Alma Ata	100	Domestic/External	O
	URS	Minsk	100	Domestic	O
	CHN	Shijiazhuang	50	CPBS	O
5 920	URS	Khabarovsk	100	Domestic/External	O
	URS	Tchita	50	Domestic/External	O
	URS	Yerevan	100	Domestic	O
	CHN	Nanning	15	CPBS	O
5 925	URS	Tallin	50	Domestic/External	O
5 930	TCH	Prague	250	R Prague	O
	URS	Tbilisi	50	Domestic	O
	URS	Alma Ata	50	Domestic	O
	URS	Murmansk	50	Domestic	O
5 935	URS	Riga	50	Domestic/External	O
	URS	Tula	50	Domestic/External	O
	CHN	Lhasa	50	CPBS	O
5 940	URS	Petropavlokam	100	Domestic/External	O
5 945	URS	Frunze	100	Domestic/External	O
	URS	Komsomolskamur	240	Domestic/External	O
	AUT	Vienna	100	R Austria Intl	O
	F	Allouis	100	R France Intl	O
	URS	Tashkent	100	Domestic/External	O
5 950	URS	Minsk	100	Domestic/External	O
	URS	Petropavlokam	100	Domestic/External	O

Frequency [kHz]	Country	Station Site	Power [kW]	Programme/ Network	O or R
5 950	YEM	San'a	300	R San'a	O
(cont'd)	USA	Okeechobee	100	WYFR/VoFC	O
	GUY	Georgetown	10	Guyana BC Corp	O
	CHN	Harbin	50	CPBS	O
	CHN	Lhasa	50	CPBS	O
5 955	URS	Moscow	100	Domestic/External	R
	D/USA	Holzkirchen	250	RFE/RL	R
	D/USA	Biblis	250	RFE/RL	R
	D/USA	Lampertheim	100	RFE/RL	R
	HOL	Flevo	500	R Netherlands	R,O
	ROU	Bucharest	250	R Romania Intl	R
	F	Allouis	100/500	R France Intl	R
	GRC	Kavalla	250	Voice of America	R
	POR	Lisbon	250	RFE/RL	R
	UAE	Abu Dhabi	500	UAE R	R
	BOT	Sebele	50	R Botswana	R
	ZAI	Lubumbashi	10		R
	CUB	Havana	250	R Havana Cuba	R
	GTM	Guatemala	10		R
	PRU	Huancayo	1		R
	BOL	Llallagua	1		R
	B	Sao Paulo	10		R
	CHL	Santiago	1		R
	URS	Tashkent	100	Domestic/External	R,O
	CHN	Lhasa	50	Domestic/External	R,O
	CHN	Harbin	50	Domestic/External	R,O
	PHL	Tinang	250	Voice of America	R
	INS	Surakarta	50		R
	YUG	Bijeljina	500	R Belgrade	O
5 958	CHN	Kunming	50	CPBS	O
5 960	D	Jeulich	100	Deutsche Welle	R
	D	Wertachtal	500	Deutsche Welle	R
	AFS	Meyerton	250	R RSA	R
	CAN	Sackville	250	R Canada Intl/R Japan	R
	MEX	Sisoguichi	0.3		
	URS	Alma Ata	50	Domestic/External	R
	URS	Sverdlovsk	240	Domestic/External	R
	IND	Jammu	1		R
	URS	Blagovechtchen	240	Domestic/External	R
	URS	Vladivostock	100	Domestic/External	
	MNG	Ulan Bator	50	R Ulan Bator	R
	KOR	Kimjae	250	R Korea	R
	CHN	Kunming	50	Domestic/External	R
	BUL	Sofia	100	R Sofia	R
	ALB	Kruja	50	R Tirana	O

Frequency [kHz]	Country	Station Site	Power [kW]	Programme/ Network	O or R
5 965	BLR	Orcha	20	Domestic	R
	D	Nauen	50	Deutsche Welle	R
	D/USA	Werchtachtal	500	Voice of America	R
	G	Wooferton	250	Voice of America	R
	UKR	Simferopol	50	Domestic/External	R
	BEL	Wavre	100	BRT	R
	GRC	Rhodes	50	Voice of America	R
	OMA/G	Masirah	100	BBC	R
	CYP/G	Limassol	250	BBC	R
	CAN	Sackville	250	R Canada Intl/BBC	R
	CUB	Havana	250	R Havana Cuba	R
	BOL	Huanun	10		O
	URS	Komsomolskamur	20	Domestic/External	R
	CHN	Shijiazhuang	50	Domestic/External	R
	HKG/G	Tsang Tsui	250	BBC	R
	PNG	Mt Hagen	10	NBC	R
	MLA	Kuala Lumpur	100	RTM Kuala Lumpur 1	O
5 970	URS	Kazan	100	Domestic/External	R
	URS	Moscow	100	Domestic/External	R
	D/USA	Biblis	100	RFE/RL	R
	GRC	Athens	100	Vo Greece	R
	E	Noblejas	350	R Exterior de Espana	R
	POR	Lisbon	250	RFE/RL	R
	YEM	Aden	100	R Aden	R
	PRU	Lima	10	R El Sol	R
	URS	Alma Ata	50	Domestic/External	R
	IND	Gauhati	50	AIR	R
	URS	Blagovechtchen	100	Domestic/External	R
	CHN	Hezuo	15		R
	INS	Bandjarmasin	10		R
5 971	CHN	Hezua	15	CPBS	O
5 975	S	Hoerby	350	R Sweden	R
	URS	Leningrad	200	Domestic/External	R
	G	Rampisham	500	BBC	R
	G	Skelton	250	BBC	R
	OMA/G	Masirah	100	BBC	R
	ZWE	Gwelo	100		R
	CUB	Havana	250	R Havana Cuba	R
	HTI	Pt au Prince	50		R
	ATG	Antigua	250	BBC	R
	BOL	Cochabamba	1		O
	PRG	Villarrica	3		R
	URS	Tashkent	100	Domestic/External	R
	IRN	Kamalabad	500	VoIRI	R

Frequency [kHz]	Country	Station Site	Power [kW]	Programme/ Network	O or R
5 975	KOR	Hwasung	100	R Korea	R
(cont'd)	CHN	Beijing	120	Domestic/External	R
	INS	Mataram	50		R
5 979	PRU	Lima	5	R Programas d Peru	O
5 980	NOR	Kvitsoy	500	R Norway/Danmarks R	R
	URS	Jigulevsk	20	Domestic/External	R
	URS	Riazan	20	Domestic	R
	D	Jeulich	100	Deutsche Welle	R
	G	Daventry	300	R Canada Intl	R
	UKR	Simferopol	250	Domestic/External	R
	YUG	Bijeljina	250	R Yugoslavia	R
	TUR	Ankara	250	TRT	R
	MEX	Linares	0.5		R
	GTM	Guatemala	5		R
	PRU	Lima	5		R
	B	Florianopolis	10	R Guaruja	R
	URS	Krasnoiarsk	100	Domestic/External	R
	CHN	Huhhot	50	Domestic/External	R
	TWN	Kao-hsiung	10	Vo Asia	O
	IRN	Kamalabad	50	VoIRI	O
5 985	D/USA	Biblis	100	RFE/RL	R
	UKR	Kiev	240	Domestic/External	R
	GRC	Kavalla	250	Voice of America	R
	POR	Lisbon	250	RDP	R
	TZA	Dar es Salaam	50	R Tanzania	R
	USA	Okeechobee	50/100	WYFR/Vo Free China	R
	USA	Delano	250	Voice of America	R
	MEX	Mexico	10		R
	CUB	Havana	75	R Havana Cuba	R
	CHL	Temuco	10		R
	URS	Dushanbe	100	Domestic/External	R
	PNG	Rabaul	10		R
	INS	Pakanbaru	50	RRI	R
	ALB	Kruja	50	R Tirana	O
5 990	G	Rampisham	500	BBC	R
	UKR	Kharkov	20	Domestic/External	R
	ROU	Bucharest	120/250	R Romania Intl	R
	F	Allouis	500	R France Intl	R
	I	Rome	100	RAI	R
	ETH	Gedja	100	V o Ethiopia	R
	GHA	Ejura	10		R
	SLV	San Salvador	50	R Nacional	R
	PRU	Tumbes	2		R

Frequency [kHz]	Country	Station Site	Power [kW]	Programme/ Network	O or R
5 990	B	Rio de Janeiro	10		R
(cont'd)	IND	Bhopal	10		R
	URS	Khavbarovsk	20	Domestic	R
	URS	Irkutsk	100	Domestic/External	R
	J	Tokyo Yamata	100	R Japan	R
	KOR	Kimjae	250	R Korea	R
	CHN	Shijiazhuang	50	Domestic/External	R
	INS	Manado	10	R	
5 995	POL	Warsaw	8	R Polonia	R
	D	Wertachtal	500	Deutsche Welle	R
	D/USA	Wertachtal	500	Voice of America	R
	G	Daventry	300	R Canada Intl	R
	G	Woofferton	250	Voice of America	R
	YUG	Bijeljina	250	R Yugoslavia	R
	F	Allouis	100	R France Intl	R
	CYP/G	Limassol	100	BBC	R
	MLI	Bamako	50		R
	ZAI	Mbandaka	10		R
	USA	Greenville	250	Voice of America	R
	BOL	Sucre	1		R
	PRG	P J Caballero	2		R
	URS	Tashkent	100	Domestic/External	R
	URS	Kenga	50	Domestic/External	R
	BGD	Dhaka	50	R Bangladesh	R
	CHN	Lhasa	50	Domestic/External	R
	INS	Yogyakarta	100		R
	AUS	Shepparton	100	R Australia	R
6 000	URS	Moscow	240	Domestic/External	R
	D	Jeulich	100	Deutsche Welle	R
	D	Wertachtal	500	Deutsche Welle	R
	LBY	Sebha	100	Tripoli	R
	ARS	Diriyya	50	BSKSA	R
	CUB	Havana	75	R Moscow	R
	B	Pt Alegre	10		R
	URG	Montevideo	5		R
	URS	Sverdlovsk	250	Domestic/External	R
	URS	Tchita	100	Domestic/External	R
	MNG	Ulan Bator	100	R Ulan Bator	R
	KRE	Pyongyang	200	R Pyongyang	R
	CHN	Fuzhou	50	Vo the Strait	R
	SNG	Singapore	50	SBC	R
6 005	URS	Voronej	100	Domestic/External	R
	URS	Volgograd	20	Domestic	R
	URS	Armavir	100	Domestic/External	R
	D/USA	Berlin	100	RIAS	R

Frequency [kHz]	Country	Station Site	Power [kW]	Programme/ Network	O or R
6 005	UKR	Kiev	20	Domestic/External	R
(cont'd)	YUG	Bijeljina	500	R Yugoslavia	R
	YEM	Aden	100		R
	ASC	Ascension	250	BBC	R
	SEY/G	Mahe	250	BBC	R
	CUB	Havana	100	R Havana Cuba	R
	BOL	La Paz	10	R Horizonte	R
	URS	Tashkent	50	Domestic/External	R
	IRN	Zahedan	500	VoIRI	R
	CLN	Ekala	10		R
	CHN	Lanzhou	15	Domestic	R
	CLN	Colombo	10	SLBC	O
	CAN	Montreal	0.5	CFCX	O
	J	Sapporo	0.6	NHK Sapporo	O
6 007	CHN	Kunming	50	V o Dem Malaysia	O
6 008	J	Nagoya	0.3	NHK Nagoya	O
6 010	URS	Moscow	20	Domestic	R
	URS	Kiev	100	Domestic/External	O
	D	Wertachtal	500	Deutsche Welle	R
	G	Skelton	250	BBC	R
	G	Daventry	300	BBC/R Canada Intl	R
	G	Rampisham	500	BBC	R
	UKR	Vinnitsa	100	Domestic/External	R
	YUG	Bijeljina	500	R Yugoslavia	R
	GRC	Kavalla	250	Voice of America	R
	I	Rome	100	RAI	R
	MEX	Mexico	5		R
	PRU	Lima	10		R
	B	Belo Horizonte	25		R
	NIG	Inabab	38		O
	URG	Montevideo	10		R
	URS	Krasnoiarsk	240	Domestic/External	R
	PAK	Islamabad	10	R Pakistan	R
	IND	Calcutta	10	AIR	O
6 011	PRU	Lima	5	R America	O
	VEN	Merida	0.25	R Los Andes	O
	MEX	Mexico City	0.25	R Mil	O
6 012		McMurdo Base	1	AFAN Radio	O
6 015	BLR	Orcha	100	Domestic/External	R
	URS	Jigulevsk	100	Domestic/External	R
	D	Wertachtal	500	Deutsche Welle	R
	D/USA	Holzkirchen	250	RFE/RL	R
	GRC	Kavalla	250	Voice of America	R
	CYP/G	Limassol	250	BBC	R

Frequency [kHz]	Country	Station Site	Power [kW]	Programme/ Network	O or R
6 015	IRQ	Babel	500	R Baghdad	R
(cont'd)	CTI	Abidjan	500	R Abidjan	R
	KEN	Langata	10		R
	CAN	Sackville	250	R Austria Intl	R
	CUB	Havana	250	R Havana Cuba	R
	BOL	S Cruz	5		R
	B	Foz do Iguacu	5		R
	PRG	Asuncion	1		R
	KOR	Kwasung	100	R Korea	R
	CHN	Beijing	50	Domestic/External	R
	INS	Amboina	50		R
6 020	URS	Moscow	100	Domestic/External/ R Kabul	R
	HOL	Flevo	500	R Netherlands	R
	UKR	Kiev	100	Domestic/External	R
	E	Arganda	100	R Exterior	R
	MCO	Monte Carlo	100	Trans World Radio	R
	ARS	Jeddah	50	BSKSA	R
	ZWE	Gwelo	20		R
	SWZ	Manzini	25	TWR	R
	USA	Greenville	250	Voice of America	R
	MEX	Veracruz	5		R
	ATN	Bonaire	300	R Netherlands	R
	PRU	Lima	5		R
	B	Pt Alegre	10		R
	B	Salvador	10		R
	CHL	Calama	30		R
	URS	Novosibirsk	50	Domestic/External	R
	URS	Khabarovsk	50	Domestic/External	R
	IND	Simla	2.5	AIR	R
	PNG	Kieta	10	NBC	R
	AUS	Brandon	10	R Australia	R
6 025	URS	Tbilisi	100	Domestic/External	R
	D	Juelich	100	Deutsche Welle	R
	G	Rampisham	500	BBC	R
	HNG	Szekesfehervar	100	R Budapest	R
	POR	Sines	250	R Canada Intl	R
	MLT	Cyclops	250	Deutsche Welle	R
	MOZ	Beira	10		R
	CUB	Havana	100	R Havana Cuba	R
	PRU	Iquitos	1		R
	PRG	Asuncion	100	R Nacional	R
	CHN	Kunming	50	V of Dem Cambodia	R
	CHN	Bayenhaote	15	Domestic	R
	INS	Bandjarmasin	50		R

Frequency [kHz]	Country	Station Site	Power [kW]	Programme/ Network	O or R
6 025	SWZ	Manzini	25	TWR	O
(cont'd)	IRN	Kamalabad	500	VoIRI	O
	BOL	La Paz	10	R Illimani	O
6 030	URS	Moscow	20/100	Domestic/External	R
	URS	Kazan	240	Domestic/External	R
	D	Muehlacker	20	Suddeustcherundfunk	R
	G	Daventry	300	R Canada Intl	R
	G	Rampisham	500	BBC	R
	UKR	Kiev	20	Domestic	R
	OMA/G	Masirah	100	BBC	R
	CYP/G	Limassol	250	BBC/Cyprus BC	R
	UGA	Kampala	250	R Uganda	R
	KEN	Koma Rock	250		R
	USA	Bethany	250	Voice of America	R
	USA	Greenville	250	Voice of America	R
	CHL	Coyhaique	1	R Santa Maria	R
	IRN	Kamalabad	500	VoIRI	R
	PHL	Tinang	250	Voice of America	R
	PHL	Bocaue	50	FEBC	R
	B	Rio de Janeiro	7.5	R Globo	O
	SYR	Adra	500	R Al Quds	O
	CAN	Calgary	0.1	CFVP	O
6 035	POL	Warsaw	60	R Polonia	R
	D	Jeulich	100	Deutsche Welle	R
	D	Wertachtal	500	Deutsche Welle	R
	UKR	Simferopol	240	Domestic/External	R
	BEL	Wavre	100	BRT	R
	SUI	Schwarzenburg	150	SRI	R
	LBR	Careysburg	250	Voice of America	R
	MEX	Mexico	100		R
	PRU	Arequipa	1		R
	BOL	La Paz	10		R
	URG	Montevideo	1	La Radio	R
	IRN	Kamalabad	500	VoIRI	R
	IND	Madras	10	AIR	R
	URS	Vladivostock	100	Domestic/External	R
	KOR	Kimjae	250	R Korea	R
	CHN	Kunming	50	Domestic/External	R
	AUS	Brandon	10	R Australia	R
	BHU	Thimphu	100	R Bhutan	O
6 040	URS	Tula	100	Domestic/External	
	URS	Murmansk	20	Domestic	R
	URS	Armavir	20	Domestic	R
	D	Nauen	50/500	Deutsche Welle	R
	D/USA	Biblis	100	RFE/RL	R

Frequency [kHz]	Country	Station Site	Power [kW]	Programme/ Network	O or R
6 040	G	Woofferton	250/300	Voice of America	R
(cont'd)	F	Allouis	100	R France Intl	R
	OMA/G	Masirah	100	BBC	R
	USA	Greenville	500	Voice of America	R
	CUB	Havana	500	R Havana Cuba	R
	B	Curitiba	7.5	R Clube Paranaense	R
	CHN	Nanchang	50	Domestic/External	R
	PNG	Alotau	10	NBC Boroko Karai	R
	TWN	Taipei	7.5	CBS	O
6 045	URS	Volgograd	20	Domestic	R
	URS	Moscow	240	Domestic/External	R
	D	Wertachtal	500	Deutsche Welle	R
	G	Skelton	250	BBC	R
	F	Allouis	100/500	R France Intl	R
	GRC	Athens	5	Vo Greece	R
	SEN	Tambacounda	4	R Tambacounda	R
	KEN	Koma Rock	250	Kenya BC	R
	ZWE	Gwelo	100		R
	MEX	S Luis Potosi	0.3	R Univ de San Luis	R
	PRU	Lima	10	R Santa Rosa	R
	URG	Montevideo	2.5	R Libertad Sport	R
	IND	Delhi	100	AIR	R
	URS	Tchita	240	Domestic/External	R
	CHN	Huhhot	15	Domestic	R
	CUB	Havana	100	R Moscow	O
6 050	URS	Leningrad	150	Domestic/External	R
	D/USA	Biblis	100	RFE/RL	R
	G	Daventry	300	BBC/R Canada Intl	R
	CYP/G	Limassol	250	BBC	R
	EQA	Quito	100	HCJB	R
	B	Belo Horizonte	10	R Guarani	R
	URS	Khabarovsk	100	Domestic/External	R
	CHN	Lhasa	50	Domestic	R
	PHL	Palauig	250	Voice of America	R
	MLA	Sibu	10	RTM Sarawak	R
	NIG	Ibadan	50	R Nigeria	O
6 055	BLR	Minsk	20	Domestic	R
	URS	Kazan	100	Domestic/External	R
	UKR	Starobelsk	100	Domestic/External	R
	TCH	Litomysl	400	R Prague	R
	TCH	Rimavska	250	R Prague	R
	F	Allouis	500	R France Intl	R
	E	Noblejas	350	REE	R
	KWT	Sulaibiyah	250	R Kuwait	R
	RRW	Kigali	50	RTV Rwandaise	R

Frequency [kHz]	Country	Station Site	Power [kW]	Programme/ Network	O or R
6 055	GUF	Montsinery	500	R France Intl	R
(cont'd)	PRU	Arequipa	1	R Continental	R
	BOL	La Paz	100		R
	URG	Melo	5		R
	URS	Sverdlovsk	240	Domestic/External	R
	IND	Aligarh	250	AIR	R
	KRE	Pyongyang	200	R Pyongyang	R
	CHN	Kunming	50	Domestic/External	R
	INS	Medan	100		R
	INS	Palembang	100		R
	J	Tokyo Nagara	50	NSB Radio Tanpa 1	O
6 060	URS	Moscow	100	Domestic/External	R
	D/USA	Wertachtal	500	RFE/RL	R
	G	Rampisham	500	BBC	R
	G	Woofferton	250	Voice of America	R
	UKR	Kharkov	20	Domestic	R
	UKR	Ivanofrankovsk	20	Domestic	R
	GRC	Kavalla	250	Voice of America	R
	I	Caltanissetta	50	RAI	R
	I	Rome	50	RAI	R
	CYP/G	Limassol	250	BBC	R
	NGR	Niamey	20	ORTV du Niger 1	R
	KEN	Langata	100		R
	ZMB	Lusaka	10	Zambian NBC	R
	CUB	Havana	50	R Havana Cuba	R
	PRU	Lima	2.5		R
	B	Curtiba	10	R Universo	R
	CHL	Concepcion	10		R
	ARG	Gral Pacheco	50	RAE	R
	URS	Alma Ata	20	Domestic	R
	URS	Irkutsk	50	Domestic/External	R
	KOR	Kimjae	100	R Korea	R
	CHN	Xichang	15	Domestic	R
	MLA	Miri	10	RTM Sarawak	R
	AUS	Shepparton	100	R Australia	R
	CME	Yaounde	30	Cameroon RTV	O
6 065	S	Karlsborg	350	R Sweden	R
	URS	Erevan	100	Domestic/External	R
	OMA/G	Masirah	100	BBC	R
	ETH	Gedja	100		R
	USA	Okeechobee	50/100	WYFR/VoFC	R
	MEX	Texmelucan	1		R
	CHL	Pt Aysen	0.3		R
	URS	Khabarovsk	100	Domestic/External	R

Frequency [kHz]	Country	Station Site	Power [kW]	Programme/ Network	O or R
6 065	SNG/G	Kranji	250	BBC	R
(cont'd)	IND	Kohima	50	AIR	O
6 070	D/USA	Biblis	100	RFE/RL	R
	UKR	Simferopol	50	Domestic/External	R
	BUL	Sofia	250	R Sofia	R
	CYP/G	Limassol	250	BBC	R
	GHA	Tema	100		R
	LBR	Monrovia	50	ELWA	R
	SWZ	Manzini	25	Trans World Radio	R
	BOL	Oruro	5	R El Condor	R
	B	Rio de Janeiro	7.5	R Capital	R
	URS	Novosibirsk	100	Domestic/External	R
	PAK	Islamabad	100	R Pakistan	R
	CHN	Changchun	15	Domestic	R
	THA	Bangkok	10	R Thailand	R
	INS	Jayapura	20	RRI Jayapura	R
	CAN	Toronto	1	CFRX	O
	MRL	Majuro	10	WSZO R Marshall	O
6 075	URS	Tula	20	Domestic	R
	D	Julich	100	Deutsche Welle	R
	D	Wertachtal	500	Deutsche Welle	R
	POR	Sines	250		R
	USA	Bethany	250	Voice of America	R
	URG	Montevideo	2.5		R
	B/D	Brasilia	250	Deutsche Welle	R
	URS	Alma Ata	20	Domestic	R
	CLN	Ekala	10	SLBC	R
	KOR	Kimjae	250	R Korea	R
	CHN	Beijing	50	Domestic/External	R
	CLM	Bogota	10	R Caracol	O
	KEN	Koma Rock	250	Kenya BC	O
6 080	URS	Jigulevsk	20	Domestic	R
	URS	Tbilisi	100	Domestic/External	R
	D	Nauen	50/100	Deutsche Welle	R
	G	Woofferton	250	Voice of America	R
	UKR	Lvov	20	Domestic	R
	KEN	Langata	10	Kenya BC	R
	USA	Greenville	500	Voice of America	R
	EQA	Quito	10	HCJB	R
	PRU	Lima	40		R
	B	Goiania	5		R
	B	Curitiba	10	R Novas da Paz	R
	CHL	Coyhaique	1	R Patagonia	R
	URS	Frunze	240	Domestic/External	R
	IRN	Kamalabad	500	VoIRI	R

Frequency [kHz]	Country	Station Site	Power [kW]	Programme/ Network	O or R
6 080	URS	Komsomolskamur	100	Domestic/External	R
(cont'd)	J	Tokyo Yamata	100	R Japan	R
	CHN	Hailar	2	Domestic	R
	SNG/G	Kranji	250	BBC	R
	PNG	Daru	10	NBC Boroko Karai	R
	INS	Yogyakarta	100		R
	AUS	Shepparton	100	R Australia	R
	ALB	Lushnje	50	R Tirana	O
	CAN	Vancouver	0.01	CKFX	
6 085	URS	Tbilisi	100	Domestic/External	R
	D	Ismaning	100	Bayerischer Rundfunk	R
	D	Wertachtal	500	Deutsche Welle	R
	BUL	Sofia	100	R Sofia	R
	GRC	Kavalla	250	Voice of America	R
	OMA	Seeb	100	R Oman	R
	CYP/G	Limassol	250	BBC	R
	ZAI	Kisangani	10		R
	CAN	Sackville	250	R Canada Intl/BBC	R
	USA	Okeechobee	50/100	WYFR/VoFC	R
	SLV	San Salvador	50		R
	CHN	Nanning	15		R
	IND	Andaman Islands	10	AIR	O
	TWN	Taipei	3	CBS	O
6 090	URS	Orenburg	100	Domestic/External	R
	G	Woofferton	250	Voice of America	R
	UKR	Kiev	100	Domestic/External	R
	LUX	Junglinster	500	R Luxembourg	R
	MEX	Cd Mante	1	R Musica Romantica	R
	CUB	Havana	100	R Havana Cuba	R
	B	Sao Paulo	10	R Bandeirantes	R
	CHL	Temuco	10	R Esperanza	R
	IRN	Mashad	500	VoIRI	R
	PAK	Islamabad	250	R Pakistan	R
	URS	Niko	50	Domestic/External	R
	CHN	Baoding	120	Domestic/External	R
	POR	Sines	250	VoA	O
	ARG	Buenos Aires	1	R Belgrano	O
	LBR	Monrovia	50	ELWA	O
	CBG	Phnom-Penh	15	VOPO Cambodia	O
6 095	POL	Warsaw	100	R Polonia	R
	BLR	Minsk	20	Domestic	R
	URS	Murmansk	20	Domestic	R
	URS	Serpukhov	100	Domestic/External	R
	G	Woofferton	250	Voice of America	R

Frequency [kHz]	Country	Station Site	Power [kW]	Programme/ Network	O or R
6 095	SUI	Schwarzenburg	150	Swiss R Intl	R
(cont'd)	MRC	Tangier	50	Voice of America	R
	ALS	Anchor Point	100	KNLS	R
	SLV	San Salvador	50		R
	PRU	Lima	10		R
	URS	Petropavlo Kam	100	Domestic/External	R
	KOR	Kimjae	100/250	R Korea/RCI	R
	CHN	Nanchang	50	Domestic/External	R
	INS	Pontianak	100		R
	SOM	Mogadishu	50	R Somalia	O
6 100	URS	Kaunas	50	Domestic/External	R
	D	Wertachtal	500	Deutsche Welle	R
	YUG	Bijeljina	250	R Yugoslavia	R
	CAF	Bangui	20		R
	KEN	Koma Rock	250		R
	CUB	Havana	100/250	R Havana Cuba	R
	CHL	Calama	1		R
	URS	Kenga	100	Domestic/External	R
	AFG	Kabul	100	R Afghanistan	R
	NPL	Kathmandu	100	R Nepal	R
	KRE	Kanggye	250	R Pyongyang	R
	CHN	Urumqi	50	Domestic/External	R
	PHL	Poro	50	Voice of America	R
	MLA	Kuala Lumpur	100	Vo Malaysia	O
6 105	URS	Kaliningrad	100	Domestic/External	R
	D/USA	Lampertheim	100	RFE/RL	R
	D/USA	Holzkirchen	250	RFE/RL	R
	UKR	Lvov	240	Domestic/External	R
	ROU	Bucharest	250	R Romania	R
	TZA	Dar es Salaam	50	TWR	R
	USA	Okeechobee	100	WYFR/VOFC	R
	MEX	Merida	1	R Tus Panteras	R
	PRU	Tacna	1		R
	B	Cachoeira Paul	5	R Cancao Nova	R
	KOR	Kimjae	250	R Korea	R
	PHL	Poro	50	Voice of America	R
	BOL	La Paz	7.5	R Panamericana	O
6 110	URS	Riga	240	Domestic/External	R
	URS	Baku	200	Domestic/External	R
	G	Skelton	250	BBC	R
	UKR	Ivan	20	Domestic	R
	HNG	Szekesfehervar	20/100	R Budapest	R
	HNG	Diosd	100	R Budapest	R
	HNG	Jaszbereny	250	R Budapest	R

Frequency [kHz]	Country	Station Site	Power [kW]	Programme/ Network	O or R
6 110	GRC	Athens	100	Vo Greece	R
(cont'd)	GRC	Kavalla	250	Voice of America	R
	MLT	Cyclops	250	R Mediterranean	R
	ASC	Ascension	250	BBC	R
	MEX	Mexico	100		R
	ATG	Antigua	125	BBC	R
	EQA	Quito	100	HCJB	R
	PRG	Asuncion	3		R
	IND	Aligarh	250	AIR	R
	IND	Srinagar	7.5	AIR	R
	KOR	Kimjae	100	R Korea	R
	CHN	Beijing	50	Domestic/External	R
	PHL	Tinang	250	Voice of America	R
	BUL	Sofia	150	R Sofia	O
6 115	BLR	Orcha	20	Domestic	R
	URS	Petropavlo Kam	20	Domestic	R
	URS	Kazan	20	Domestic	R
	D	K Wusterhausen	50	Deutsche Welle	R
	D/USA	Lampertheim	100	RFE/RL	R
	D/USA	Biblis	100	RFE/RL	R
	POR	Lisbon	250	RFE/RL	R
	POR	Sines	250	RFE/RL	R
	KEN	Langata	100		R
	COG	Brazzaville	50	V Rev Congolaise	R
	MEX	Hermosillo	1	R Univ de Sonora	R
	CUB	Havana	100/500	R Havana Cuba	R
	PRU	Lima	100	R Union	R
	URG	Montevideo	5		R
	URS	Kenga	500	Domestic/External	R
	IND	Madras	100	AIR	R
	IND	Aligarh	250	AIR	R
	UKR	Khabarovsk	100	Domestic/External	R
	CHN	Fuzhou	50	Domestic/External	R
	INS	Biak	100		R
	J	Tokyo Nagara	50	NSB R Tanpa 2	O
6 120	FNL	Pori	100/250/ 500	R Finland	R
	BLR	Minsk	20	Domestic	R
	URS	Moscow	250	Domestic/External	R
	D	Julich	100	Deutsche Welle	R
	D	Wertachtal	500	Deutsche Welle	R
	TUR	Ankara	250	TRT	R
	CAN	Sackville	250	R Canada Intl/R Japan	R
	MEX	Tapachula	0.3		R

Frequency [kHz]	Country	Station Site	Power [kW]	Programme/ Network	O or R
6 120	PRU	Lima	1		R
(cont'd)	B	Sao Paulo	7.5	R Globo	R
	ARG	S Fernando	5	RN Buenos Aires	R
	URS	Novosibirsk	100	Domestic/External	R
	IND	Hyderabad	10	AIR	R
	CHN	Xian	120	Domestic/External	R
	PHL	Iba	100	FEBC	R
	ALB	Lushnje	100	R Tirana	O
6 125	G	Woofferton	250	Voice of America	R
	G	Daventry	300	R Canada Intl	R
	G	Skelton	250	BBC	R
	E	Noblejas	350	REE	R
	CYP/G	Limassol	250	BBC	R
	ZAI	Kananga	10		R
	USA	Bethany	250	Voice of America	R
	URG	Montevideo	10		R
	URS	Tashkent	20	Domestic	R
	URS	Irkutsk	20	Domestic	R
	KRE	Pyongyang	200	R Pyongyang	R
	KOR	Kimjae	250	R Korea	R
	CHN	Shijiazhuang	50	Domestic/External	R
	INS	Nabire	25	RRI Nabire	R
	ALB	Kruja	50	R Tirana	O
	AFG	Kabul	100	Kabul City Service	O
	POR	Sines	250	R Canada Intl	O
6 130	URS	Murmansk	20	Domestic	R
	URS	Moscow	240	Domestic/External	R
	D	Wertachtal	500	Deutsche Welle	R
	D/USA	Biblis	100	RFE/RL	R
	UKR	Lvov	240	Domestic/External	R
	UKR	Starobelsk	20	Domestic	R
	E	Arganda	100	REE	R
	POR	S Gabriel	100	RDP	R
	GHA	Accra	50	R Ghana	R
	USA	Greenville	250	Voice of America	R
	USA	Delano	250	Voice of America	R
	MEX	Mexico	10		R
	EQA	Quito	500	HCJB	R
	URS	Novosibirsk	100	Domestic/External	R
	IND	Delhi	20	AIR	R
	IND	Gauhati	10	AIR	R
	CLN	Ekala	10	SLBC	R
	BGD	Dhaka	100	R Bangladesh	R
	LAO	Vientiane	10	Lao National R	R
	CAN	Halifax	0.5	CHNS Halifax	O

Frequency [kHz]	Country	Station Site	Power [kW]	Programme/ Network	O or R
6 135	POL	Warsaw	100	R Polonia	R
	URS	Baku	100	Domestic/External	R
	D/USA	Biblis	100	RFE/RL	R
	D/USA	Holzkirchen	250	RFE/RL	R
	SUI	Schwarzenburg	150	Swiss R Intl	R
	BUL	Sofia	500	R Sofia	R
	BOL	S Cruz	1	R Santa Cruz	R
	B	Aparecida	25	R Aparecida	R
	CHL	Concepcion	30	R Universidad	R
	URS	Novosibirsk	100	Domestic/External	R
	URS	Alma Ata	100	Domestic/External	R
	KOR	Hwasung	10	R Korea	R
	CHN	Shijiazhuang	500	External	R
	INS	Samarinda	7.5/50	RRI Samarinda	R
	J	Fukuoka	0.6	NHK Fukuoka	O
	MDG	Antananarivo	30	R Madagascar	O
	YEM	San'a	20	R San'a	O
	OCE	Papeete	4	RFO Tahiti	O
6 140	URS	Voronej	240	Domestic/External	R
	URS	Leningrad	20	Domestic	R
	D	Wertachtal	500	Deutsche Welle	R
	G	Woofferton	250	Voice of America	R
	G	Daventry	300	R Canada Intl	R
	UKR	Vinnitsa	20	Domestic	R
	TUR	Ankara	250	TRT	R
	GRC	Kavalla	250	Voice of America	R
	E	Arganda	100	REE	R
	BDI	Gitega	100		R
	CAN	Sackville	250	R Canada Intl/R Korea	R
	MEX	Chihuahua	0.3		R
	CUB	Havana	100	R Havana Cuba	R
	URG	Mont	10	R Monte Carlo	R
	IRN	Kamalabad	500	VoIRI	R
	IND	Ranchi	2	AIR	R
	IND	Delhi	50	AIR	R
	NPL	Kathmandu	100	R Nepal	R
	CHN	Baoding	120	External	R
	CHN	Kunming	50	External	R
	PNG	Wewak	10	NBC Boroko Karai	R
	AUS	Perth	10	R Australia	R
	ZAI	Kinshasa	10	Voix du Zaire	O
6 145	D	Julich	100	Deutsche Welle	R
	D	Wertachtal	500	Deutsche Welle	R
	UKR	Kiev	240	Domestic/External	R
	ALG	Ouled Fayet	50		R

Frequency [kHz]	Country	Station Site	Power [kW]	Programme/ Network	O or R
6 145	MEX	Tlaxiaco	0.3		R
(cont'd)	PRU	La Oroya	1		R
	BOL	Tarija	1	R Luis de Fuentes	R
	URS	Omsk	100	Domestic/External	R
	BGD	Dhaka	50	R Bangladesh	R
	URS	Khab	100	Domestic/External	R
	KOR	Kimjae	250	R Korea	R
	CHN	Beijing	50	Domestic/External	R
	PHL	Bocaue	50	FEBC	R
	INS	Jakarta	120		R
	ALB	Kruja	50	R Tirana	O
6 150	URS	Serpukhov	20	Domestic	R
	G	Daventry	300	R Canada Intl	R
	G	Woofferton	300	Voice of America	R
	ROU	Bucharest	250	R Romania	R
	YUG	Zagreb	10	R Yugoslavia	R
	F	Allouis	500	R France Intl	R
	GRC	Kavalla	250	Voice of America	R
	CVA	S M Galeria	500	Vatican R	R
	MRC	Tangier	100	Voice of America	R
	KEN	Koma Rock	250	Kenya BC	R
	CAN	Sackville	250	R Canada Intl	R
	CUB	Havana	100	R Havana Cuba	R
	B	Sao Paulo	7.5	R Record	R
	CHL	Santiago	100		R
	IRN	Kamalabad	500	VoIRI	R
	CLN	Ekala	10	SLBC	R
	J	Tokyo Yamata	300	R Japan/R Canada Intl	R
	KOR	Kimjae	250	R Korea/R Canada Intl	R
	CHN	Qiqihar	50	Domestic/External	R
	PHL	Palauig	250	Voice of America	R
	CHN	Xian	150	R Canada Intl	O
	SDN	Al Fitahab	50	R Omdurman	O
	CLM	Bogota	10	R Caracol	O
6 155	POL	Warsaw	100	R Polonia	R
	URS	Kaunas	150/240	Domestic/External	R
	ROU	Bucharest	250	R Romania	R
	AUT	Vienna	300	ORF	R
	LBY	Tripoli	500	Tripoli	R
	GUI	Conakry	100	R N Guinee	R
	ASC	Ascension	250	BBC	R
	BOL	La Paz	1	R Fides	R
	URG	Montevideo	10		R
	IND	Delhi	100	AIR	R
	URS	Niko	50	Domestic/External	R

Frequency [kHz]	Country	Station Site	Power [kW]	Programme/ Network	O or R
6 155	J/USA	Tokyo	10	Far East Network	R
(cont'd)	CHN	Lanzhou	15	Domestic	R
	SNG	Singapore	50	SBC	R
	INS	Bandjarmasin	100		R
	SWZ	Sandlane	100	Swazi R	O
6 160	D/USA	Wertachtal	500	RFE/RL	R
	G	Woofferton	300	Voice of America	R
	BUL	Sofia	250	R Sofia	R
	GRC	Kavalla	250	Voice of America	R
	ALG	Ouled Fayet	50		R
	B	Pt Alegre	10	R Nueva Esperanza	R
	CHL	Chile Chico	0.1		R
	CHN	Shij	50	Domestic/External	R
	PHL	Palauig	250	Voice of America	R
	CAN	St John's	1	CKZN St John's	O
	CAN	Vancouver	0.5	CKZU Vancouver	O
6 165	URS	Moscow	200	Domestic/External	R
	URS	Tbilisi	100	Domestic/External	R
	UKR	Khabarovsk	20	Domestic	R
	UKR	Kiev	100	Domestic/External	R
	SUI	Sarnen	250	Swiss R Intl/R Beijing	R
	ZMB	Lusaka	50	Zambian NBC	R
	MEX	Mexico	10	R XEW 900	R
	ATN	Bonaire	300	Radio Netherlands	R
	URS	Sverdlovsk	20	Domestic	R
	IRN	Ahwaz	500	VoIRI	R
	URS	Khab	100	Domestic/External	R
	KOR	Hwasung	100	R Korea	R
	CHN	Kunming	50	Domestic/External	R
	INS	Ujungpandang	50		R
	YUG	Bijeljina	250	R Yugoslavia	O
6 170	D/USA	Lampertheim	100	RFE/RL	R
	D/USA	Holzkirchen	250	RFE/RL	R
	UAE	Abu Dhabi	500	UAE R	R
	GAB	Moyabi	250	Africa No 1	R
	KEN	Langata	10		R
	CUB	Havana	250	R Havana Cuba	R
	B	Sao Paulo	7.5	R Cultura	R
	URG	Montevideo	1	R Fenix	R
	URS	Novosibirsk	500	Domestic/External	R
	URS	Sverdlovsk	240	Domestic/External	R
	IND	Lucknow	10	AIR	R
	IND	Delhi	50	AIR	R
	CLN	Perkara	250	DW	R

Frequency [kHz]	Country	Station Site	Power [kW]	Programme/ Network	O or R
6 170	BGD	Dhaka	50	R Bangladesh	R
(cont'd)	CHN	Fuzhou	15	Domestic	R
	PHL	Marulas	10		R
	MDG	Antananarivo	10	R Madagascar	O
	GUF	Cayenne	4	RFO Cayenbe	O
6 175	URS	Kazan	100	Domestic/External	R
	URS	Moscow	250	Domestic/External	R
	F	Allouis	100	R France Intl	R
	IRQ	Abu Ghraib	250	VoMasses	R
	CAN	Sackville	250	BBC	R
	USA	Okeechobee	100	WYFR/VOFC	R
	GUF	Montsinery	500	R France Intl	R
	PRU	Cuzco	5		R
	BOL	Potosi	5		R
	URS	Khab	50	Domestic/External	R
	KOR	Kimjae	100	R Korea	R
	CHN	Xian	15	Domestic	R
	INS	Semarang	50		R
	MLA	Kuala Lumpur	100	Vo Malayasia	O
	IRN	Kamalabad	500	VoIRI	O
6 180	BLR	Minsk	20	Domestic	R
	URS	Armavir	100	Domestic/External	R
	D	Julich	100	Deutsche Welle	R
	G	Woofferton	250	Voice of America	R
	CVA	S M Galeria	250	Vatican R	R
	CYP/G	Limassol	100/300	BBC	R
	ISR	Jerusalem	50/300	Kol Israel	R
	SEN	Ziguinchor	4	R Ziguinchor	R
	LBR	Careysburg	250	Voice of America	R
	ATN	Bonaire	100	TWR	R
	GTM	Guatemala	2	V de Guatemala	R
	B	Brasilia	250	R Bras	R
	URS	Alma Ata	100	Domestic/External	R
	NPL	Kathmandu	100	R Nepal	R
	URS	Khab	100	Domestic/External	R
	CHN	Baoding	120	Domestic/External	R
	J	Tokyo Shobu	0.9	NHK Tokyo	O
	KRE	Pyongyang	100	R Pyongyang	O
	POR	Sines	250	VoA	O
6 185	URS	Riazan	240	Domestic/External	R
	CVA	S M Galeria	100/250	Vatican R	R
	LBY	Tripoli	100	Tripoli	R
	USA	New Orelans	100	WRNO	R
	MEX	Mexico	1	R Educacion	R

Frequency [kHz]	Country	Station Site	Power [kW]	Programme/ Network	O or R
6 185	BOL	La Paz	10	R Batallon Color	R
(cont'd)	CLN	Ekala	10	SLBC	R
	KOR	Kimjae	250	R Korea	R
	INS	Manokwari	1	RRI Manokwari	R
	INS	Manado	50		R
	INS	Biak	300		R
	D	Julich	100	DW	O
	ALB	Kruja	50	R Tirana	O
6 190	D	Bremen	10	Sender Freies Berlin	R
	ROU	Bucharest	250	R Bucharest	R
	SUI	Schwarzenburg	150	Swiss R Intl	R
	CVA	Cite Vatican	100	Vatican R	R
	CVA	S M Galeria	100	Vatican R	R
	LSO/G	Lancers	100	BBC	R
	USA	Greenville	250	Voice of America	R
	CUB	Havana	250	R Havana Cuba	R
	PRU	Iquitos	3		R
	CHL	Santiago	100		R
	URS	Omsk	100	Domestic/External	R
	URS	Tashkent	100	Domestic/External	R
	IND	Delhi	10	AIR	R
	CHN	Baoji	50	Domestic	R
	INS	Padang	10	RRI Padang	R
	J	Osaka Mihara	0.3	NHK Osaka	O
	MRC	Sevaa-Aioun	10	RTVM Rabat	O
6 195	POL	Warsaw	1	R Polonia	R
	URS	Baku	50	Domestic	R
	URS	Jigulevsk	100	Domestic/External	R
	G	Daventry	300	BBC	R
	G	Skelton	250	BBC	R
	G	Rampisham	500	BBC	R
	UKR	Kiev	20	Domestic	R
	EGY	Abis	250	R Cairo	R
	UAE	Abu Dhabi	500	UAE R	R
	HTI	Pt au Prince	50		R
	ATG	Antigua	250	BBC	R
	PRU	Cuzco	1		R
	BOL	La Paz	5/10	R Metropolitana	R
	PAK	Islamabad	100	R Pakistan	R
	BGD	Dhaka	50	R Bangladesh	R
	URS	Tchita	50	Domestic/External	R
	KRE	Pyongyang	200	R Pyongyang	R
	CHN	Huhhot	50	Domestic	R
	SNG/G	Kranji	125	BBC	R

Frequency [kHz]	Country	Station Site	Power [kW]	Programme/ Network	O or R
6 195	INS	Surabaja	50		R
(cont'd)	CUB	Havana	250	R Moscow	O
6 200	TWN	Panchiau	25	VoFC	O
6 205	EQA	Quito	100	HCJB	O
6 220	MCO	Monte Carlo	100	TWR	O
6 230	EGY	Abis	250	R Cairo	O
	AFG	Kabul	100	Iran Toilers	O
6 245v	CVA	Vatican City	80	Vatican R	O
6 250	KRE	Pyongyang	100	Pyongyang BCS	O
6 260	CHN	Xining	15	PBS	O
6 280	LBN	Marjayoun	10	King of Hope	O
6 290	CHN	Beijing	15	R Beijing	O
6 300	TWN	Taipei	100	WYFR	O
6 325	CHN	Kunming	50	Vo the Khmer	O
6 400	KRE	Kanggye	100	Pyongyang BCS	O
6 448	VTN	Hanoi	15	R Hanoi	O
6 480	KOR	Kimjae	250	R Korea	O
6 500	CHN	Xining	15	PBS	O
6 540	KRE	Pyongyang	100	R Pyongyang	O
6 576	KRE	Pyongyang	200	R Pyongyang	O
6 590	CHN	Beijing	15	R Beijing	O
6 607	KOR	Seoul	10	Vo the People	O
6 700	CHN	Kunming	50	Vo Dem Malaysia	O
6 750	CHN	Shijiazhuang	50	CPBS	O
6 770	URS	Noginsk	15	R Moscow	O
6 805	URS			Feeder	O
6 810	CHN	Beijing	15	R Beijing	O
6 822.5	URS			Domestic [feeder]	O
6 825	URS			Domestic/External [feeder]	O
	CHN	Beijing	15	CPBS	O
6 840	CHN	Beijing	50	CPBS	O

Frequency [kHz]	Country	Station Site	Power [kW]	Programme/ Network	O or R
6 860	CHN	Beijing	100/240	Domestic/External	O
6 873	USA			VoA [feeder]	O
6 890	CHN	Xian	120	CPBS	O
	URS			Domestic	O
6 895	PRU	Huancabamba	0.25	R Sensation	O
6 900	TUR	Ankara	5	Turkiye Meterol R	O
6 910	IRL	Dublin		R Dublin	O
6 920	URS			Domestic/External [feeder]	O
	CHN	Beijing	120	Domestic/External	O
6 933	CHN	Beijing	120	External	O
6 955	CHN	Baoding	120	R Beijing	O
6 974	CHN	Beijing	500	R Beijing	O
6 987.5	URS			External [feeder]	O
6 995	D			RFE/RL [feeder]	O
7 017	VTN	Hanoi	1	R Hanoi City Service	O
7 080	BGD	Dhaka	7.5	R Bangladesh	O
7 098	INS	Yogyakarta	7.5	RRI	O
7 105	BLR	Orcha	500	Domestic/External	R
	URS	Orenburg	240/500	Domestic/External	R
	D/USA	Wertachtal	500	VoA	R
	G	Rampisham	500	BBC	R
	UKR	Simferopol	100	Domestic/External	R
	ROU	Bucharest	250	R Romania	R
	GRC	Kavalla	250	VoA	R
	E	Arganda	100	REE	R
	COG	Brazzaville	25	V Rev Congolaise	R
	ASC	Ascension	250	BBC	R
	URS	Frunze	100	Domestic/External	R
	IRN	Ahwaz	500	VoIRI	R
	NPL	Kathmandu	100	R Nepal	R
	CHN	Huhhot	50	Domestic/External	R
	PHL	Tinang	250	VoA	R
	SNG/G	Kranji	100	BBC	R
	INS	Banda Aceh	50		R
	INS	Yogyakarta	7.5	R	
7 108	CHN	Hohhot	100	CPBS	O

Frequency [kHz]	Country	Station Site	Power [kW]	Programme/ Network	O or R
7 110	POL	Warsaw	60	R Polonia	R
	TUR	Ankara	250	TRT	R
	GRC	Kavalla	250	VoA	R
	MLT	Cyclops	250	IBRA	R
	ETH	Gedja	100		R
	MOZ	Maputo	25		R
	URS	Novo	250	Domestic/External	R
	IRN	Kamalabad	500	VoIRI	R
	IND	Delhi	50	AIR	R
	CHN	Lhasa	50	Domestic/External	R
	CHN	Xian	150	Domestic/External	R
	INS	Ujungpandang	100	Domestic	R
	ALB	Kruja	50	R Tirana	O
	MLI	Bamako	50	RTV Malienne	O
	UGA	Kampala	502	R Uganda	O
7 115	BLR	Minsk	20	Domestic	R
	D/USA	Biblis	100	RFE/RL	R
	UKR	Ivan	200/500	Domestic/External	R
	BUL	Sofia	500	R Sofia	R
	POR	Lisbon	250	RFE/RL	R
	ZAI	Bandundu	10		R
	URS	Dushanbe	20	Domestic	R
	CLN	Colombo	10	VoA	R
	BGD	Dhaka	100	R Bangladesh	R
	URS	Irkutsk	500		R
	CHN	Beijing	50	Domestic	R
	THA	Bangkok	10	R Thailand	R
	INS	Surakarta	50		R
	IRN	Kamalabad	500	VoIRI	O
	LAO	Vientiane	10	Lao National R	O
7 120	URS	Kazan	150	Domestic/External	R
	D	Julich	100	DW	R
	D/USA	Wertachtal	500	VoA	R
	G	Rampisham	500	BBC	R
	G	Skelton	250	BBC	R
	F	Allouis	500	RFI	R
	GRC	Athens	100	Vo Greece	R
	LBY	Tripoli	500	Tripoli	R
	TCD	N'Djamena	100		R
	KEN	Koma Rock	250		R
	URS	Ashkabad	500	External	R
	IND	Delhi	100	AIR	R
	NPL	Kathmandu	100	R Nepal	R
	CHN	Huhhot	50	Domestic/External	R
	PHL	Tinang	250	VoA	R

Frequency [kHz]	Country	Station Site	Power [kW]	Programme/ Network	O or R
7 120	PHL	Poro	50	VoA	R
(cont'd)	ALB	Lushnja	100	R Tirana	O
7 125	POL	Warsaw	100	R Polonia	R
	URS	Moscow	20	Domestic	R
	D	Wertachtal	500	DW	R
	GRC	Kavalla	250	VoA	R
	CVA	S M Galeria	500	Vatican R	R
	CYP/G	Limassol	250	BBC	R
	GUI	Conakry	100		R
	KEN	Langata	10		R
	PAK	Peshawar	10	R Pakistan	R
	IND	Ranchi	2	AIR	R
	CLN	Colombo	10	VoA	R
	URS	Khabarovsk	100	Domestic	R
	CHN	Xian	150	RFI	R
	CHN	Baoding	120	Domestic/External	R
	INS	Bengkulu	50		R
	INS	Jakarta	2.5		R
	INS	Padang Cermin	250	Vo Indonesia	R
	GAB	Moyabi	500	R Japan	O
	TWN	Taipei		R Democracy	O
7 130	URS	Yerevan	100	Domestic/External	R
	URS	Orenburg	100	Domestic/External	R
	D	Julich	100	DW	R
	D	Wertachtal	500	DW	R
	D/USA	Holzkirchen	250	RFE/RL	R
	D/USA	Biblis	100	VoA	R
	HOL	Flevo	500	R Netherlands	R
	UKR	Vinnitsa	100	Domestic/External	R
	GRC	Kavalla	250	VoA	R
	CVA	S M Galeria	100	Vatican R	R
	E	Noblejas	350	REE	R
	IRQ	Salah El Deen	500	R Baghdad	R
	KOR	Kimjae	100	R Korea	R
	MLA	Stapok	10		R
	MCO	Monte Carlo	100	TWR	O
	TWN	Minhsiung	50	VoFC	O
7 135	URS	Moscow	240	Domestic/External	R
	D	Julich	100	DW	R
	UKR	Lvov	240	Domestic/External	R
	ROU	Bucharest	250	R Romania	R
	F	Allouis	100/500	RFI	R
	CYP/G	Limassol	300	BBC	R
	LBR	Careysburg	50	VoA	R

Frequency [kHz]	Country	Station Site	Power [kW]	Programme/ Network	O or R
7 135	GAB	Moyabi	250		R
(cont'd)	PAK	Islamabad	100	R Pakistan	R
	UKR	Irkutsk	240	Domestic/External	R
	URS	Komsomolsk	500	Domestic/External	R
	CHN	Linghsi	50	Domestic/External	R
	AUS	Darwin	250	R Australia	O
	G	Daventry	300	RCI	O
	ALB	Lushnja	100	R Tirana	O
7 140	BLR	Minsk	20	Domestic	R
	URS	Kazan	150	Domestic/External	R
	URS	Moscow	250	Domestic/External	R
	URS	Jig	240	Domestic/External	R
	G	Daventry	100	BBC	R
	CYP/G	Limassol	100	BBC	R
	KEN	Langata	100		R
	URS	Kenga	100	Domestic/External	R
	IND	Hyderabad	100	AIR	R
	IND	Delhi	50	AIR	R
	J	Tokyo Yamata	300	R Japan	R
	CHN	Xian	150	Domestic/External	R
	INS	Amboina	100		R
	BEL	Wavre	100	RTBF	O
	I	Spoleto	0.05	R Italia Intl	O
7 145	POL	Warsaw	100	R Polonia	R
	BLR	Orcha	20	Domestic	R
	URS	Kazan	100	Domestic/External	R
	URS	Tula	20	Domestic	R
	D	Julich	100	DW	R
	D/USA	Holzkirchen	250	RFE/RL	R
	D/USA	Lampertheim	100	RFE/RL	R
	ROU	Bucharest	250	R Romania	R
	F	Allouis	500	RFI	R
	POR	Lisbon	250	RFE/RL	R
	ALG	Bouchaqui	100		R
	ARS	Riyadh	350	BSKSA	R
	MOZ	Queliman	0.3		R
	URS	Tashkent	100	Domestic/External	R
	IND	Delhi	50	AIR	R
	CHN	Beijing	509	Domestic/External	R
	LAO	Vientiane	250		R
	MLA	Stapok	10		R
	SNG/G	Kranji	100	BBC	R
	NIG	Ilorin	10	Kwara State BC	O
7 150	URS	Arm	500	Domestic/External	R
	D	Julich	100	DW	R

Frequency [kHz]	Country	Station Site	Power [kW]	Programme/ Network	O or R
7 150	D	Wertachtal	500	DW	O
(cont'd)	G	Skelton	250	BBC	R
	BUL	Sofia	500	R Sofia	R
	LBY	Tripoli	500	Tripoli	R
	ARS	Riyadh	350	BSKSA	R
	KEN	Langata	10		R
	MOZ	Pemba	0.3		R
	AFS	Umtata	50	Capital R	R
	URS	Alma Ata	500	Domestic/External	R
	URS	Kras	500	Domestic/External	R
	IND	Gauhati	50	AIR	R
	IND	Aligarh	250	AIR	R
	CHN	Linghi	50	Domestic/External	R
	ZAI	Bunia	10	R Candip	O
	CME	Douala	100	R Douala	O
7 152	AGL	Lobito	1	R Lobito	O
7 155	URS	Kazan	100	Domestic/External	R
	URS	Tbilisi	240	Domestic/External	R
	D/USA	Holzkirchen	250	VoA	R
	G	Daventry	300	RCI	R
	BUL	Sofia	250	R Sofia	R
	E	Playa de Pals	250	RFE/RL	R
	JOR	Al Karanah	500		R
	NGR	Niamey	20		R
	URS	Dushanbe	100	Domestic/External	R
	INS	Jayapyra	50		R
	ALB	Lushnja	100	R Tirana	O
7 160	URS	Kazan	240	Domestic/External	R
	URS	Tula	250	Domestic/External	R
	UKR	Kharkov	20	Dom	R
	YUG	Zagreb	10	R Yuogslavia	R
	F	Allouis	100/500	RFI	R
	MCO	Mt Carlo	100/500	TWR	R
	GRC	Kavalla	250	VoA	R
	OMA/G	Masirah	100	BBC	R
	GAB	Moyabi	250	Kalam al Haiyat/RFI	R
	URS	Omsk	100	Domestic/External	R
	URS	Sverdlovsk	240	Domestic/External	R
	IND	Madras	10	AIR	R
	IND	Aligarh	250	AIR	R
	URS	Petropavlokam	240	Domestic/External	R
	URS	Khabarovsk	100	Domestic/External	R
	CHN	Shijazhuang	500	External	R
	PHL	Palauig	250	R Veritas Asia	R

Frequency [kHz]	Country	Station Site	Power [kW]	Programme/ Network	O or R
7 160	MLA	Stapok	10		R
(cont'd)	SNG/G	Kranji	250	BBC	R
	NOR	Kvitsoy	500	R Norway/Danmarks R	O
7 165	URS	Serpukhov	250	Domestic/External	R
	D/USA	Lampertheim	100	RFE/RL	R
	D/USA	Biblis	100	RFE/RL	R
	UKR	Kiev	500	Ext	R
	YUG	Bijelina	500	R Yugoslavia	R
	POR	Lisbon	250	RFE/RL	R
	LBY	Tripoli	500	Tripoli	R
	ETH	Gedja	100		R
	TZA	Dar es Salaam	10		R
	NMB	Hoffnung	100	R Namibia	R
	NPL	Kathmandu	100	R Nepal	R
	URS	Irkutsk	100	Domestic/External	R
	CHN	Beijing	120	Domestic/External	R
	INS	Jambi	50		R
	SNG	Singapore	10	SBC	O
	CME	Bertoua	20	R Bertoua	O
7 170	URS	Moscow	240	Domestic/External	R
	URS/ CHN	Moscow	240	R Beijing	O
	D	K Wusterhausen	50	DW	R
	D/USA	Wertachtal	500	VoA	R
	G	Woofferton	300	VoA	R
	GRC	Kavalla	250	VoA	R
	SEN	Dakar	100		R
	URS	Novo	500	Domestic/External	R
	PAK	Quetta	10	R Pakistan	R
	IND	Delhi	10	AIR	R
	URS	Komsomolsk	100	Domestic/External	R
	CHN	Lhasa	50	Domestic	R
	CHN	Beijing	120	Domestic/External	R
	SNG	Singapore	10	SBC	R
	ALB	Kruja	50	R Tirana	O
	POR	Lisbon	250	VoA	O
	NCL	Sainte-Marie	20	RFO Noumea	O
7 175	URS	Leningrad	240	Domestic/External	R
	URS	Moscow	20	Domestic	R
	D	Wertachtal	500	DW	R
	G	Rampisham	500	BBC	R
	ROU	Bucharest	250	R Romania	R
	F	Allouis	500	RFI	R
	I	Caltanissetta	50	RAI R 2	R

Frequency [kHz]	Country	Station Site	Power [kW]	Programme/ Network	O or R
7 175	COG	Brazzaville	25	V Rev Congolaise	R
(cont'd)	ZWE	Gwelo	100		R
	URS	Dushanbe	500	Domestic/External	R
	URS	Novo	500	Domestic/External	R
	URS	Khabarovsk	120	Domestic/External	R
	CHN	Xian	150	Domestic	R
	INS	Dili	50		R
7 180	POL	Warsaw	60	R Polonia	R
	D/USA	Lampertheim	100	VoA	R
	D/USA	Holzkirchen	250	VoA	R
	D/USA	Biblis	100	VoA	R
	G	Woofferton	300	VoA	R
	TUR	Ankara	250	TRT	R
	CYP/G	Limassol	250	BBC/Cyprus BC	R
	IRQ	Abu Ghraib	250	R Baghdad	R
	ETH	Gedja	100		R
	URS	Tashkent	100	Domestic/External	R
	IND	Bhopal	10	AIR	R
	BGD	Dhaka	50	R Bangladesh	R
	CHN	Beijing	120	Domestic/External	R
	HKG/G	Tsang Tsui	250	BBC	R
	SNG/G	Kranji	250	BBC	R
	IND	Port Blair	10	AIR	O
7 185	BLR	Minsk	20	Domestic	R
	URS	Volgograd	20	Domestic	R
	URS	Moscow	250	Domestic/External	R
	D	Nauen	500	DW	R
	D	K Wusterhausen	50	DW	R
	UKR	Vinnitsa	240	Domestic/External	R
	URS	Sverdlovsk	20	Domestic	R
	URS	Petropavlokam	100	Domestic/External	R
	URS	Blag	500	Domestic/External	R
	CHN	Baoding	120	Domestic/External	R
	INS	Tanjungkaran	50		R
7 190	URS	Armavir	100	Domestic/External	R
	D/USA	Biblis	100	RFE/RL	R
	POR	Lisbon	250	RFE/RL	R
	MRC	Tangier	50	VoA	R
	BEN	Parakou	20		R
	NMB	Hoffnung	100	R Namibia	R
	CLN	Ekala	10	SLBC	R
	CHN	Kunming	50	Domestic/External	R
	ALB	Kruja	50	R Tirana	O
	IRN	Kamalabad	500	VoIRI	O

Frequency [kHz]	Country	Station Site	Power [kW]	Programme/ Network	O or R
7 190	YMS	Al-Hiswah	100	R Aden	O
(cont'd)	INS	Yogyakarta	50	RRI	O
7 195	URS	Tula	100	Domestic/External	R
	UKR	Simferopol	500	Domestic/External	R
	ROU	Bucharest	250	R Romania	R
	MCO	Monte Carlo	100/500	TWR	R
	LBR	Careysburg	50	VoA	R
	URS	Novo	100	Domestic/External	R
	IND	Delhi	100	AIR	R
	BGD	Dhaka	250/50	R Bangladesh	R
	URS	Komsomolsk	100	Domestic/External	R
	CHN	Urumqui	15	Domestic	R
	INS	Semarang	50		R
	F	Allouis	100	RFI	O
	UGA	Kampala	20	R Uganda	O
7 200	BLR	Minsk	20	Domestic	R
	URS	Jigulevsk	20	Domestic	R
	URS	Yerevan	100	Domestic/External	R
	URS	Moscow	240	Domestic/External	R
	URS	Moscow	100	R Afghanistan	O
	D/USA	Holzkirchen	250	RFE/RL	R
	G	Woofferton	250	VoA	R
	UKR	Ivan	20	Domestic	R
	YUG	Belgrade	100	R Belgrade P1	R
	POR	Lisbon	250	RFE/RL	R
	SWZ	Manzini	25	TWR	R
	AFG	Kabul	50	R Kabul 1	R
	URS	Irkutsk	100	Domestic/External	R
	KRE	Pyongyang	200	R Pyongyang	R
	PHL	Poro	100	VoA	R
7 203	SOM	Mogadishu	50	R Somalia	O
7 205	POL	Warsaw	1	R Polonia	R
	URS	Armavir	500	Domestic/External	R
	URS	Moscow	100	Domestic/External	R
	UKR	Kiev	100	Domestic/External	R
	GRC	Kavalla	250	VoA	R
	GRC	Rhodes	50	VoA	R
	ZAI	Lubumbashi	10		R
	URS	Vladivostock	240	Domestic/External	R
	CHN	Xian	150	Domestic/External	R
	INS	Medan	50		R
	AUS	Carnarvon	300	R Australia	R
	IND	Madras	100	AIR	O

Frequency [kHz]	Country	Station Site	Power [kW]	Programme/ Network	O or R
7 205	ALB	Lushnja	100	R Tirana	O
(cont'd)	CME	Yaounde	30	Cameroun RTV	O
7 210	NOR	Kvitsoy	500	R Norway/Danmarks R	R
	NOR	Sveio	500	R Norway/Danmarks R	R
	BLR	Minsk	20	Domestic	R
	URS	Kazan	240	Domestic/External	R
	URS	Moscow	240	Domestic/External	R
	G	Rampisham	500	BBC	R
	G	Daventry	300	BBC	R
	G	Woofferton	250	VoA	R
	SUI	Beromunster	250	SRI/RCBS	R
	ARS	Riyadh	350	BSKSA	R
	KEN	Langata	100		R
	IND	Delhi	100	AIR	R
	IND	Calcutta	10	AIR	R
	URS	Khabarovsk	100	Domestic/External	R
	J	Tokyo Yamata	100	R Japan	R
	CHN	Kunming	15	Domestic	R
	SEN	Dakar	4	R Senegal	O
7 211	INS	Biak	1	RRI	O
7 215	URS	Tula	100	Domestic/External	R
	URS	Moscow	200	R Havana Cuba	R
	URS	Moscow	100	R Afghanistan	O
	UKR	Vinnitsa	240	Domestic/External	R
	YUG	Bijeljina	500/250	R Yugoslavia	R
	UAE	Abu Dhabi	500	UAE R	R
	CTI	Abidjan	20		R
	SEY	Mahe	100	FEBA	R
	IRN	Kamalabad	100/500	VoIRI	R
	CHN	Nanjing	50	Vo Jinling	R
	CHN	Baoji	50	Domestic	R
	INS	Mataram	50		R
	AUS	Shepparton	100	R Australia	R
	ALB	Lushnja	100	R Tirana	O
	AGL	Luanda	10	R N Angola	O
7 220	D/USA	Lampertheim	100	RFE/RL	R
	D/USA	Holzkirchen	250	RFE/RL	R
	YUG	Bijeljina	500	R Yugoslavia	R
	HNG	Jazbereny	20/250	R Budapest	R
	HNG	Szekesfehervar	20	R Budapest	R
	E	Playa de Pals	500	RFE/RL	R
	ARS	Diriyya	50	BSKSA	R
	ZMB	Lusaka	50		R
	URS	Sverdlovsk	100	Domestic/External	R

Frequency [kHz]	Country	Station Site	Power [kW]	Programme/ Network	O or R
7 220	URS	Tchita	500	Domestic/External	R
(cont'd)	KOR	Kimjae	250	R Korea	R
	CHN	Lingshi	50	Domestic	R
	CAF	Bangui	100	R Centralafricaine	O
7 225	URS	Tula	240	Domestic/External	R
	ROU	Bucharest	250	R Romania	R
	MLT	Cyclops	250	DW	R
	TUN	Sfax	100		R
	RRW	Kigali	250	DW	R
	IRN	Mashhad	500	VoIRI	R
	IND	Aligarh	250	AIR	R
	CLN	Perkara	250	SLBC	R
	CHN	Chengdu	15	Domestic	R
	PHL	Tinang	250	VoA	R
	INS	Bukittinggi	50		R
	INS	Padang Cermin	250		R
	CLN	Trincomalee	250	DW	O
7 230	URS	Armavir	100	Domestic	R
	G	Rampisham	500	BBC	R
	G	Skelton	250	BBC	R
	G	Daventry	300	RCI	R
	CYP/G	Limassol	250	BBC	R
	BFA	Ouagadougou	50		R
	AFS	Meyerton	250/500	R RSA	R
	URS	Krasnioarsk	100	Domestic/External	R
	IRN	Kamalabad	100	VoIRI	R
	IND	Kurseong	20		R
	URS	Vladivostock	200	Domestic/External	R
	KRE	Pyongyang	200	R Pyongyang	R
	KOR	Kimjae	250	R Korea	R
	I	Forli	10	AWR	O
7 235	URS	Jigulevsk	250	Domestic/External	R
	URS	Riga	100	Domestic/External	R
	D	Julich	100	DW	R
	D	Wertachtal	500	DW	R
	G	Daventry	300	RCI	R
	UKR	Ivan	20	Domestic	R
	F	Allouis	500	RFI	R
	I	Rome	100	RAI	R
	OMA/G	Masirah	100	BBC	R
	CYP/G	Limassol	250	BBC	R
	MLT	Cyclops	250	DW	R
	ETH	Gedja	100		R
	ZMB	Lusaka	50		R

Frequency [kHz]	Country	Station Site	Power [kW]	Programme/ Network	O or R
7 235	URS	Tashkent	20	Domestic	R
(cont'd)	URS	Kenga	500	Domestic/External	R
	MNG	Ulan Bator	50/100		R
	CHN	Kunming	50	Domestic	R
	INS	Fakfak	25		R
	URS	Moscow	100	R Afghanistan	O
	URS	Alma Ata	20	Dom	O
7 240	URS	Petozavodsk	20	Domestic	R
	URS	Tula	240	Domestic/External	R
	YUG	Bijeljina	250	R Yugoslavia	R
	MOZ	Maputo	100		R
	URS	Sverdlovsk	150	Domestic/External	R
	IND	Bombay	10	AIR	R
	NPL	Kathmandu	100	R Nepal	R
	KOR	Kimjae	250	R Korea	R
	PHL	Palauig	250	R Veritas Asia	R
	AUS	Carnarvon	100/250	R Australia	R
	CME	Garoua	100	R Garoua	O
7 245	D/USA	Lampertheim	100	RFE/RL	R
	D/USA	Wertachtal	500	VoA	R
	UKR	Kharkov	20	Domestic	R
	UKR	Simferopol	100	Domestic/External	R
	POR	Lisbon	250	RFE/RL	R
	ALG	Auled Fayet	50		R
	LBY	Tripoli	500	Tripoli	R
	MTN	Nouakchott	100	ORTV de Mauritanie	R
	AGL	Luanda	100	RN Angola	R
	URS	Tashkent	100	Domestic/External	R
	URS	Khabarovsk	240	Domestic/External	R
	URS	Irkutsk	500	Domestic/External	R
	CHN	Xian	150	Domestic/External	R
	INS	Bandung	50		R
	URS	Dushanbe	50	Domestic	O
7 250	URS	Serpukhov	100	Domestic/External	R
	URS	Tbilisi	100	Domestic/External	R
	URS	Kazan	100	Domestic/External	R
	YUG	Bijeljina	250/500	R Yugoslavia	R
	CVA	S M Galeria	100	Vatican R	R
	ARS	Jeddah	50		R
	ZMB	Lusaka	120		R
	URS	Kras	100	Domestic/External	R
	IND	Lucknow	10	AIR	R
	KOR	Kimjae	250	R Korea	R
	CHN	Kunming	120	Domestic/External	R

Frequency [kHz]	Country	Station Site	Power [kW]	Programme/ Network	O or R
7 250	CHN	Beijing	120	Domestic/External	R
(cont'd)	SNG	Singapore	50	SBC	R
	INS	Ujungpandang	300		R
7 255	S	Hoerby	350	R Sweden	R
	BLR	Minsk	150	Domestic/External	R
	D/USA	Biblis	100	RFE/RL	R
	D/USA	Lampetheim	100	RFE/RL	R
	D/USA	Holzkirchen	250	RFE/RL	R
	BUL	Sofia	150	R Sofia	R
	NIG	Ikorodu	500	Vo Nigeria	R
	BOT	Sebele	50	R Botswana	R
	ZAI	Kinshasa	10		R
	MOZ	Nampula	0.3		R
	URS	Alma Ata	240	Domestic/External	R
	IND	Aligarh	250	AIR	R
	URS	Irkutsk	240	Domestic/External	R
	KOR	Kimjae	100	R Korea	R
	CHN	Beijing	500	External	R
	D	Nauen	500	DLF/DW	O
7 260	BLR	Orcha	20	Domestic	R
	URS	Jigulevsk	100	Domestic/External	R
	D	Nauen	500	DW	R
	G	Daventry	300	RCI	R
	G	Rampisham	500	BBC	R
	URS	Alma Ata	100	Domestic/External	R
	URS	Sverdlovsk	240	Domestic/External	R
	IRN	Mashhad	500	VoIRI	R
	IND	Bombay	100	AIR	R
	IND	Kohima	2	AIR	R
	URS	Iujnsakhalinsk	100	Domestic/External	R
	URS	Petropavlokam	100	Domestic/External	R
	MNG	Ulan Bator	25	R Ulan Bator	R
	CHN	Baoding	120	Domestic/External	R
	VUT	Port Vila	10	R Vanuatu	R
	COM	Moroni	4	R Comoro	O
7 265	S	Hoerby	350	R Sweden	R
	BLR	Orcha	20	Domestic	R
	BLR	Orcha	240	Domestic/External	R
	URS	Volgograd	20	Domestic	R
	URS	Leningrad	20	Domestic	R
	D	Rohrdorf	20	SWF	R
	MLT	Cyclops	250	DW	R
	LBR	Careysburg	250	VoA	R
	PAK	Islamabad	100	R Pakistan	R

Frequency [kHz]	Country	Station Site	Power [kW]	Programme/ Network	O or R
7 265	IND	Aligarh	250	AIR	R
(cont'd)	URS	Iakutsk	100	Domestic/External	R
	URS	Tchita	250	Domestic/External	R
	KOR	Kimjae	250	RCI	R
	CHN	Beijing	120	Domestic/External	R
	INS	Surabaja	50		R
	PAK	Rawalpindi	100	Azad Kashmir Radio	O
	TGO	Lome	100	RTV Togolaise	O
7 270	POL	Warsaw	100	R Polonia	R
	D/USA	Wertachtal	500	VoA	R
	GRC	Kavalla	250	VoA	R
	POR	Sines	250	VoA	R
	MLT	Cyclops	250	DW	R
	SEN	Dakar	100		R
	KEN	Koma Rock	250		R
	AFS	Meyerton	250	R RSA	R
	URS	Kenga	100	Domestic/External	R
	URS	Petropavlokam	250	Domestic/External	R
	KRE	Pyongyang	200	R Pyongyang	R
	DHN	Huhhot	50	Domestic/External	R
	MLA	Stapok	10		R
	INS	Jakarta	50	RRI	O
	GAB	Libreville	100	RTV Gabonaise	O
7 275	URS	Serpukhov	240	Domestic/External	R
	I	Rome	100	RAI	R
	E	Arganda	100	REE	R
	POR	Lisbon	250	RFE/RL	R
	ARS	Riyadh	350	BSKSA	R
	URS	Dushanbe	50	Domestic/External	R
	KOR	Kimjae	250	R Korea	R
	CHN	Guiyang	7.5	CPBS	R
	SNG/G	Kranji	100	BBC	R
	INS	Biak	300		R
	URS	Tashkent	100	Domestic/External	O
7 280	BLR	Minsk	20	Domestic	R
	URS	Moscow	250	Domestic/External	R
	URS	Jigulevsk	240	Domestic/External	R
	F	Allouis	100/500	RFI	R
	GRC	Kavalla	250	VoA	R
	E	Noblejas	350	RFE/RL	R
	ARS	Jeddah	50	BSKSA	R
	LBR	Careysburg	250	VoA	R
	TZA	Dar es Salaam	30		R
	URS	Kenga	50	Domestic/External	R

Frequency [kHz]	Country	Station Site	Power [kW]	Programme/ Network	O or R
7 280	IND	Gauhati	50	AIR	R
(cont'd)	IND	Delhi	100	AIR	R
	IND	Aligarh	250	AIR	R
	URS	Komsomolsk	240	Domestic/External	R
	KOR	Kimjae	250	R Korea	R
	CHN	Fuzhou FJ	50	Vo Strait	R
	CHN	Beijing	500	Ext	R
	PHL	Palauig	250	VoA	R
7 285	POL	Warsaw	100	R Polonia	R
	URS	Leningrad	240	Domestic/External	R
	D	Wertachtal	500	DW	R
	G	Rampisham	500	BBC	R
	POR	Sines	250	DW/RCI	R
	MLI	Bamako	100	RTV Malienne	R
	ETH	Gedja	100		R
	ZWE	Gwelo	20	Vo Zimbabwe	R
	AFS	Meyerton	100	R Oranje	R
	SWZ	Manzini	25	TWR	R
	URS	Tashkent	100	Domestic/External	R
	URS	Tchita	100	Domestic/External	R
	CHN	Lanzhou	15	Domestic	R
	CHN	Xian	150	Domestic/External	R
	PHL	Poro	100	VoA	R
	INS	Fakfak	0.5		R
	TWN	Kaohsiung	10	Vo Asia	O
	IRN	Kamalabad	500	VoIRI	O
	NIG	Lagos	50	R Nigeria	O
7 290	MCO	Mt Carlo	100	TWR	R
	I	Rome	100	RAI	R
	ARS	Jeddah	50	BSKSA	R
	KEN	Langata	10		R
	URS	Kenga	100	Domestic/External	R
	URS	Alma Ata	500	Domestic/External	R
	PAK	Islamabad	100/250	R Pakistan	R
	URS	Vladivostock	240	Domestic/External	R
	KRE	Pyongyang	200	R Pyongyang	R
	CHN	Kunming	50	Domestic/External	R
	IRQ	Salah-el-Deen	500	R Baghdad	O
	F	Allouis	100	RFI	O
	HKG	Hong Kong	30	RTV Hong Kong	O
	S	Horby	350	R Sweden	O
7 294	I	Milan	0.2	R Europe	O
7 295	URS	Moscow	240	Domestic/External	R
	URS	Kazan	100	Domestic/External	R

Frequency [kHz]	Country	Station Site	Power [kW]	Programme/ Network	O or R
7 295	D	Nauen	100	DW	R
(cont'd)	D/USA	Holzkirchen	250	RFE/RL	R
	D/USA	Biblis	100	RFE/RL	R
	D/USA	Lampertheim	100	RFE/RL	R
	G	Woofferton	300	VoA	R
	G	Daventry	300	RCI	R
	GRC	Kavalla	250	VoA	R
	GHA	Accra	50	R Ghana 2	R
	ZAI	Mbujimay	10		R
	IRN	Zahedan	500	VoIRI	R
	IND	Aizawl	10	AIR	R
	CHN	Baoding	120	Domestic/External	R
	CHN	Xian	150	Domestic/External	R
	INS	Manado	50		R
	TWN	Taipei	250	CBC Taipei	O
	MLA	Kuala Lumpur	100	RTM Kuala Lumpur	O
7 300	URS	Minsk	100	R Moscow	O
	URS	Moscow	100	Domestic/External	O
	ALB	Lushnja	100	R Tirana	O
	CHN	Kunming	50	Vietnam Resistance R	O
7 305	URS	Armavir	100	Domestic/External	O
	URS	Irkutsk	100	Domestic/External	O
7 310	ALB	Lushnja	100	R Tirana	O
7 315	URS	Irkutsk	500	Domestic/External	O
	MCO	Monte Carlo	100	TWR	O
	USA	Noblesville	100	WHRI	O
	MNG	Ulan Bator	25	R Ulan Bator	O
7 320	URS	Armavir	240	Domestic/External	O
7 325	G	Daventry	300	BBC	O
	G	Rampisham	500	BBC	O
	URS	Moscow	100	Domestic/External	O
	G	Woofferton	300	VoA	O
	PAK	Islamabad	100	R Pakistan	O
7 330	URS	Moscow	500	Domestic/External	O
	URS	Khabarovsk	100	Domestic/External	O
7 335	CHN	Xian	150	R Beijing	O
	URS	Vladivostock	100	Domestic/External	O
	MCO	Monte Carlo	500	TWR	O
	CHN	Shijiazhuang	50	R Beijing	O
	CAN	Ottawa	10	CHU	O
7 340	URS	Kazan	100	Domestic/External	O
	URS	Armavir	100	Domestic/External	O

Frequency [kHz]	Country	Station Site	Power [kW]	Programme/ Network	O or R
7 340	GTM	Guatemala City	50	Voz del C.I.D.	O
(cont'd)	IND	Madras	100	AIR	O
7 345	TCH	Litomysl	200	R Prague	O
	TCH	Rimavska Sobota	250	R Prague	O
	URS	Petropavlokam	100	Domestic/External	O
7 350	URS	Kazan	100	Domestic/External	O
	CHN	Kunming	50	Domestic/External	O
7 355	MCO	Monte Carlo	100	TWR	O
	URS	Novosibirsk	500	Domestic/External	O
	USA	New Orleans	100	WRNO	O
	USA	Noblesville	100	WHRI	O
	ALS	Anchor Point	100	KNLS	O
	USA	Okeechobee	100	WYFR	O
7 360	URS	Armavir	500	Domestic/External	O
	CHN	Kunming	50	R Beijing	O
7 365	CVA	S M Galeria	100	Vatican R	O
	ALS	Anchor Point	100	KNLS	O
7 370	URS	Moscow	100/240	Domestic/External	O
	TUR	Ankara	1	Turkish Police R	O
7 375	CHN	Beijing	500	R Beijing	O
7 380	URS	Irkutsk	500	Domestic/External	O
	UKR	Simferopol	240	Domestic/External	O
7 383	LAO	Savannakhet	1	R Savannakhet	O
7 385	MCO	Monte Carlo	500	TWR	O
	CHN	Kunming	120	R Beijing	O
7 390	URS	Moscow	240	Domestic/External	O
	URS	Yerevan	100	Domestic/External	O
7 395	MCO	Monte Carlo	100	TWR	O
	USA	Cypress Creek	500	Christian Science Mon	O
7 400	UKR	Simferopol	500	R Moscow	O
7 405	CHN	Jinhua	500	R Beijing	O
7 410	ISR	Jerusalem	300	Kol Israel	O
7 412	IND	Aligarh	250	AIR	O
	IND	Delhi	100	AIR	O
7 416	VTN	Hanoi	15	Vo Vietnam	O
7 420	URS	Kazan	100	Domestic/External	O
	URS	Minsk	100	Domestic/External	O

Frequency [kHz]	Country	Station Site	Power [kW]	Programme/ Network	O or R
7 420	CHN	Xian	150	Domestic/External	O
(cont'd)	URS	Noginsk	15	Tass	O
7 430	GRC	Athens	100	ERT	O
7 435	CHN	Beijing	150	R Beijing	O
7 440	URS	Moscow	240	Domestic/External	O
	CHN	Lingshi	50	CPBS	O
7 445	TWN	Panchiau	50	VoFC/Vo Asia	O
7 450	E	Arganda	300	REE	O
	URS	Moscow	20	Domestic	O
7 465	ISR	Jerusalem	300	Kol Israel	O
7 470	CHN	Baoding	120	Domestic/External	O
7 475	TUN	Sfax	100		O
7 480	CHN/ SUI	Beijing	120	SRI	O
	CHN	Xian	150	R Beijing	O
7 505	CHN	Xian	150	CPBS	O
7 516	CHN	Lingshi	50	CPBS	O
7 520	USA	Nashville	100	WWCR	O
7 525	CHN	Beijing	50	CPBS	O
7 538	I	Pordenone	0.6	Vo Europe	O
7 550	KOR	Kimje	100/250	R Hanguk/R Korea	O
7 580	KRE	Pyongyang	100	R Pyongyang	O
7 590	CHN	Kunming	50	R Beijing	O
7 600	EQA	Guayaquil	1	Iodela	O
7 620	CHN	Beijing	50	CPBS	O
7 645	URS			Domestic/External [feeder]	O
7 648.5	USA	Greenville	40	VoA [feeder]	O
7 660	CHN	Xian	150	Domestic/External	O
7 670	BUL	Stolnik	15	R Sofia	O
7 700	CHN	Xian	150	R Beijing	O
7 770	CHN	Beijing	50	CPBS2	O

Frequency [kHz]	Country	Station Site	Power [kW]	Programme/ Network	O or R
7 780	CHN	Beijing	500	Domestic/External	O
7 800	CHN	Baoding	120	R Beijing	O
7 820	CHN	Xian	150	Domestic/External	O
7 935	CHN	Lingshi	50	CPBS	O
7 992	ISL	Reykjavik	10	IBS	O
8 000	J	Tokyo Nazaki	2	JJY	O
8 007	CHN	Baoji	50	CPBS 2	O
8 345	CHN	Beijing	15	R Dem Cambodia	O
8 425	CHN	Beijing	15	R Beijing	O
8 461	AFS	Milnerton	10	ZSC Cape Town	O
8 473	CLN	Ekala	1	Colombo R	O
8 490	CHN	Beijing	15	Domestic/External	O
8 492	B	Rio de Janeiro	1	PPR	O
8 539	HKG	Kowloon	1	VPS Hong Kong	O
8 542	INS	Jakarta	1	PKI	O
8 566	CHN	Beijing	15	CPBS	O
8 634	B	Rio de Janeiro	1	PPR	O
8 650	PRU	Callao	1	OBC Peru	O
8 660	CHN	Beijing	15	R Beijing	O
8 721	B	Rio de Janeiro	1	PPR	O
8 828	HKG	Kowloon	1	VPA	O
9 022	IRN	Kamalabad	500	VoIRI	O
9 030	CHN	Beijing	50	CPBS	O
9 045	EGY	Abis	250	Kaviyani Banner	O
9 064	CHN	Lingshi	50	CPBS1	O
9 080	CHN	Beijing	50	CPBS2	O
9 090	URS	Alma Ata	15	Kazakh Telegraph	0
9 105	URS			Domestic/External [feeder]	O
9 115	ARG	Buenos Aires	0.5	R Continental [feeder]	O

Frequency [kHz]	Country	Station Site	Power [kW]	Programme/ Network	O or R
9 145	URS			R Moscow [feeder]	O
9 150	URS			R Moscow [feeder]	O
9 170	CHN	Beijing	50	Domestic/External	O
9 180	URS			Domestic/External [feeder]	O
9 210	URS			Domestic/External [feeder]	O
9 220	KRE	Pyongyang	200	R Pyongyang	O
9 240	URS			Domestic/External [feeder]	O
9 250	URS			Domestic/External [feeder]	O O
9 272	ISL	Reykjavik	20	IBS	O
9 280	TWN	Taipei	100	WYFR	O
9 320	URS			Domestic/External [feeder]	O
9 325	KRE	Pyongyang	400	R Pyongyang	O
9 345	KRE	Pyongyang	400	R Pyongyang	O
	EQA	Quito	500	HCJB	O
9 360	E	Noblejas	350	REE	O
9 365	FNL	Pori	500	R Finland	O
	CHN	Kunming	120	R Beijing	O
9 375	ALB	Kruja	50	R Tirana	O
9 380	CHN	Beijing	50	CPBS	O
9 385	ISR	Jerusalem	50/300	Kol Israel	O
9 390	CHN	Beijing	50	Domestic/External	O
9 395	GRC	Athens	100	ERT	O
9 400	CHN	Beijing	50	Domestic/External	O
9 410	G	Daventry	100/300	BBC	O
	G	Rampisham	500	BBC	O
	G	Skelton	250	BBC	O
9 420	GRC	Athens	100	ERT	O
9 425	GRC	Athens	100	ERT	O
	GRC	Kavala	250	R Macedonias	O

Frequency [kHz]	Country	Station Site	Power [kW]	Programme/ Network	O or R
9 430	ALB	Lushnja	100	R Tirana	O
9 435	ISR	Jerusalem	300	Kol Israel	O
9 440	CHN	Baoding	120	R Beijing	O
	CHN	Kunming	50	Vo Dem Cambodia	O
9 445	TUR	Ankara	500	TRT	O
9 450	URS	Moscow	100	Domestic/External	O
	URS	Novosibirsk	100	Domestic/External	O
9 455	USA	Greenville	500	VoA	O
	USA	Cypress Creek	500	Christian Science Mon	O
	USA	Okeechobee	100	WYFR	O
	CHN	Nanchang	50	Domestic/External	O
9 457	CHN	Xian	150	R Beijing	O
9 460	PAK	Islamabad	100	R Pakistan	O
	TUR	Ankara	500	TRT	O
9 465	USA	Delano	250	VoA	O
	USA			WCSN	O
	USA	Noblesville	100	WHRI	O
	USA	Bethel	50	WMLK	O
		Saipan	100	KFBS	O
	USA	Cypress Creek	500	Christian Science Mon	O
9 470	URS	Moscow	100/250	Domestic/External	O
9 475	EGY	Abis	250	R Cairo	O
9 480	URS	Novosibirsk	100	Domestic/External	O
	ALB	Lushnja	100	R Tirana	O
	MCO	Monte Carlo	100	TWR	O
	CHN	Baoding	120	Domestic/External	O
	CHN	Beijing	120	Domestic/External	O
9 485	MCO	Monte Carlo	100	TWR	O
	PRU	Tacna	0.5	R Tacna	O
9 490	URS	Moscow	100/500	Domestic/External	O
	MCO	Monte Carlo	100	TWR	O
	CHN	Lhasa	50	Domestic/External	O
9 495	MCO	Monte Carlo	100/500	TWR	O
	PAK	Islamabad	100	R Pakistan	O
	USA	Noblesville	100	WHRI	O
	USA	Cypress Creek	500	Christian Science Mon	O
	MRA	Marpi	100	KFBS	O
	PHL	Iba	100	FEBC	O
	GUM	Agat	100	AWR/KSDA	O

Frequency [kHz]	Country	Station Site	Power [kW]	Programme/ Network	O or R
9 500	ALB	Lushnja	100	R Tirana	O
9 505	URS	Tula	240	Domestic/External	R
	D/USA	Biblis	100	RFE/RL	R
	D/USA	Holzkirchen	250	RFE/RL	R
	TCH	Velkekostolany	120	R Prague	R
	YUG	Belgrade	100	R Yugoslavia	R
	GRC	Kavalla	250	VoA	R
	GRC	Thessaloniki	35	Voice of Greece	R
	E	Playa de Pals	250	RFE/RL	R
	POR	Lisbon	250	RFE/RL	R
	ZMB	Lusaka	50		R
	USA	Okeechobee	100	WYFR	R
	CUB	Havana	50	R Havana Cuba	R
	PRU	Tacna	1		R
	BOL	La Paz	100		R
	B	Sao Paulo	7.5	R Record	R
	URS	Alma Ata	100	Domestic	R
	URS	Komsomolsk	120	Domestic/External	R
	J	Tokyo Yamata	300	R Japan	R
	KRE	Pyongyang	200/400	R Pyongyang	R
	CHN	Fuzhou FJ	50	Vo the Strait	R
	CHN	Jinhua	500	R Beijing	R
	INS	Medan	100		R
	AUS	Darwin	250	R Australia	R
	UAE	Abu Dhabi	500	UAE R	O
9 510	POL	Warsaw	100	R Polonia	R
	BLR	Orcha	150	Domestic/External	R
	URS	Armavir	100	Domestic/External	R
	G	Rampisham	500	BBC	R
	ROU	Bucharest	250	R Romania	R
	ALG	Ouled Fayet	50		R
	PRU	Lima	5	R America	R
	CHL	Santiago	100		R
	URS	Tashkent	100	Domestic/External	R
	IND	Madras	100	AIR	R
	URS	Vladivostock	120	Domestic/External	R
	KRE	Pyongyang	200	R Pyongyang	R
	KOR	Kimjae	250	R Korea	R
	CHN	Beijing	50	Domestic/External	R
	PHL	Tinang	250	VoA	O
	NCL	Sainte Marie	4	RFO Noumea	O
9 515	URS	Moscow	250	Domestic/External	R
	GRC	Athens	100	Voice of Greece	R
	I	Caltanissetta	50	RAI	R
	MLT	Cyclops	250	DW	R

Frequency [kHz]	Country	Station Site	Power [kW]	Programme/ Network	O or R
9 515	UGA	Kampala	250		R
(cont'd)	ASC	Ascension	250	BBC	R
	SWZ	Manzini	25	TWR	R
	CAN	Sackville	250	BBC	R
	USA	Delano	250	BBC	R
	MEX	Mexico	20	R XEW 900	R
	ATN	Bonaire	100	TWR	R
	B	Curitiba	10	R Novas de Paz	R
	URG	Montevideo	10		R
	PAK	Islamabad	100	R Pakistan	R
	KOR	Kimjae	100	R Korea	R
	CHN	Beijing	50	Domestic/External	R
	PHL	Poro	50	FEBA	R
	INS	Kupang	50		R
	IRQ	Salah-el-Deen	500	R Baghdad	O
	ATG	Antigua	250	BBC	O
9 520	URS	Armavir	240	Domestic/External	R
	D/USA	Lampertheim	100	RFE/RL	R
	HNG	Diosd	100	R Budapest	R
	HNG	Jaszbereny	250	R Budapest	R
	BUL	Sofia	250	R Sofia/R Moscow	R
	E	Playa de Pals	500	RFE/RL	R
	CUB	Havana	50	R Havana Cuba	R
	SLV	San Salvador	50		R
	PRU	Lima	5	R La Cronica	R
	IRN	Kamalabad	500	VoIRI	R
	PAK	Islamabad	100	R Pakistan	R
	IND	Aligarh	250	AIR	R
	J	Tokyo Yamata	300	R Japan	R
	CHN	Huhhot	50	Domestic/External	R
	PHL	Palauig	100	R Veritas Asia	R
	ALB	Lushnja	100	R Tirana	O
	PNG	Port Moresby	10	R Central	O
9 525	POL	Warsaw	100	R Polonia	R
	URS	Serpukhov	100	Domestic/External	R
	D/USA	Wertachtal	500	RFE/RL	R
	IRQ	Babel	500	R Baghdad	R
	LBR	Careysburg	250	VoA	R
	MOZ	Maputo	25	R Mozambique	R
	USA	Bethany	250	VoA	R
	USA	Greenville	250	VoA	R
	CUB	Havana	500	R Havana Cuba	R
	IRN	Kamalabad	500	VoIRI	R
	KRE	Pyongyang	200	R Pyongyang	R
	PHL	Palauig	250	R Veritas Asia	R

Frequency [kHz]	Country	Station Site	Power [kW]	Programme/ Network	O or R
9 525	PHL	Poro	100	VoA	R
(cont'd)	INS	Jakarta	100		R
	CHN	Xian	150	R Beijing	O
9 530	ISL	Reykjavik	10	IBS	R
	URS	Moscow	100/500	Domestic/External	R
	D/USA	Wertachtal	500	VoA	R
	G	Woofferton	300	VoA	R
	G	Rampisham	500	BBC	R
	UKR	Starobelsk	100	Domestic/External	R
	ROU	Bucharest	250	R Bucharest	R
	GRC	Kavalla	250	VoA	R
	E	Noblejas	350	REE	R
	MRC	Tangier	100	VoA	R
	JOR	Al Karanah	500	R Jordan	R
	USA	Greenville	500	VoA	R
	PRU	Tacna	5		R
	URS	Sverdlovsk	100	Domestic/External	R
	URS	Okhotsk	100	Domestic/External	R
	IND	Calcutta	10	AIR	R
	URS	Vladivostock	100	Domestic/External	R
	CHN	Xian	150	Domestic/External	R
	MRA	Agingan Point	100	Christian Science Mon	R
	SNG	Singapore	50	SBC	R
9 535	SUI	Lenk	250	SRI	R
	F	Allouis	100/500	RFI	R
	ALG	Bouchaqui	100	R Algiers	R
	AGL	Luanda	100	R N Angola	R
	CAN	Sackville	250	RCI	R
	CUB	Havana	75	R Havana Cuba	R
	ATN	Bonaire	50	TWR	R
	GUF	Montsinery	500	RFI	R
	URS	Dushanbe	100	Domestic/External	R
	IND	Madras	100	AIR	R
	IND	Aligarh	250	AIR	R
	CLN	Trincomalee	250	DW	R
	J	Tokyo Yamata	300	R Japan	R
	J	Harita	0.6	NHK Matsuyama	O
	J	Osaka	0.3	NHK Osaka	O
	CHN	Xian	150	Domestic/External	R
	INS	Biak	50		R
	GRC	Kavalla	250	VoA	O
9 538	J	Fukuoka	0.6	NHK Fukuoka	O
9 540	POL	Warsaw	100	R Polonia	R
	URS	Moscow	100	Domestic/External	R

Frequency [kHz]	Country	Station Site	Power [kW]	Programme/ Network	O or R
9 540	D/USA	Lampertheim	100	RFE/RL	R
(cont'd)	UKR	Ivan	240	Domestic/External	R
	TCH	Velkekostolany	120	R Prague	R
	LBR	Careysburg	250	VoA	R
	B	Salvador	10	R Educacion da Bahia	R
	URS	Tashkent	100	Domestic/External	R
	NPL	Kathmandu	100	R Nepal	R
	URS	Petropavlokam	250	Domestic/External	R
	J	Tokyo Yamata	300	R Japan	R
	KRE	Pyongyang	200	R Pyongyang	R
	CHN	Beijing	50	Domestic	R
	SDN	Omdurman	50	R Omdurman	O
	VEN	Caracas	50	R N Venezuela	O
9 545	D	Wertachtal	500	DW	R
	D	Julich	100	DW	R
	MLT	Cyclops	250	DW	R
	IRQ	Babel	500	R Baghdad	R
	GHA	Tema	100		R
	CAN	Sackville	250	DW	R
	MEX	Veracruz	0.5		R
	HTI	Pt au Prince	100		R
	PAK	Islamabad	10	R Pakistan	R
	IND	Delhi	100	AIR	R
	URS	Khabarovsk	50	Domestic	R
	CHN	Xining	50	Domestic	R
	CHN	Beijing	50	Domestic	R
	PHL	Tinang	250	VoA	R
	INS	Palangkaraya	25		R
	B/D	Brasilia	250	DW	O
	J	Tokyo Yamata	300	R Japan	O
	SLM	Honiara	10	Solomon Isles BC	O
9 550	FNL	Pori	500	YLE	R
	URS	Volgograd	20	Domestic	R
	URS	Jigulevsk	250	Domestic/External	R
	URS	Moscow	240	Domestic/External	R
	ROU	Bucharest	250	R Romania	R
	F	Allouis	100/500	RFI	R
	MCO	Mt Carlo	100	TWR	R
	GRC	Thessaloniki	35	Voice of Greece	R
	LBR	Monrovia	50	ELWA	R
	TZA	Dar es Salaam	50		R
	CUB	Havana	100/250/ 500	R Havana Cuba	R
	B	Pt Alegre	5	R Nuevo Esperanza	R
	CHL	Santiago	100	R Nacional Chile	R

Frequency [kHz]	Country	Station Site	Power [kW]	Programme/ Network	O or R
9 550	URS	Tashkent	20	Domestic	R
(cont'd)	URS	Tashkent	100	Domestic/External	R
	IND	Aligarh	250	AIR	R
	IND	Bombay	100	AIR	R
	IND	Delhi	100	AIR	R
	CHN	Jinhua	500	R Beijing	R
	INS	Ujungpandang	7.5	RRI	R
9 553	J	Tokyo Shobo	0.9	NHK Tokyo	O
9 555	URS	Tula	100	Domestic/External	R
	D/USA	Holzkirchen	250	RFE/RL	R
	G	Daventry	300	RCI	R
	POR	Lisbon	250	RFE/RL	R
	IRQ	Salah el Deen	500	R Baghdad	R
	USA	Okeechobee	100	WYFR	R
	MEX	Mexico	1	La Hora Exacta	R
	BOL	La Paz	10		R
	URS	Sverdlovsk	100	Domestic/External	R
	KRE	Pyongyang	200	R Pyongyang	R
	KOR	Kimjae	100	R Korea	R
	CHN	Xian	300	R Beijing	R
	PHL	Palauig	100/250	R Veritas Asia	R
	INS	Wamena	25		R
	AFS	Meyerton	250	R RSA	O
9 560	FNL	Pori	500	YLE	R
	URS	Kazan	240	Domestic/External	R
	URS	Serpukhov	20	Domestic	R
	UKR	Lvov	240	Domestic/External	R
	D	Nauen	500	DW	R
	UKR	Starobelsk	100	Domestic/External	R
	SUI	Schwarzenburg	150	SRI	R
	CYP/G	Limassol	250	BBC	R
	JOR	Al Karanah	500	R Jordan	R
	ETH	Gedja	100	Vo Ethiopia	R
	PRU	Lima	20		R
	CHL	Santiago	10/100		R
	IND	Delhi	100	AIR	R
	URS	Khaborovsk	20	Domestic	R
	KRE	Pyongyang	200/400	R Pyongyang	R
	CHN	Urumqi	50	Domestic	R
	PHL	Palauig	250	R Veritas Asia	R
9 565	ISL	Reykjavik	10	IBS	R
	D	Julich	100	DW	R
	D/USA	Holzkirchen	250	RFE/RL	R
	D/USA	Biblis	100	RFE/RL	R

Frequency [kHz]	Country	Station Site	Power [kW]	Programme/ Network	O or R
9 565	G	Woofferton	250	VoA	R
(cont'd)	UKR	Ivan	250	Domestic/External	R
	GRC	Athens	100	Voice of Greece	R
	E	Playa de Pals	250	RFE/RL	R
	MLT	Cyclops	250	DW	R
	RRW	Kigali	250	DW	R
	SEY	Mahe	75	FEBA	R
	USA	Greenville	500	VoA	R
	USA	Bethany	250	Vo OAS	R
	CUB	Havana	100	R Havana Cuba	R
	B	Curitiba	7.5	R Universo	R
	URS	Frunze	240	Domestic/External	R
	IND	Delhi	100	AIR	R
	IND	Aligarh	250	AIR	R
	URS	Irkutsk	240	Domestic/External	R
	KOR	Kimjae	100	R Korea	R
	CHN	Nanchang	50	Domestic	R
	CHN	Xian	150	R Beijing	R
	PHL	Poro	50	VoA	R
	INS	Ujungpandang	100	RRI	R
	NOR	Sveio	500	R Norway/Danmarks R	O
9 570	POL	Warsaw	60	R Polonia	R
	BLR	Minsk	240	Domestic/External	R
	ROU	Bucharest	250	R Romania	R
	GRC	Kavalla	250	VoA	R
	ARS	Jeddah	50	BSKSA	R
	PAK	Quetta	10	R Pakistan	R
	KOR	Kimjae	250	R Korea	R
	CHN	Xian	300	R Beijing	R
	SNG/G	Kranji	250	BBC	R
	BGD	Dhaka	250	R Bangladesh	O
	AFS	Meyerton	250	R RSA	O
	PHL	Tinang	30	VoA	O
	D/USA	Wertachtal	500	VoA	O
9 575	URS	Serpukhov	240	Domestic/External	R
	D/USA	Lampertheim	100	RFE/RL	R
	F	Allouis	100	RFI	R
	GRC	Kavalla	250	VoA	R
	I	Rome	100	RAI	R
	POR	Muge	100	R Renascensa	R
	IRQ	Abu Ghraib	250	R Baghdad	R
	JOR	Al Karanah	500	R Jordan	R
	GAB	Moyabi	250		R
	USA	Bethany	250	VoA	R
	MEX	Mexico	100		R

Frequency [kHz]	Country	Station Site	Power [kW]	Programme/ Network	O or R
9 575	URS	Alma Ata	500	Domestic/External	R
(cont'd)	IND	Madras	10	AIR	R
	IND	Aligarh	250	AIR	R
	URS	Irkutsk	50	Domestic	R
	CHN	Xian	150	R Beijing	R
	MRA	Marpi	100		R
	PHL	Tinang	250	VoA	R
	INS	Medan	50		R
	MLT	Nador	250	Medi 1	O
	TWN	Chingmei	10	VoFC	O
	IRN	Kamalabad	500	VoIRI	O
9 580	ISL	Reykjavik	10	IBS	R
	URS	Kazan	100/250	Domestic/External	R
	G	Woofferton	250	VoA	R
	E	Arganda	100	REE	R
	OMA/G	Masirah	100	BBC	R
	CYP/G	Limassol	100/250	BBC	R
	GAB	Moyabi	500	Africa No 1	R
	GAB/J	Moyabi	500	R Japan	R
	ZMB	Lusaka	50		R
	CUB	Havana	250	R Havana Cuba	R
	URS	Blag	240	Domestic/External	R
	J	Tokyo Yamata	100	R Japan	R
	KOR	Kimjae	100	R Korea	R
	CHN	Beijing	50	R Beijing	R
	SNG/G	Kranji	100	BBC	R
	AUS	Shepparton	100	R Australia	R
9 585	NOR	Sveio	500	R Norway/Danmarks R	R
	URS	Moscow	100	Domestic/External	R
	G	Woofferton	300	VoA	R
	HNG	Szekesfehervar	20	R Budapest	R
	HNG	Diosd	100	R Budapest	R
	I	Rome	100	RAI	R
	AFS	Meyerton	250	R RSA	R
	EQA	Quito	500	HCJB	R
	B	Sao Paulo	10	R Excelsior	R
	INS	Pakanbaru	50	RRI	R
	GNE	Bata	50	R East Africa	O
9 590	NOR	Fredrikstad	350	R Norway/Danmarks R	R
	NOR	Kvitsoy	500	R Norway/Danmarks R	R
	POL	Warsaw	100	R Polonia	R
	URS	Leningrad	100	Domestic/External	R
	ROU	Bucharest	250	R Romania	R
	OMA/G	Masirah	100	BBC	R

Frequency [kHz]	Country	Station Site	Power [kW]	Programme/ Network	O or R
9 590	CYP/G	Limassol	100	BBC	R
(cont'd)	SEY/G	Mahe	100	BBC	R
	CAN	Sackville	250	RCI	R
	USA	Greenville	250	VoA	R
	USA	Bethany	250	VoA	R
	CUB	Havana	50	R Havana Cuba	R
	ATN	Bonaire	300	R Netherlands	R
	CHN	Xian	150	R Beijing	R
	GUM	Agana	100	TWR	R
	PHL	Tinang	250	VoA	R
9 595	D/USA	Biblis	100	RFE/RL	R
	BUL	Sofia	500	R Sofia	R
	POR	Lisbon	250	RFE/RL/VoA	R
	UAE	Dubai	300	UAE R	R
	UAE	Abu Dhabi	500	UAE R	R
	ETH	Gedja	100		R
	SEY/G	Mahe	250	BBC	R
	URG	Montevideo	10	R Monte Carlo	R
	URS	Sverdlovsk	50	Domestic/External	R
	IND	Aligarh	250	AIR	R
	CHN	Urumqi	50	Domestic	R
	INS	Manokwari	25	RRI	R
	J	Tokyo Nagara	50	NSB/Radio Tanpa 1	O
9 600	URS	Moscow	250	Domestic/External	R
	G	Skelton	250	BBC	R
	E/CHN	Noblejas	350	R Beijing	R
	POR	Muge	100	R Renascensa	R
	POR	S Gabriel	100	RDP	R
	MLT	Cyclops	250	DW	R
	LBY	Benghazi	100	Tripoli	R
	UAE	Abu Dhabi	500	UAE R	R
	ETH	Gedja	100		R
	ASC	Ascension	250	BBC	R
	MEX	Mexico	1	R Universidad	R
	CUB	Havana	100	R Moscow	R
	B	Rio de Janeiro	7.5	R Mec	R
	URS	Tashkent	100/250	Domestic/External	R
	CLN	Trincomalee	250	DW	R
	URS	Okhotsk	100	Domestic/External	R
	KRE	Pyongyang	200/400	R Pyongyang	R
	CHN	Kunming	50	R Beijing	R
	ALB	Lushnja	100	R Tirana	O
	IND	Port Blair	10	AIR	O
9 605	D	Wertachtal	500	DW	R
	D	Julich	100	DW	R

Frequency [kHz]	Country	Station Site	Power [kW]	Programme/ Network	O or R
9 605	TCH	Litomysl	120	R Prague	R
(cont'd)	F	Allouis	100	RFI	R
	CVA	S M Galeria	500	Vatican R	R
	POR	Sines	250	AWR	R
	OMA/G	Masirah	100	BBC	R
	MLT	Cyclops	250	DW	R
	LBR	Careysburg	15	ELWA	R
	LBR	Careysburg	250	VoA	R
	USA	Okeechobee	100	WYFR	R
	BOL	S Cruz	5		R
	CHN	Kunming	50	R Beijing	R
	SNG/G	Kranji	100/250	BBC	R
	INS	Palu	50		R
9 610	NOR	Kvitsoy	500	R Norway/Danmarks R	R
	URS	Moscow	100/200	Domestic/External	R
	G	Rampisham	500	BBC	R
	G	Skelton	250	BBC	R
	MCO	Monte Carlo	100	TWR	R
	ISR	Jerusalem	50/300	IBA	R
	MTN	Nouakchott	100	ORTB de Mauritanie	R
	ETH	Gedja	100		R
	COG	Brazzaville	50	Vo Rev Congolaise	R
	ASC	Ascenion	250	BBC	R
	EQA	Quito	500	HCJB	R
	PRU	Iquitos	2		R
	URS	Alma Ata	240/500	Domestic/External	R
	IRN	Kamalabad	500	VoIRI	R
	IND	Delhi	50/100	AIR	R
	CHN	Beijing	50	Domestic/External	R
	PHL	Tinang	250	VoA	R
	AUS	Perth	10	ABC, Perth	R
	TWN	Taipei	250	CBC Taipei	O
	SEY	Mahe	75	FEBA	O
9 615	NOR	Sveio	500	R Norway Intl/ R Danmarks	R
	NOR	Fredrikstad	350	R Norway Intl/ R Danmarks	R
	S	Hoerby	350	R Sweden	R
	URS	Kinghisepp	240	Domestic/External	R
	D	Julich	100	DW	R
	GRC	Kavalla	250	VoA	R
	CVA	S M Galeria	500	Vatican R	R
	POR	Sines	250	DW/RDP/RCI	R
	MLT	Cyclops	250	DW	R
	MRC	Tangier	100		R

Frequency [kHz]	Country	Station Site	Power [kW]	Programme/ Network	O or R
9 615	LBY	Tripoli	500	Tripoli	R
(cont'd)	ETH	Gedja	100		R
	USA	Redwood City	50	KGEI	R
	B	Sao Paulo	7.5		R
	PAK	Peshawar	10	R Pakistan	R
	IND	Bombay	100	AIR	R
	CLN	Trincomalee	250	DW	R
	MNG	Ulan Bator	50	R Ulan Bator	R
	PHL	Marulas	250	R Veritas Asia	R
	INS	Samarinda	50	RRI	R
9 620	URS	Armavir	240	Domestic/External	R
	URS	Jigulevsk	200	Domestic/External	R
	URS	Starobelsk	100	Domestic/External	R
	YUG	Bijeljina	250/500	R Yugoslavia	R
	E	Arganda	100	REE	R
	EGY	Abu Zaabal	100	R Cairo	R
	MOZ	Maputo	100	R Mozambique	R
	CUB	Havana	250	R Havana Cuba	R
	URG	Montevideo	20	Sodre Montevideo	R
	IND	Delhi	100	AIR	R
	IND	Aligarh	250	AIR	R
	URS	Vladivostock	100	Domestic/External	R
	CHN	Beijing	120	R Beijing	R
	PHL	Poro	50	VoA	R
	PHL	Tinang	250	VoA	R
9 625	ISL	Reykjavik	10	IBS	R
	URS	Kazan	240	Domestic/External	R
	D	Julich	100	DW	R
	D/USA	Lampertheim	100	RFE/RL	R
	D/USA	Biblis	100	RFE/RL	R
	ROU	Bucharest	120/250	R Romania	R
	MLT	Cyclops	250	DW	R
	CAN	Sackville	100	CBC Northern Service	R
	URS	Frunze	500	Domestic/External	R
	URS	Sverdlovsk	100	Domestic/External	R
	URS	Tchita	500	Domestic/External	R
	MNG	Ulan Bator	250	R Ulan Bator	R
	CHN	Kunming	120	R Beijing	R
	INS	Yogyakarta	100		R
	GAB	Moyabi	250	AWR Africa	O
9 630	URS	Serpukhov	250	Domestic/External	R
	E	Noblejas	350	REE	R
	POR	Sines	250	RDP	R
	IRQ	Salah el Deen	500	R Baghdad	R

Frequency [kHz]	Country	Station Site	Power [kW]	Programme/ Network	O or R
9 630	SEY/G	Mahe	250	BBC	R
(cont'd)	ATN	Bonaire	300	R Netherlands	R
	B	Aparecida	10	R Aparecida	R
	CHN	Santiago	10	R Agricultura	R
	IND	Aligarh	250	AIR	R
	IND	Delhi	10	AIR	R
	CHN	Kunming	50	R Beijing	R
	PHL	Tinang	250	VoA	R
	CHN	Minshiung	3	CPBS	O
9 635	URS	Jigulevsk	100	Domestic/External	R
	D	Nauen	500	DW	R
	G	Daventry	100	BBC	R
	G	Rampisham	500	BBC	R
	G	Skelton	250	BBC	R
	GRC	Kavalla	250	VoA	R
	CVA	S M Galeria	500	Vatican R	R
	POR	S Gabriel	100	RDP	R
	CYP/G	Limassol	300	BBC	R
	MLI	Bamako	50	RTV Malienne	R
	GAB	Moyabi	250	Africa No 1	R
	MOZ	Beira	100	E P de Sofala	R
	CAN	Sackville	100	RCI	R
	PRU	Cuzco	1.2		R
	URS	Frunze	100	Domestic/External	R
	AFG	Kabul	100	R Afghanistan	R
	URS	Vladivostock	50	Domestic/External	R
	CHN	Baoding	120	R Beijing	R
	SNG	Singapore	50	SBC	R
	INS	Ujungpandang	50		R
	IRN	Kamalabad	500	VoIRI	O
9 640	FNL	Pori	250	R Finland	R
	D	Wertachtal	500	DW	R
	D	Julich	100	DW	R
	UKR	Starobelsk	100/500	Domestic/External	R
	ALG	Bouchaqui	50	Vo Res Chilena	R
	ARS	Riyadh	350	BSKSA	R
	SEY	Mahe	75	FEBC	R
	SWZ	Manzini	100	TWR	R
	USA	Greenville	250	VoA	R
	CUB	Havana	100	R Havana Cuba	R
	ATG	Antigua	125/250	BBC	R
	URG	Montevideo	10		R
	URS	Sverdlovsk	100	Domestic/External	R
	KRE	Pyongyang	200	R Pyongyang	R
	KOR	Kimjae	250	R Korea	R

Frequency [kHz]	Country	Station Site	Power [kW]	Programme/ Network	O or R
9 645	FNL	Pori	500	R Finland	R
	NOR	Fredrikstad	350	R Norway/Danmarks R	R
	NOR	Sveio	500	R Norway/Danmarks R	R
	NOR	Kvitsoy	500	R Norway/Danmarks R	R
	BLR	Minsk	50	Domestic	R
	D/USA	Biblis	100	RFE/RL	R
	CVA	S M Galeria	100/500	Vatican R	R
	MRC	Tangier	100		R
	GAB	Moyabi	500	Africa No 1	R
	GAB/J	Moyabi	500	R Japan	R
	B	Sao Paulo	7.5	R Bandeirantes	R
	PAK	Islamabad	100/250	R Pakistan	R
	CLN	Colombo	35	VoA	R
	MNG	Ulan Bator	50/100	R Ulan Bator	R
	KRE	Pyongyang	200/400	R Pyongyang	R
	CHN	Baoji	50	R Beijing	R
	PHL	Iba	100	R Veritas Asia	R
	INS	Banda Aceh	50		R
	AUS	Darwin	250	R Australia	R
	CTR	San Jose	0.5	Faro del Caribe	O
9 650	NOR	Kvitsoy	500	R Norway/Danmarks R	R
	URS	Jigulevsk	240	Domestic/External	R
	D	Wertachtal	500	DW	R
	D/USA	Wertachtal	500	VoA	R
	G	Daventry	300	BBC	R
	G	Rampisham	500	BBC	R
	SUI	Sottens	500	SRI	R
	MCO	Monte Carlo	100/500	TWR	R
	CVA	S M Galeria	100/250/ 500	Vatican R	R
	E	Noblejas	350	REE	R
	POR	Sines	250	DW	R
	CYP/G	Limassol	100/250	BBC	R
	MRC	Tangier	100	VoA	R
	GUI	Conakry	100		R
	SWZ	Manzini	25	TWR	R
	CAN	Sackville	250	RCI/R Korea	R
	URG	Montevideo	10		R
	URS	Frunze	100/500	Domestic/External	R
	IND	Gauhati	10	AIR	R
	IND	Bombay	100	AIR	R
	BGD	Dhaka	100	R Bangladesh	R
	J	Tokyo Yamata	300	R Japan	R
	KRE	Pyongyang	200	R Pyongyang	R
	KOR	Kimjae	250	R Korea	R
	GUM	Agat	100	AWR	R

Frequency [kHz]	Country	Station Site	Power [kW]	Programme/ Network	O or R
9 655	NOR	Kvitsoy	500	R Norway/Danmarks R	R
	S	Hoerby	350	R Sweden	R
	BLR	Orcha	20	Domestic	R
	URS	Volgograd	20	Domestic	R
	URS	Moscow	240	Domestic/External	R
	URS	Armavir	100	Domestic/External	R
	BUL	Sofia	500	R Sofia	R
	LBY	Tripoli	500	Tripoli	R
	UAE	Abu Dhabi	500	UAE R	R
	SWZ	Manzini	100	TWR	R
	CUB	Havana	50-500	R Havana Cuba	R
	CHN	Lhasa	50	R Beijing	R
	PHL	Bocaue	50		R
	THA	Bangkok	100	R Thailand	R
	INS	Nabire	25	RRI	R
	AUS	Shepparton	100	R Australia	R
	B	Brasilia	250	R N B Brasilia	O
9 660	D/USA	Holzkirchen	250	RFE/RL	R
	G	Woofferton	300	VoA	R
	YUG	Bijeljina	500	R Yugoslavia	R
	E	Playa de Pals	250	RFE/RL	R
	POR	Lisbon	250	RFE/RL	R
	CYP/G	Limassol	300	BBC	R
	ZAI	Kinshasa	50		R
	EQA	Quito	500	HCJB	R
	IRN	Sirjan	500	VoIRI	R
	J	Tokyo Yamata	300	R Japan	R
	CHN	Baoding	120	R Beijing	R
	AUS	Brisbane	10	ABC, Brisbane	R
	ETH	Addis Ababa	100	Vo Ethiopia	O
	VEN	Caracas	10	R Rumbos	O
9 665	URS	Voronej	240	Domestic/External	R
	D	K Wusterhausen	100	DW	R
	ROU	Bucharest	250	R Romania	R
	TUR	Ankara	250	TRT	R
	ARS	Riyadh	350	BSKSA	R
	AFS	Meyerton	100	R Suid Afrika	R
	USA	Vado	50	KJES El Paso	R
	CUB	Havana	100	R Havana Cuba	R
	B	Florianopolis	10	R Marumby	R
	URS	Dushanbe	500	Domestic/External	R
	IND	Delhi	100	AIR	R
	IND	Aligarh	250	AIR	R
	KRE	Pyongyang	200	KCBS Pyongyang	R
	CHN	Shijiazhuang	500	R Beijing	R

Frequency [kHz]	Country	Station Site	Power [kW]	Programme/ Network	O or R
9 665	PHL	Iba	100	R Veritas Asia	R
(cont'd)	INS	Semarang	50	RRI	R
	URS	Moscow	100	R Afghanistan	O
	MLT	Cyclops	250	IBRA R	O
9 670	G	Daventry	300	BBC	R
	GRC	Kavalla	250	VoA	R
	GRC	Rhodes	50	VoA	R
	POR	Sines	250	AWR	R
	CYP/G	Limassol	100/300	BBC/Cyprus BC	R
	MRC	Tangier	100	VoA	R
	EGY	Abis	250	R Cairo	R
	USA	Greenville	250/500	VoA	R
	CUB	Havana	100	R Havana Cuba	R
	EQA	Quito	100	HCJB	R
	URG	Montevideo	10		R
	CLN	Trincomalee	250	DW	R
	URS	Komsomolsk	100	Domestic/External	R
	CHN	Kunming	50	Domestic/External	R
	MRA	Marpi	100	KFBS	R
	PHL	Tinang	250	VoA	R
	PHL	Bocaue	50	FEBC Manila	R
	ATG	Antigua	250	DW	O
	IRN	Kamalabad	500	VoIRI	O
9 675	POL	Warsaw	100	R Polonia	R
	URS	Voronej	20	Domestic	R
	E	Arganda	100	REE	R
	TUN	Sfax	100		R
	EGY	Abis	250	R Cairo	R
	GUF	Montsinery	500	R Japan	R
	PRU	Lima	7.5	R del Pacifico	R
	B	Cachoeira Paul	10	R Cancao Nova	R
	URS	Tashkent	240/500	Domestic/External	R
	IND	Delhi	100	AIR	R
	IND	Aligarh	100	AIR	R
	URS	Komsomolsk	100	Domestic/External	R
	CHN	Xian	300	R Beijing	R
	CHN	Kunming	50	R Beijing	R
	INS	Serui	25		R
	INS	Padang Cermin	250	Vo Indonesia	R
	INS	Jakarta	100		R
9 680	URS	Leningrad	20	Domestic	R
	D/USA	Lampertheim	100	RFE/RL	R
	D/USA	Biblis	100	RFE/RL	R
	SUI	Schwarzenburg	150	SRI	R

Frequency [kHz]	Country	Station Site	Power [kW]	Programme/ Network	O or R
9 680	GRC	Kavalla	250	VoA	R
(cont'd)	POR	Lisbon	250	RDP	R
	POR	Muge	100	R Renascenca	R
	POR	S Gabriel	100	RDP	R
	USA	Okeechobee	100	WYFR/VoFC	R
	CUB	Havana	50	R Havana Cuba	R
	URG	Montevideo	10		R
	IRN	Kamalabad	500	VoIRI	R
	CHN	Lhasa	50	R Beijing	R
	INS	Jakarta	50	RRI	O
	MEX	Mexico City	0.5	R XEQ 940	O
9 685	URS	Moscow	240	Domestic/External	R
	UKR	Lvov	500	Domestic/External	R
	TUR	Ankara	250	TRT	R
	E	Arganda	100	REE	R
	ALG	Ouled Fayet	100	Vo Palestine	R
	UGA	Kampala	250	R Uganda	R
	TZA	Dar es Salaam	50	R Tanzania	R
	GUF	Montsinery	500	RFI	R
	PRU	Arequipa	1		R
	B	Sao Paulo	7.5	R Gazeta	R
	IRN	Kamalabad	500	VoIRI	R
	URS	Irkutsk	500	Domestic/External	R
	CHN	Baoding	120	R Beijing	R
	INS	Kendari	50	RRI	R
9 690	URS	Tula	20	Domestic	R
	D	Wertachtal	500	DW	R
	D	Julich	100	DW	R
	ROU	Bucharest	250	R Romania	R
	E/CHN	Noblejas	350	R Beijing/REE	R
	GRC	Kavalla	250	VoA	R
	USA	Delano	250	BBC	R
	CUB	Havana	250	R Havana Cuba	R
	HTI	Pt au Prince	100		R
	ARG	Gral Pacheco	100	RAE	R
	URS	Alma Ata	20	Domestic	R
	PAK	Islamabad	100	R Pakistan	R
	IND	Bhopal	10	AIR	R
	URS	Komsomolsk	20	Domestic	R
	CHN	Kunming	50/120	R Beijing	R
	ATG	Antigua	250	DW	O
	TWN	Taipei	10	CBS Taipei	O
	MDG	Antananarivo	10	R Madagascar 1	O
9 693	CBG	Phnom Penh	50	Vo the People	O

Frequency [kHz]	Country	Station Site	Power [kW]	Programme/ Network	O or R
9 695	S	Hoerby	350	R Sweden	R
	S	Karlsborg	350	R Sweden	R
	URS	Kazan	160/250	Domestic/External	R
	URS	Moscow	20	Domestic	R
	D/USA	Biblis	100	RFE/RL	R
	POR	Lisbon	250	RFE/RL	R
	UAE	Abu Dhabi	120	UAE R	R
	B	Manaus	7.5	R Rio Mar	R
	URS	Frunze	240	Domestic/External	R
	INS	Sorong	50		R
	NZL	Taupo	100	R New Zealand Intl	O
	IRN	Kamalabad	500	VoIRI	O
	USA	Okeechobee	100	WYFR	O
9 700	URS	Moscow	100/120	Domestic/External	R
	D	Wertachtal	500	DW	R
	D	Julich	100	DW	R
	BUL	Sofia	150/250	R Sofia	R
	GRC	Kavalla	250	VoA	R
	EGY	Abu Zaabal	100	R Cairo	R
	BGD	Dhaka	250	R Bangladesh	R
	KOR	Kimjae	250	R Korea	R
	CHN	Xian	150	R Beijing	R
	IND	Delhi	50	AIR	O
9 705	D/USA	Biblis	100	RFE/RL	R
	GRC	Kavalla	250	VoA	R
	CVA	S M Galeria	500	Vatican R	R
	POR	Lisbon	250	RFE/RL	R
	POR	S Gabriel	100	RDP	R
	IRQ	Abu Ghraib	250	R Baghdad	R
	LBY	Tripoli	500	Tripoli	R
	ARS	Jeddah	50	BSKSA	R
	NGR	Niamey	50	ORTV du Niger 2	R
	ETH	Gedja	100	Vo Ethiopia	R
	USA	Okeechobee	50	WYFR	R
	MEX	Mexico	10	R Mexico Intl	R
	B	S Goncalo	7.5		R
	URS	Tashkent	20/100	Domestic/External	R
	IND	Delhi	50/100	AIR	R
	IND	Aligarh	250	AIR	R
	URS	Iakutsk	20	Domestic	R
	URS	Vladivostock	500	Domestic/External	R
	URS	Irkutsk	100	Domestic/External	R
	INS	Pontianak	50	RRI	R
	IRN	Kamalabad	500	VoIRI	O

Frequency [kHz]	Country	Station Site	Power [kW]	Programme/ Network	O or R
9 705	USA	Okeechobee	50/100	WYFR	O
(cont'd)	B	Rio de Janeiro	7.5	R Nacional	O
9 710	URS	Kaunas	50	Domestic/External	R
	UKR	Kiev	250	Domestic/External	R
	UKR	Simferopol	240	Domestic/External	R
	I	Rome	100	RAI	R
	CUB	Havana	50	R Havana Cuba	R
	PRU	Tarapoto	1		R
	ARG	S Gernando	5		R
	CHN	Lanzhou	15	Domestic	R
	PHL	Palauig	100	R Veritas Asia	R
	AUS	Shepparton	100	R Australia	R
	AUS	Carnarvon	250	R Australia	O
9 715	BLR	Orcha	240	Domestic/External	R
	URS	Tula	240	Domestic/External	R
	D	Wertachtal	500	DW	R
	D/USA	Holzkirchen	250	RFE/RL	R
	HOL	Flevo	500	R Netherlands	R
	F	Allouis	100	RFI	R
	GRC	Kavalla	250	VoA	R
	CYP/G	Limassol	250	BBC	R
	IRQ	Abu Ghraib	250	R Baghdad	R
	COG	Brazzaville	50	V Rev Congolaise	R
	USA	New Orelans	100	WRNO	R
	USA	Okeechobee	50	WYFR	R
	ATN	Bonaire	300	R Netherlands	R
	GUF	Montsinery	500	RFI	R
	EQA	Quito	100	HCJB	R
	BOL	Sucre	2	R La Plata	R
	PHL	Tinang	250	VoA	R
	INS	Biak	100	RRI	R
	G	Daventry	300	BBC	O
	URS	Tashkent	100	Domestic/External	O
9 720	URS	Volgograd	20	Domestic	R
	URS	Moscow	250	Domestic/External	R
	UKR	Vinnitsa	240	Domestic/External	R
	YUG	Bijeljina	500	R Yugoslavia	R
	ARS	Diriyya	50	BSKSA	R
	ARS	Jeddah	50	BSKSA	R
	AGL	Luanda	100	R N Angola	R
	CUB	Havana	250	R Moscow	R
	URS	Frunze	250	Domestic/External	R
	IRN	Kamalabad	500	VoIRI	R
	IND	Hyderabad	10	AIR	R

Frequency [kHz]	Country	Station Site	Power [kW]	Programme/ Network	O or R
9 720	CLN	Ekala	100	SLBC	R
(cont'd)	MNG	Ulan Bator	250	R Ulan Bator	R
	KOR	Kimjae	100	R Korea	R
	CHN	Beijing	120	R Beijing	R
9 725	URS	Serpukhov	240	Domestic/External	R
	D/USA	Lampertheim	100	RFE/RL	R
	D/USA	Biblis	100	RFE/RL	R
	SUI	Sottens	500	SRI	R
	POR	Lisbon	250	RFE/RL	R
	B	Curitiba	7.5	R Clube Paranaense	R
	URS	Sverdlovsk	100	Domestic/External	R
	CHN	Huhhot	50	Domestic/External	R
	SNG/G	Kranji	100	BBC	R
	INS	Amboina	100	RRI	R
	CTR	Alajuela	40	AWR/R Lira	O
9 730	URS	Tula	240/500	Domestic/External	R
	URS	Armavir	20	Domestic	R
	D	Nauen	500	DW	R
	D	K Wusterhausen	50/100	DW	R
	ARS	Riyadh	350	BSKSA	R
	CUB	Havana	100/250/ 500	R Havana Cuba	R
	IND	Delhi	100	AIR	R
	BRM	Yangon	50	Vo Myanmar	R
	URS	Khab	100	Domestic/External	R
	CHN	Baoding	120	Domestic/External	R
	VTN	Hanoi	15	Vo Vietnam	R
	FNL	Pori	500	R Finland	R
	URS	Noginsk	15	Tass News	O
9 735	URS	Tula	20	Domestic	R
	URS	Armavir	100	Domestic/External	R
	URS	Petrozavodsk	500	Domestic/External	R
	D	Wertachtal	500	DW	R
	D	Julich	100	DW	R
	D/USA	Wertachtal	500	VoA	R
	G	Woofferton	250	VoA	R
	UKR	Simferopol	100	Domestic/External	R
	OMA	Seeb	100	R Oman	R
	OMA	Thumrait	100	R Oman	R
	CYP/G	Limassol	250	BBC	R
	MLT	Cyclops	250	DW	R
	RRW	Kigali	250	DW	R
	PRG	Asuncion	100	R N Paraguay	R
	URS	Irkutsk	500	Domestic/External	R

Frequency [kHz]	Country	Station Site	Power [kW]	Programme/ Network	O or R
9 735	URS	Komsomolsk	500	Domestic/External	R
(cont'd)	PHL	Bocaue	50	R Veritas Asia	R
	INS	Merauke	100	RRI	R
9 740	G	Daventry	300	RCI	R
	BUL	Sofia	250	R Sofia	R
	GRC	Kavalla	250	VoA	R
	GRC	Rhodes	50	VoA	R
	POR	Lisbon	250	RFE/RL	R
	POR	S Gabriel	100	RDP	R
	CYP/G	Limassol	250	BBC	R
	ISR	Jerusalem	50/300	IBA	R
	EGY	Abis	250	R Cairo	R
	IRN	Sirjan	500	VoIRI	R
	CHN	Kunming	50	Domestic/External	R
	SNG/G	Kranji	100/250	BBC	R
9 742	INS	Sorong	10	RRI	R
9 745	URS	Kazan	240	Domestic/External	R
	URS	Moscow	100	Domestic/External	R
	D	Julich	100	DW	R
	D/USA	Wertachtal	500	VoA	R
	UKR	Simferopol	100	Domestic/External	R
	F	Allouis	100	RFI	R
	E	Noblejas	350	REE	R
	LBY	Tripoli	500	Tripoli	R
	CUB	Havana	50	R Moscow	R
	EQA	Quito	50/100	HCJB	R
	URS	Kenga	100	Domestic/External	R
	KRE	Pyongyang	200/400	R Pyongyang	R
	INS	Bandjarmasin	50	RRI	R
	IRN	Kamalabad	500	VoIRI	R
9 750	URS	Kaunas	150	Domestic/External	R
	D	Wertachtal	500	DW	R
	D/USA	Lampertheim	100	RFE/RL	R
	G	Rampisham	500	BBC	R
	G	Skelton	250	BBC	R
	G	Daventry	300	BBC	R
	UKR	Lvov	100	Domestic/External	R
	ROU	Bucharest	250	R Romania	R
	GRC	Athens	100	Voice of Greece	R
	E	Playa de Pals	250	RFE/RL	R
	OMA/G	Masirah	100	BBC	R
	CYP/G	Limassol	250	BBC	R
	KWT	Sulaibyah	500	R Kuwait	R
	TZA	Dar es Salaam	50	R Tanzania	R

Frequency [kHz]	Country	Station Site	Power [kW]	Programme/ Network	O or R
9 750	MEX	Mexico	100		R
(cont'd)	CUB	Havana	100	R Havana Cuba	R
	CHL	Santiago	10	R Mineria	R
	KRE	Pyongyang	200	R Pyongyang	R
	KOR	Kimjae	250	R Korea	R
	CHN	Huhhot	50	Domestic/External	R
	ALB	Lushnja	100	R Tirana	O
	MLA	Kajang	100	Vo Malaysia	O
	OCE	Tahiti	4	RFO Tahiti	O
9 755	POL	Warsaw	60	R Polonia	R
	URS	Jigulevsk	100	Domestic/External	R
	URS	Serpukhov	240	Domestic/External	R
	BUL	Sofia	250	R Sofia	R
	CVA	S M Galeria	100/250	Vatican R	R
	EGY	Mokattam	100	R Cairo	R
	CAN	Sackville	250	RCI	R
	IND	Delhi	50/100	AIR	R
	URS	Petropavlokam	250	Domestic/External	R
	CHN	Baoji	50	Domestic/External	R
	PHL	Tinang	250	VoA	R
	INS	Surakarta	50		R
	URS	Kazan	100	R Afghanistan	O
	VTN	Hanoi	15	Vo Vietnam	O
9 760	URS	Kazan	150	Domestic/External	R
	D	K Wusterhausen	100	DW	R
	D	Julich	100	DW	R
	G	Skelton	250	BBC	R
	G	Woofferton	250	VoA	R
	BEL	Wavre	100	BRT	R
	GRC	Kavalla	250	VoA	R
	CYP/G	Limassol	250	BBC	R
	MRC	Tangier	100	VoA	R
	CAN	Sackville	250	RCI	R
	B	Brasilia	250	R Bras	R
	PAK	Quetta	10	R Pakistan	R
	PHL	Tinang	250	VoA	R
	AUS	Shepparton	100	R Australia	R
	AUS	Carnarvon	100	R Australia	R
	ALB	Lushnja	100	R Tirana	O
	J	Tokyo Nagara	50	NSB/R Tanpa 2	O
	GTM	Guatemala City	1	V de Guatemala	O
9 765	URS	Armavir	250	Domestic/External	R
	URS	Leningrad	240	Domestic/External	R
	D	Wertachtal	500	DW	R

Frequency [kHz]	Country	Station Site	Power [kW]	Programme/ Network	O or R
9 765	D	Julich	100	DW	R
(cont'd)	UKR	Lvov	250	Domestic/External	R
	E	Arganda	100	REE	R
	MLT	Cyclops	250	Vo Mediterranean	R
	UAE	Abu Dhabi	500	UAE	R
	EQA	Quito	50	HCJB	R
	URS	Sver	100	Domestic/External	R
	CHN	Beijing	500	R Beijing	R
	INS	Pontianak	100		R
	URS	Kazan	100	R Afghanistan	O
	S	Horby	350	R Sweden	O
	S	Karlsborg	350	R Sweden	O
	TWN	Pa-li	50	VoFC	O
	TWN	Taipei	250	VoFC	O
	IRN	Kamalabad	500	VoIRI	O
9 770	S	Horby	350	R Sweden	R
	D	Julich	100	DW	R
	D	Wertachtal	500	DW	R
	G	Rampisham	500	BBC	R
	F	Allouis	100/500	RFI	R
	EGY	Abis	250	R Cairo	R
	ZAI	Kinshasa	10		R
	SEY	Mahe	100	FEBC	R
	CUB	Havana	100/250	R Havana Cuba	R
	ATN	Bonaire	300	R Netherlands	R
	GUF	Montsinery	500	RFI	R
	URG	Montevideo	10		R
	IRN	Kamalabad	500	VoIRI	R
	PAK	Islamabad	100	R Pakistan	R
	IND	Delhi	100	AIR	R
	KRE	Pyongyang	200	R Pyongyang	R
	CHN	Baoji	50	Domestic/External	R
	PHL	Tinang	250	VoA	R
	AUS	Shepparton	100	R Australia	R
	MLI	Bamako	50	R Beijing	O
	USA	Okeechobee	100	WYFR	O
9 775	URS	Moscow	100/240	Domestic/External	O
	URS	Kazan	50	Domestic/External	O
	ATN	Bonaire	300	R Netherlands	O
	LBR	Careysburg	250	VoA	O
	USA	Greenville	250/500	VoA	O
	CHN	Baoji	50	CPBS	O
9 778	DOM	Santa Domingo	1	R Santiago	O

Frequency [kHz]	Country	Station Site	Power [kW]	Programme/ Network	O or R
9 780	URS	Kazan	100	Domestic/External	O
	URS	Khabarovsk	100	Domestic/External	O
	YMS	San'a	50	R San'a	O
	UAE	Abu Dhabi	500	UAE R	O
	URS	Alma Ata	50	Domestic/External	O
	CHN	Zining	50	CPBS	O
9 785	UKR	Vinnitsa	100	Domestic/External	O
	GUM	Agana	100	TWR	O
	USA	Vado	100	KJES El Paso	O
9 790	URS	Moscow	100	Domestic/External	O
	URS	Tashkent	100	Domestic/External	O
	F	Allouis	100/500	RFI	O
	ALB	Lushnja	100	R Tirana	O
9 795	URS	Sverdlovsk	100	Domestic/External	O
	URS	Vladivostock	500	Domestic/External	O
	MCO	Monte Carlo	500	TWR	O
	TUR	Ankara	2250	TRT	O
	GUF	Montsinery	500	RFI	O
	MNG	Ulan Bator	50	R Ulan Bator	O
9 800	PHL	Bocaue	50	FEBC	O
	F	Allouis	100	RFI	O
	ISR	Jerusalem	300	Kol Israel	O
	URS	Kazan	500	Domestic/External	O
	UKR	Kiev	100	Domestic/External	O
	GRC	Athens	100	Voice of Greece	O
9 805	F	Allouis	100/500	RFI	O
	URS	Moscow	100	Domestic/External	O
	URS	Khabarovsk	500	Domestic/External	O
	SUI	Schwarzenburg	150	SRI	O
9 810	I	Milan	10	IRRS	O
	ISR	Jerusalem	20	Kol Israel	O
	USA	Salt Lake City	100	KUSW	O
	F	Allouis	100	RFI	O
	USA	Delano	250	VoA	O
	ALS	Anchor Point	100	KNLS	O
9 820	URS	Leningrad	100	Domestic/External	O
	URS	Sverdlovsk	100	Domestic/External	O
	URS	Irkutsk	100	Domestic/External	O
	GUM	Piti	100	KHBN	O
9 825	G	Daventry	100/300	BBC	O
	G	Rampisham	500	BBC	O

Frequency [kHz]	Country	Station Site	Power [kW]	Programme/ Network	O or R
9 825	URS	Petropavlokam	100	Domestic/External	O
(cont'd)	URS	Vladivostock	100	Domestic/External	O
9 830	F	Allouis	100	RFI	O
	URS	Irkutsk	250	Domestic/External	O
	URS	Tashkent	100	Domestic/External	O
	GUM	Piti	100	KHBN	O
	MRA	Marpi	100	KFBS	O
9 835	HNG	Jaszbereny	250	R Budapest	O
9 840	URS	Tashkent	100	Domestic/External	O
	USA	Greenville	250	VoA	O
	VTN	Hanoi	120	Vo Vietnam	O
	USA	Scotts Corners	500	Christian Science Mon	O
9 845	URS	Novosibirsk	500	Domestic/External	O
	URS	Khabarovsk	100	Domestic/External	O
	F	Allouis	100	R Beijing	O
	PHL	Iba	100	FEBC	O
	TWN	Panchiau	50	VoFC	O
9 850	EGY	Abis	250	R Cairo	O
	EGY	Abu Zaabal	100	R Cairo	O
	F	Allouis	100	RFI	O
	GAB	Moyabi	250	RFI	O
	USA	Scotts Corners	500	Christian Science Mon	O
	PHL	Iba	100	FEBC	O
	URS	Noginsk	15	TASS	O
9 852	USA	Okeechobee	100	VoFC	O
9 855	URS	Irkutsk	500	Domestic/External	O
	URS	Novosibirsk	100	Domestic/External	O
	URS	Vladivostock	100	Domestic/External	O
	HOL	Flevo	500	R Netherlands	O
	NZL	Taupo	100	R New Zealand Intl	O
9 860	HOL	Flevo	500	R Netherlands	O
	URS	Simferopol	500	Domestic/External	O
	PAK	Islamabad	100	R Pakistan	O
	BEL	Wavre	180	BRT	O
	AUS	Carnarvon	100	R Australia	O
	AUS	Darwin	250	R Australia	O
9 865	URS	Kazan	100	Domestic/External	O
	URS	Leningrad	100	Domestic/External	O
	URS	Moscow	100	Domestic/External	O
9 870	AUT	Moosbrunn	100/300	R Austria Intl	O
	URS	Vinnitsa	500	Domestic/External	O

Frequency [kHz]	Country	Station Site	Power [kW]	Programme/ Network	O or R
9 870	ARS	Riyadh	350	BSKSA	O
(cont'd)	KOR	Kimjae	250	R Korera	O
	GUM	Agana	100	TWR	O
	USA	Salt Lake City	100	KUSW	O
9 875	AUT	Moosbrunn	500	R Austria Intl	O
	URS	Novosibirsk	500	Domestic/External	O
	URS	Khab	100	Domestic/External	O
	E	Arganda	100	REE	O
	E	Noblejas	350	REE	O
	PHL	Bocaue	50	FEBC	O
9 880	URS	Moscow	100/500	Domestic/External	O
	URS	Kazan	250	Domestic/External	O
	CHN	Kunming	50	R Beijing	O
9 885	URS	Moscow	100	Domestic/External	O
	URS	Vladivostock	100	Domestic/External	O
	URS	Dushanbe	240	Domestic/External	O
	SUI	Schwarzenburg	150	SRI	O
	SUI	Sottens	500	SRI	O
9 890	URS	Leningrad	100	Domestic/External	O
	URS	Kazan	100	Domestic/External	O
9 895	URS	Yerevan	100	Domestic/External	O
	URS	Petropavlokam	100	Domestic/External	O
	HOL	Flevo	500	R Netherlands	O
	MRA	Aginan Point	100	Christian Science Mon	O
9 900	EGY	Abis	250	R Cairo	O
	CHN	Baoding	120	R Beijing	O
9 910	IND	Aligarh	250	AIR	O
	G	Rampisham	500	BBC	O
	G	Skelton	250	BBC	O
	G	Woofferton	250	BBC	O
9 920	CHN	Beijing	120	Domestic/External	O
	CHN	Xian	150	R Beijing	O
9 925	BEL	Wavre	180	BRT/RTBF	O
9 930	ISR	Jerusalem	100	IBA	O
9 935	GRC	Thessaloniki	35	Thessaloniki R	O
	GRC	Athens	100	Voice of Greece	O
9 940	EGY	Abis	250	R Cairo	O
9 945	CHN	Baoding	120	R Beijing	O

Frequency [kHz]	Country	Station Site	Power [kW]	Programme/ Network	O or R
9 950	SYR	Damascus	100	R Damascus	O
	IND	Delhi	250	AIR	O
	EGY	Abis	250	R Cairo	O
9 955	USA	Okeechobee	100	WYFR	O
	TWN	Taipei	250	WYFR/VoFC	O
9 965	GTM	Guatemala City	1	R Caiman	O
	CHN	Baoding	120	R Beijing	O
9 977	KRE	Pyongyang	200	R Pyongyang	O
9 985	CHN	Kunming	50	Domestic/External	O
10 010	VTN	Hanoi	15	Vo Vietnam	O
	CHN	Beijing	50	CPBS	O
10 235	USA			VoA [feeder]	O
10 245	CHN	Shijiazhuang	50	CPBS	O
10 260	CHN	Baoji	50	CPBS	O
10 330	IND	Delhi	50	AIR	O
10 344	URS			R Moscow [feeder]	O
10 420	USA			RFE/RL [feeder]	O
10 510	ALB	Kruja	50	R Tirana	O
10 740	URS			R Moscow [feeder]	O
10 869	USA			VoA [feeder]	O
	LBR			Careysburg VoA [feeder]	O
10 870	AFG	Kabul	50	Iran Toilers	O
10 955	URS			Moscow Domestic [feeder]	O
11 000	CHN	Beijing	50	CPBS	O
11 040	CHN	Xian	120	CPBS	O
11 100	CHN	Beijing	50	CPBS	O
11 330	CHN	Beijing	50	CPBS	O
11 375	CHN	Beijing	50	CPBS	O
11 390	I	Taranto	0.3	R Marconi Intl	O
11 418	ISL	Reykjavik	10	IBS [feeder]	O
11 440	INS	Jakarta	3	PLC Jakarta	O

Frequency [kHz]	Country	Station Site	Power [kW]	Programme/ Network	O or R
11 445	CHN	Kunming	120	R Beijing	O
11 480	URS			R Moscow [feeder]	O
11 490	EGY	Abis	250	Vo Unity	O
11 500	CHN	Beijing	120	R Beijing	O
11 505	CHN	Beijing	50	CPBS	O
11 515	CHN	Beijing	120	R Beijing	O
11 550	TUN	Sfax	100	Tunis	O
	TWN	Taipei	100/250	WYFR	O
11 560	EGY	Abu Zaabal	250	R Cairo	O
11 570	PAK	Islamabad	10	R Pakistan	O
11 575	CHN	Xian	150	R Beijing	O
11 580	USA	Greenville	250	VoA	O
	USA	Okeechobee	100	WYFR	O
	GUM	Agana	100	TWR	O
	MRA	Aginan Point	100	Christian Science Mon	O
11 585	ISR	Jerusalem	100	IBA	O
11 595	GRC	Thessaloniki	35	Thessaloniki R	O
11 600	CHN	Baoding	120	R Beijing	O
	PAK	Islamabad	100	R Pakistan	O
11 605	ISR	Jerusalem	300	IBA	O
11 610	CHN	Linghsi	50	CPBS	O
	PAK	Islamabad	100	R Pakistan	O
11 615	EGY			Kaviyani Banner	O
	URS			R Moscow [feeder]	O
11 620	IND	Bangalore	500	AIR	O
11 625	EQA	Quito	500	HCJB	O
	MCO	Monte Carlo	500	TWR	O
11 630	URS	Moscow	100/240	Domestic/External	O
	CHN	Baoji	50	CPBS	O
11 635	SLV	San Jose	50	La Voz del CID	O
11 645	GRC	Athens	100	Voice of Greece	O
	GRC	Kavalla	250	Voice of Greece	O
11 650	GUM	Agana	100	KTWR	O
	CHN	Xian	250	R Beijing	O

Frequency [kHz]	Country	Station Site	Power [kW]	Programme/ Network	O or R
11 650	PHL	Bocaue	150	FEBC	O
(cont'd)	MRA	Marpi	100	KFBS	O
11 655	ISR	Jerusalem	300	Kol Israel	O
	URS	Moscow	100	Domestic/External	O
	UKR	Simferopol	500	Domestic/External	O
	MCO	Monte Carlo	100	TWR	O
11 660	HOL	Flevo	500	R Netherlands	O
	ATN	Bonaire	300	R Netherlands	O
	F	Allouis	100/500	RFI	O
	BEL	Wavre	100	RTBF	O
	BUL	Kostinbrod	250	R Sofia	O
11 665	EGY	Abu Zaabal	100	R Cairo	O
	URS	Armavir	500	Domestic/External	O
	URS	Irkutsk	500	Domestic/External	O
	URS	Khabarovsk	100	Domestic/External	O
	GUM	Agana	100	KTWR	O
11 670	F	Allouis	100/500	RFI	O
	GUF	Montsinery	500	RFI	O
	UKR	Vinnitsa	500	Domestic/External	O
	URS	Novosibirsk	100	Domestic/External	O
11 680	G	Rampisham	500	BBC	O
	G	Skelton	250	BBC	O
	BUL	Kostinbrod	250	R Sofia	O
	USA	Greenville	500	VoA	O
	USA	Redwood City	250	KGEI	O
	KRE	Kangye	50	R Pyongyang	O
11 685	URS	Khabarovsk	100	Domestic/External	O
	URS	Tashkent	100	Domestic/External	O
	URS	Moscow	100/240	Domestic/External	O
	TCH	Rimavska Sobota	250	R Prague Intl	O
	ARS	Riyadh	350	BSKSA	O
	CHN	Xian	150	R Beijing	O
11 694	VEN	Caracas	30	R N Venezuela	O
11 695	BEL	Wavre	100	BRT	O
	URS	Irkutsk	100/500	Domestic/External	O
	URS	Novosibirsk	100	Domestic/External	O
	F	Allouis	100/500	RFI	O
	CHN/ SUI	Beijing	120	SRI	O
	USA	Greenville	500	VoA	O
11 700	POR	Sines	250	IBRA R	O
	URS	Sverdlovsk	100	Domestic/External	O

Frequency [kHz]	Country	Station Site	Power [kW]	Programme/ Network	O or R
11 700	F	Allouis	100	RFI	O
(cont'd)	BUL	Plovdiv	500	R Sofia/R Moscow	O
	GUM	Agana	100	KTWR	O
	ALS	Anchor Point	100	KNLS	O
11 705	S	Hoerby	350	R Sweden	R
	D	Nauen	50	DW	R
	UKR	Kiev	100	Domestic/External	R
	F	Allouis	100/500	RFI	R
	MCO	Monte Carlo	100	TWR	R
	ISR	Jerusalem	50	IBA	R
	GAB	Moyabi	250	Africa No 1	R
	CUB	Havana	250	R Havana Cuba	R
	GUF	Montsinery	500	RFI	R
	URS	Dushanbe	100	Domestic/External	R
	CLN	Colombo	35	VoA	R
	BGD	Dhaka	100	R Bangladesh	R
	J/CAN	Tokyo Yamata	300	RCI	R
	KRE	Kujang	200	R Pyongyang	R
	CHN	Huhhot	50	Domestic/External	R
	PHL	Palauig	100	R Veritas Asia	R
	PHL	Tinang	250	VoA	R
	USA	Cypress Creek	500	Christian Science Mon	O
11 710	ISL	Reykjavik	10	IBS	R
	URS	Moscow	240	Domestic/External	R
	HOL	Flevo	500	R Netherlands	R
	G	Woofferton	250	VoA	R
	BUL	Sofia	250	R Sofia	R
	E/CHN	Noblejas	350	R Beijing	R
	CYP/G	Limassol	100	BBC	R
	MRC	Tangier	100	VoA	R
	CUB	Havana	250	R Moscow	R
	ARG	Gral Pacheco	100	RAE	R
	PAK	Islamabad	10	R Pakistan	R
	BGD	Dhaka	250	R Bangladesh	R
	URS	Petropavlokam	250	Domestic/External	R
	CHN	Lingshi	50	CPBS	R
	GUM	Agana	100	KTWR	R
	SUD	Al Fitahab	120	R Omdurman	O
	COG	Brazzaville	100	V Rev Congolaise	O
11 715	ISL	Reykjavik	10	IBS	R
	S	Hoerby	350	R Sweden	R
	URS	Tula	100	Domestic/External	R
	HOL	Flevo	500	R Netherlands	R
	UKR	Ivanofranovsk	240	Domestic/External	R
	GRC	Athens	100	Voice of Greece	R

Frequency [kHz]	Country	Station Site	Power [kW]	Programme/ Network	O or R
11 715 *(cont'd)*	CVA	S M Galeria	100/250/ 500	Vatican R	R
	E	Noblejas	350	REE	R
	ALG	Bouchaqui	50	R Algiers	R
	EGY	Abis	250	R Cairo	R
	MLI	Bamako	50	R Beijing	R
	LBR	Careysburg	250	VoA	R
	CAN	Sackville	250	R Korea	R
	CUB	Havana	100	R Havana Cuba	R
	ATN	Bonaire	300	R Netherlands	R
	IRN	Ahwaz	500	VoIRI	R
	IND	Delhi	100	AIR	R
	IND	Aligarh	250	AIR	R
	PHL	Poro	50	VoA	R
	INS	Medan	100		R
	URS	Moscow	100	R Afghanistan	O
	J	Yamata	300	RFI	O
11 720	URS	Yerevan	100	Domestic/External	R
	BUL	Sofia	150/250	R Sofia	R
	OMA/G	Masirah	100	BBC	R
	CYP/G	Limassol	100/250	BBC	R
	IRQ	Salah el Deen	500	R Baghdad	R
	ARS	Riyadh	350	BSKSA	R
	ZAI	Kinshasa	10		R
	MEX	Mexico	100		R
	ATN	Bonaire	300	R Netherlands	R
	CHL	Santiago	25		R
	URS	Kenga	100	Domestic/External	R
	CHN	Beijing	50	Domestic	R
	PHL	Poro	50	VoA	R
	AUS	Shepparton	100	R Australia	R
11 725	URS	Tbilisi	240	Domestic/External	R
	URS	Serpukhov	200	Domestic/External	R
	D/USA	Lampertheim	100	RFE/RL	R
	CVA	S M Galeria	500	Vatican R	R
	POR	Lisbon	250	RFE/RL	R
	USA	Okeechobee	100	WYFR	R
	CUB	Havana	50/250	R Havana Cuba	R
	KOR	Kimjae	250	R Korea	R
	INS	Biak	300		R
	TWN	Taipei	250	CBC Taipei	O
11 730	BLR	Orcha	20	Domestic	R
	HOL	Flevo	500	R Netherlands	R
	UKR	Vinnista	500	Domestic/External	R

Frequency [kHz]	Country	Station Site	Power [kW]	Programme/ Network	O or R
11 730	E	Noblejas	350	REE	R
(cont'd)	OMA	Seeb	100	R Oman	R
	CYP/G	Limassol	100/250	BBC	R
	TUN	Sfax	100		R
	ARS	Riyadh	350	BSKSA	R
	SEY/G	Mahe	250	BBC	R
	CAN	Sackville	250	RCI	R
	USA	Vado	50		R
	URS	Tashkent	240	Domestic/External	R
	IND	Delhi	100	AIR	R
	URS	Tchita	240	Domestic/External	R
	CHN	Kunming	50	CPBS	R
11 735	ISL	Rekyavik	10	IBS	R
	YUG	Bijeljina	500	R Yugoslavia	R
	MCO	Monte Carlo	500	TWR	R
	BUL	Sofia	250/500	R Sofia	R
	TUR	Ankara	500	TRT	R
	CVA	S M Galeria	100	Vatican R	R
	USA	Dallas	50	KCBI	R
	CUB	Havana	500	R Havana Cuba	R
	URG	Montevideo	5	R Oriental	R
	J	Tokyo Yamata	300	R Japan	R
	KRE	Kujang	200/400	R Pyongyang	R
	INS	Ujungpandang	100		R
	IND	Delhi	50	AIR	O
	GAB	Moyabi	500	R Japan	O
	USA	Dallas	50	KCBI	O
	URS	Stolnik	250	Domestic/External	O
	NOR	Kvitsoy	500	R Norway/Danmarks R	O
	GRC	Rhodes	50	VoA	O
11 740	G	Daventry	300	BBC	R
	ROU	Bucharest	250	R Romania	R
	GRC	Kavalla	250	VoA	R
	CVA	S M Galeria	100	Vatican R	R
	POR	S Gabriel	100	RDP	R
	OMA/G	Masirah	100	BBC	R
	CYP/G	Limassol	250	BBC	R
	IRQ	Salah el Deen	500	R Baghdad	R
	USA	Okeechobee	100	VoFC	R
	MEX	Mexico	5		R
	CUB	Havana	100	R Havana Cuba	R
	ATN	Bonaire	300	R Netherlands	R
	EQA	Quito	100	HCJB	R
	URS	Frunze	250	Domestic/External	R
	URS	Novosibirsk	50	Domestic	R

Frequency [kHz]	Country	Station Site	Power [kW]	Programme/ Network	O or R
11 740	CLN	Perkara	250	DW	R
(cont'd)	KRE	Kujang	200	R Pyongyang	R
	KOR	Kimjae	100	R Korea	R
	CHN	Beijing	50	R Beijing	R
	PHL	Palauig	100	R Veritas Asia	R
11 745	BLR	Minsk	20/250	Domestic/External	R
	URS	Armarvir	500	Domestic/External	R
	UKR	Vinnitsa	500	Domestic/External	R
	AFS	Meyerton	250	R RSA	R
	B	Brasilia	250	R Bras	R
	IRN	Kamalabad	100	VoIRI	R
	IND	Delhi	100	AIR	R
	MNG	Ulan Bator	50	R Ulan Bator	R
	CHN	Beijing	120	R Beijing	R
	INS	Jayapura	100		R
	ISR	Jerusalem	300	Kol Israel	O
	TWN	Panchiau	50	VoFC	O
11 750	URS	Moscow	100	Domestic/External	R
	D/USA	Wertachtal	500	VoA	R
	UKR	Lvov	250	Domestic/External	R
	CVA	S M Galeria	100/250	Vatican R	R
	POR	Lisbon	50	RDP	R
	MRC	Tangier	100	VoA	R
	ASC	Ascension	250	BBC	R
	PAK	Islamabad	250	R Pakistan	R
	J/USA	Tokyo	10	Far East Network	R
	CHN	Xian	150	R Beijing	R
	SNG/G	Kranji	100/125/ 250	BBC	R
	BUL	Plovdiv	500	R Sofia	O
11 755	FNL	Pori	500	R Finland	R
	URS	Tbilisi	100/240	Domestic/External	R
	URS	Moscow	100	R Havana Cuba	R
	IRQ	Salah el Deen	500	R Baghdad	R
	LBY	Tripoli	500	Tripoli	R
	SWZ	Manzini	25	TWR	R
	USA	Vado	50	KJES	R
	ARG	S Fernando	1	R N Buenos Aires	R
	URS	Tchita	100	Domestic/External	R
	CHN	Beijing	120	R Beijing	R
	INS	Jakarta	100	Vo Indonesia	R
	URS	Moscow	100	R Afghanistan	O
11 760	URS	Volgograd	20	Domestic	R
	G	Rampisham	500	BBC	R

Frequency [kHz]	Country	Station Site	Power [kW]	Programme/ Network	O or R
11 760	UKR	Kharkov	20	Domestic	R
(cont'd)	LBR	Careysburg	250	VoA	R
	OMA/G	Masirah	100	BBC	R
	CUB	Havana	100/250	R Havana Cuba	R
	EQA	Quito	100	HCJB	R
	BGD	Dhaka	250	R Bangladesh	R
	KRE	Pyongyang	200	R Pyongyang	R
	PHL	Tinang	250	VoA	R
	INS	Jakarta	100	RRI Jakarta	R
	IND	Delhi	250	AIR	O
	CKH	Rarotonga	1	R Cook Islands	O
11 765	D	Wertachtal	500	DW	R
	D	Julich	100	DW	R
	BUL	Sofia	250	R Sofia	R
	IRQ	Salah el Deen	500	R Baghdad	R
	ATG	Antigua	250	BBC	R
	URS	Tashkent	100	Domestic/External	R
	CLN	Perkara	250	DW	R
	URS	Irkutsk	100	Domestic/External	R
	KRE	Pyongyang	200	R Pyongyang	R
	CHN	Shijazhuang	500	R Beijing	R
	AUS	Carnarvon	300	R Australia	R
	AUS	Darwin	250	R Australia	R
	TZA	Dar es Salaam	50	R Tanzania	O
11 770	UKR	Kiev	240	Domestic/External	R
	F	Allouis	100/500	RFI	R
	POR	Lisbon	250	RFE/RL	R
	IRQ	Salah el Deen	500	R Baghdad	R
	YEM	Aden	100	R Aden	R
	NIG	Ikorodu	500		R
	GAB	Mioyabi	250	Africa No 1	R
	AFS	Meyerton	100	R Suid Afrika	R
	MEX	Mexico	10	R Mexico Intl	R
	CHL	Santiago	25		R
	IRN	Ahwaz	500	VoIRI	R
	URS	Khabarovsk	200	Domestic/External	R
	CHN	Beijing	50	R Beijing	R
	PHL	Palauig	100	VoA	R
	IND	Delhi	100	AIR	O
11 775	URS	Armavir	500	Domestic/External	R
	G	Woofferton	250	VoA	R
	ROU	Bucharest	250	R Romania	R
	BUL	Sofia	250	R Sofia	R
	TUR	Ankara	250	TRT	R

Frequency [kHz]	Country	Station Site	Power [kW]	Programme/ Network	O or R
11 775	E	Noblejas	350	REE	R
(cont'd)	ATG	Antigua	125		R
	EQA	Quito	100	HCJB	R
	URS	Irkutsk	500	Domestic/External	R
	CHN	Beijing	120	R Beijing	R
	PHL	Poro	50	VoA	R
	CAN	Sackville	250	BBC	O
	TWN	Minhsiung	100	CBS	O
11 780	URS	Kazan	100	Domestic/External	R
	D/USA	Holzkirchen	250	RFE/RL	R
	G	Rampisham	500	BBC	R
	G	Skelton	250	BBC	R
	UKR	Simferopol	100	Domestic/External	R
	AUT	Vienna	500	R Austria Intl	R
	GRC	Kavalla	250	VoA	R
	CVA	S M Galeria	100	Vatican R	R
	MRC	Tangier	35	VoA	R
	ARS	Riyadh	350	BSKSA	R
	CUB	Havana	100	R Havana Cuba	R
	B	Brasilia	250	R Nacional Amazonia	R
	ARG	Buenos Aires	1	R Belgrano	O
	IRN	Mashhad	500	VoIRI	R
	KRE	Kujang	200	R Pyongyang	R
	CHN	Kunming	50	Vo Dem Cambodia	R
	CHN	Baoding	120	R Beijing	O
11 785	NOR	Kvitsoy	500	R Norway/Danmarks R	R
	URS	Moscow	250	Domestic/External	R
	D	K Wusterhausen	100	DW	R
	D	Nauen	500	DW	R
	D	Julich	100	DW	R
	EGY	Abu Zaabal	100	R Cairo	R
	RRW	Kigali	250	DW	R
	B	Pt Alegre	7.5	R Guaiba	R
	URS	Tashkent	100	Domestic/External	R
	CLN	Perkara	250	DW	R
	INS	Jakarta	100	Vo Indonesia	R
11 790	NOR	Sveio	500	R Norway/Danmarks R	R
	ROU	Bucharest	250	R Romania	R
	F	Allouis	100	RFI	R
	E	Arganda	100	REE	R
	LBY	Tripoli	500	Tripoli R	R
	UAE	Dubai	300	UAE R	R
	MLI	Bamako	50		R
	USA	Noblesville	100	WHRI	R

Frequency [kHz]	Country	Station Site	Power [kW]	Programme/ Network	O or R
11 790	CHL	Santiago	25		R
(cont'd)	IRN	Kamalabad	500	VoIRI	R
	IND	Aligarh	250	AIR	R
	BGD	Dhaka	100	R Bangladesh	R
	URS	Blag	240	Domestic/External	R
	CHN	Beijing	50	Domestic/External	R
	PHL	Palauig	100/250	R Veritas Asia	R
	INS	Padang Cermin	250		R
11 795	ISL	Reykjavik	10	IBS	R
	URS	Tbilisi	100	Domestic/External	R
	D	Julich	100	DW	R
	MLT	Cyclops	250	DW	R
	LBY	Tripoli	500	Tripoli R	R
	RRW	Kigali	250	DW	R
	ZAI	Kinshasa	10		R
	CUB	Havana	100	R Havana Cuba	R
	EQA	Quito	100	HCJB	R
	CHN	Xian	150	Domestic/External	R
	ATG	Antigua	250	DW	O
	NOR	Sveio	500	R Norway/Danmarks R	O
	UAE	Dubai	300	UAE R	O
	PHL	Palauig	250	R Veritas Asia	O
11 800	UKR	Kiev	100	Domestic/External	R
	F	Allouis	500	RFI	R
	BUL	Sofia	150	R Sofia	R
	I	Rome	100	RAI	R
	POR	S Gabriel	100	RDP	R
	POR	Lisbon	250	RDP	R
	GHA	Ejura	250		R
	GAB	Moyabi	250	Africa No 1	R
	CUB	Havana	100/250	R Havana Cuba	R
	URS	Dushanbe	100	Domestic/External	R
	CLN	Ekala	100	SLBC	R
	AUS	Darwin	250	R Australia	R
11 805	D/USA	Wertachtal	500	VoA	R
	F	Allouis	100	RFI	R
	GRC	Kavalla	250	VoA	R
	AFS	Meyerton	250	R RSA	R
	USA	Okeechobee	100	WYFR	R
	HTI	Pt au Prince	100		R
	EQA	Quito	100	HCJB	R
	B	Rio de Janeiro	10	R Globo	R
	KOR	Kimjae	250	R Korea	R
	CHN	Baoji	50	Domestic/External	R

Frequency [kHz]	Country	Station Site	Power [kW]	Programme/ Network	O or R
11 805	GUM	Agana	100	KTWR	R
(cont'd)	PHL	Tinang	250	VoA	R
	INS	Surabaja	50		R
11 810	URS	Serpukhov	240	Domestic/External	R
	D	Wertachtal	500	DW	R
	D	Julich	100	DW	R
	UKR	Lvov	20	Domestic	R
	ROU	Bucharest	250	R Romania	R
	GRC	Kavalla	250	VoA	R
	CVA	S M Galeria	250/500	Vatican R	R
	I	Rome	100	RAI	R
	IRQ	Salah el Deen	500	R Baghdad	R
	JOR	Al Karanah	500	R Jordan	R
	RRW	Kigali	250	DW	R
	SEY	Mahe	100	FEBA	R
	B/D	Brasilia	250	DW	R
	IND	Delhi	100	AIR	R
	KOR	Kimjae	250	R Korea	R
	ATG	Antigua	250	DW	O
11 815	POL	Warsaw	100	R Polonia	R
	URS	Tbilisi	100	Domestic/External	R
	E	Noblejas	350	REE	R
	POR	Lisbon	250	RFE/RL	R
	LBY	Tripoli	500	Tripoli R	R
	UAE	Abu Dhabi	500	UAE R	R
	SEY	Mahe	100	FEBA	R
	ATN	Bonaire	50	TWR	R
	B	Goiania	7.5	R Brasil Central	R
	IND	Delhi	100	AIR	R
	URS	Khabarovsk	100	Domestic/External	R
	J	Tokyo Yamata	100/300	R Japan	R
	INS	Palembang	100		R
11 820	URS	Voronej	240	Domestic/External	R
	E	Noblejas	350	REE	R
	POR	S Gabriel	100	RDP	R
	JOR	Al Karanah	500	R Jordan	R
	GAB	Moyabi	250	Africa No 1	R
	SEY	Mahe	75	FEBA	R
	ASC	Ascension	250	BBC	R
	MOZ	Maputo	120	R Mozambique	R
	USA	Delano	250	VoA	R
	CUB	Havana	50/250	R Havana Cuba	R
	URS	Frunze	150	Domestic/External	R
	IRN	Zahedan	500	VoIRI	R

Frequency [kHz]	Country	Station Site	Power [kW]	Programme/ Network	O or R
11 820	CHN	Lhasa	50	Domestic	R
(cont'd)	PHL	Tinang	250	VoA	R
	PHL	Palauig	100	VoA	R
	URS	Moscow	100	R Afghanistan	O
	CLM	Bogota	25	R N Colombia	O
11 825	ISL	Reykjavik	10	IBS	R
	D/USA	Biblis	100	RFE/RL	R
	POR	Lisbon	50/250	VoA	R
	ARS	Riyadh	350	BSKSA	R
	URS	Kenga	100	Domestic/External	R
	KRE	Kujang	200	R Pyongyang	R
	INS	Biak	300		R
	ALB	Lushnje	100	R Tirana	O
	TWN	Panchiau	25	VoFC	O
	OCE	Papeete	20	RFO Tahiti	O
11 830	URS	Moscow	240	Domestic/External	R
	URS	Petropavlokam	20	Domestic	R
	ROU	Bucharest	250	R Romania Intl	R
	CVA	S M Galeria	250	Vatican R	R
	IRQ	Salah el Deen	500	R Baghdad	R
	LBR	Monrovia	50		R
	USA	Okeechobee	100	WYFR	R
	USA	Bethany	250	VoOAS	R
	B	Goiania	10	R Anhanguera	R
	IND	Aligarh	250	AIR	R
	IND	Bombay	100	AIR	R
	IND	Delhi	100	AIR	R
	KRE	Kujang	200	R Pyongyang	R
	KOR	Kimjae	250	R Korea	R
	CHN	Beijing	50	Domestic/External	R
	GUM	Agana	100		R
11 835	ISL	Reykjavik	10	IBS	R
	YUG	Bijeljina	500	R Yugoslavia	R
	GRC	Kavalla	250	VoA	R
	OMA/G	Masirah	100	BBC	R
	CYP/G	Limassol	250	BBC	R
	LBR	Careysburg	250	VoA	R
	GAB	Moyabi	500	R Japan	R
	MOZ	Maputo	25	R Mozambique	R
	CUB	Havana	100	R Havana Cuba	R
	EQA	Quito	500	HCJB	R
	URG	Montevideo	5	R El Espectador	R
	URS	Kenga	100	Domestic/External	R
	PAK	Islamabad	10	R Pakistan	R

Frequency [kHz]	Country	Station Site	Power [kW]	Programme/ Network	O or R
11 835	CLN	Ekala	35	SLBC	R
(cont'd)	PHL	Poro	50	VoA	R
	G	Daventry	300	BBC	O
	CUB	Havana	100	R Havana Cuba	O
	ALB	Lushnje	100	R Tirana	O
	USA	Greenville	500	VoA	O
11 840	POL	Warsaw	100	R Polonia	R
	BLR	Orcha	20	Domestic	R
	D/USA	Wertachtal	500	VoA	R
	G	Daventry	300	RCI	R
	UKR	Vinnitsa	100	Domestic/External	R
	ROU	Bucharest	250	R Romania	R
	E	Noblejas	350	REE	R
	POR	S Gabriel	100	RDP	R
	CAN	Sackville	250	RCI	R
	CUB	Havana	100	R Moscow	R
	BGD	Dhaka	250	R Bangladesh	R
	J	Tokyo Yamata	100/300	R Japan	R
	KOR	Kimjae	100	R Korea	R
	CHN	Kunming	120	Domestic/External	R
	PHL	Tinang	250	VoA	R
	NOR	Kvitsoy	500	R Norway/Danmarks R	O
	BUL	Sofia	250	R Sofia	O
11 845	S	Horby	350	R Sweden	R
	URS	Tbilisi	100	Domestic/External	R
	D	Wertachtal	500	DW	R
	F	Allouis	100	RFI	R
	GRC	Kavalla	250	VoA	R
	CYP/G	Limassol	250	BBC	R
	CAN	Sackville	250	RCI	R
	URG	Montevideo	10		R
	KRE	Kujang	200	R Pyongyang	R
	CHN	Kunming	120	Domestic/External	R
	INS	Bandung	50		R
	PHL	Bocaue	50	FEBC	O
	NOR	Kvitsoy	500	R Norway/Danmarks R	O
11 850	FNL	Pori	500	R Finland	R
	NOR	Fredrikstad	350	R Norway/Danmarks R	R
	NOR	Sveio	500	R Norway/Danmarks R	R
	URS	Konevo	240	Domestic/External	R
	URS	Riazan	240	Domestic/External	R
	URS	Moscow	240	R Havana Cuba	R
	D	Wertachtal	500	DW	R
	E/CHN	Noblejas	350	R Beijing	R

Frequency [kHz]	Country	Station Site	Power [kW]	Programme/ Network	O or R
11 850	OMA/G	Masirah	100	BBC	R
(cont'd)	CYP/G	Limassol	100	BBC	R
	GHA	Ejura	250		R
	LBR	Careysburg	250	VoA	R
	CAN	Sackville	250	RCI	R
	CUB	Havana	100	R Havana Cuba	R
	ATN	Bonaire	50	TWR	R
	PRG	Asuncion	5		R
	IND	Delhi	100	AIR	R
	BGD	Dhaka	250	R Bangladesh	R
	J	Tokyo Yamata	100	R Japan	R
	PHL	Bocaue	50	VoA	R
	SNG/G	Kranji	250	BBC	R
	MNG	Ulan Bator	50	R Ulan Bator	O
11 855	ISL	Reykjavik	10	IBS	R
	D/USA	Lampertheim	100	RFE/RL	R
	POR	Lisbon	250	RFE/RL	R
	MRC	Tangier	100	VoA	R
	ARS	Jeddah	100	BSKSA	R
	CAN	Sackville	250	RCI	R
	USA	Okeechobee	100	WYFR	R
	B	Aparecida	1	R Aparecida	R
	IND	Delhi	50/100	AIR	R
	MNG	Ulan Bator	250	R Ulan Bator	R
	KRE	Kujang	200	R Pyongyang	R
	CHN	Jinhua	500	Domestic/External	R
	INS	Ujungpandang	50		R
	AUS	Carnarvon	100	R Australia	R
11 860	ISL	Reykjavik	10	IBS	R
	NOR	Sveio	500	R Norway/Danmarks R	R
	URS	Gorki	240	Domestic/External	R
	UKR	Vinnitsa	250	Domestic/External	R
	BUL	Sofia	250	R Sofia	R
	OMA/G	Masirah	100	BBC	R
	IRQ	Salah el Deen	500	R Baghdad	R
	SEY	Mahe	100	FEBA	R
	ASC	Ascension	250	BBC	R
	SEY/G	Mahe	250	BBC	R
	CUB	Havana	100	R Havana Cuba	R
	IND	Delhi	100	AIR	R
	IND	Aligarh	250	AIR	R
	VEN	Caracas	50	R N Venezuela	O
	BUL	Sofia	50/250	R Sofia	O
	TWN	Taipei	50	VoFC	O

Frequency [kHz]	Country	Station Site	Power [kW]	Programme/ Network	O or R
11 865	NOR	Kvitsoy	500	R Norway/Danmarks R	R
	D	Julich	100	DW	R
	D	Wertachtal	500	DW	R
	G	Woofferton	300	VoA	R
	POR	Sines	250	DW	R
	MLT	Cyclops	250	DW	R
	LBY	Tripoli	500	Tripoli R	R
	SEN	Dakar	100		R
	ZAI	Lubumbashi	100		R
	SEY	Mahe	100	FEBA	R
	PAK	Islamabad	100	R Pakistan	R
	IND	Delhi	100	AIR	R
	CHN	Huhhot	50	PBS	R
	PHL	Bocaue	50	VoA	R
	SNG/G	Kranji	100	BBC	R
	J	Tokyo Yamata	300	R Japan	O
	INS	Jakarta	25	RRI Jakarta	O
11 870	NOR	Kvitsoy	500	R Norway/Danmarks R	R
	URS	Serp	240	Domestic/External	R
	BUL	Sofia	500	R Sofia	R
	ARS	Jeddah	50	BSKSA	R
	IND	Delhi	100	AIR	R
	MNG	Ulan Bator	250/308	R Ulan Bator	R
	J	Tokyo Yamata	100	R Japan	R
	CHN	Kunming	50	Vo Dem Cambodia	R
	PHL	Iba	100		R
	PHL	Tinang	250	VoA	R
	URS	Moscow	100	Lao National R	O
	ALB	Lushnja	100	R Tirana	O
11 875	D/USA	Lampertheim	100	RFE/RL	R
	D/USA	Biblis	100	RFE/RL	R
	TUR	Ankara	500	TRT	R
	GRC	Kavalla	250	VoA	R
	POR	Lisbon	250	RFE/RL	R
	ISR	Jerusalem	50/300	Kol Israel	R
	EGY	Abis	250	R Cairo	R
	CUB	Havana	100/250	R Havana Cuba	R
	IND	Delhi	100	AIR	R
	J	Tokyo Yamata	300	R Japan	R
	NOR	Kvitsoy	500	R Norway/Danmarks R	O
11 880	URS	Moscow	240	Domestic/External	R
	UKR	Ivanofranovsk	100	Domestic/External	R
	F	Allouis	100	RFI	R
	BUL	Sofia	250	R Sofia	R

Frequency [kHz]	Country	Station Site	Power [kW]	Programme/ Network	O or R
11 880	E	Noblejas	350	REE	R
(cont'd)	ZMB	Lusaka	50	R Zambia Intl	R
	CAN	Sackville	250	RCI	R
	USA	Greenville	250	VoA	R
	MEX	Mexico	5		R
	URS	Tashkent	500	Domestic/External	R
	IND	Bangalore	500	AIR	R
	KRE	Kujang	200	R Pyongyang	R
	KRE	Xujang	400	R Pyongyang	R
	CHN	Xian	150	Domestic	R
	PHL	Poro	50	VoA	R
	AUS	Brandon	10	R Australia	R
	ALS	Anchor Point	100	KNLS	O
11 885	D/USA	Holzkirchen	250	RFE/RL	R
	ROU	Bucharest	250	R Romania	R
	E	Playa de Pals	250	RFE/RL	R
	POR	Lisbon	250	RFE/RL	R
	ATN	Bonaire	100	TWR	R
	URG	Montevideo	10		R
	INS	Ujungpandang	250		R
	ROU	Bacau	250	R Romania Intl	O
	PHL	Palauig	100	R Veritas Asia	O
	MLA	Kuala Lumpur	100	Vo Malaysia	O
11 890	URS	Riazan	250	Domestic/External	R
	D	Nauen	100	DW	R
	E	Noblejas	350	REE	R
	OMA	Seeb	50	Oman R	R
	OMA	Thumrait	100	Oman R	R
	USA	Bethany	250	VoA	R
	USA	Greenville	250/500	VoA	R
	ATN	Bonaire	300	R Netherlands	R
	CHL	Santiago	100		R
	URS	Frunze	240/500	Domestic/External	R
	BGD	Dhaka	100/250	R Bangladesh	R
	CHN	Beijing	120	Domestic/External	R
11 895	POR	Lisbon	50/250	RFE/RL	R
	USA	Greenville	500	VoA	R
	B	Pt Alegre	1		R
	URS	Frunze	150	Domestic/External	R
	IND	Delhi	100	AIR	R
	CLN	Ekala	35	SLBC	R
	INS	Yogyakarta	100		R
	GUM	Agana	100	KTWR	O
	IRN	Kamalabad	500	VoIRI	O

Frequency [kHz]	Country	Station Site	Power [kW]	Programme/ Network	O or R
11 900	S	Horby	350	R Sweden	R
	URS	Armavir	500	Domestic/External	R
	URS	Serpukhov	250	Domestic/External	R
	AFS	Meyerton	250	R RSA	R
	EQA	Quito	100	HCJB	R
	URG	Montevideo	20		R
11 905	S	Horby	350	R Sweden	R
	D	Julich	100	DW	R
	D	Wertachtal	500	DW	R
	I	Rome	100	RAI	R
	MRC	Tangier	35	VoA	R
	EGY	Abu Zaabal	100	R Cairo	R
	B	Curitiba	10	R Universo	R
	CLN	Perkara	250	SLBC	R
	KRE	Kujang	200	R Pyongyang	R
	CHN	Beijing	120	Domestic/External	R
	CHN	Baoding	120	Domestic/External	R
	THA	Bangkok	50	R Thailand	R
	D/USA	Munich	100	VoA	O
	GRC	Rhodes	50	VoA	O
	GRC	Kavalla	250	VoA	O
	TWN	Taipei	35	CBS Taipei	O
	TWN	Minhsiung	35	Vo Free Asia	O
11 910	URS	Moscow	100	Domestic/External	R
	HNG	Jaszbereny	250	R Budapest	R
	HNG	Diosd	100	R Budapest	R
	SYR	Adra	500	R Damascus	O
	IRQ	Salah el Deen	500	R Baghdad	R
	CUB	Havana	50	R Havana Cuba	R
	EQA	Quito	250/500	HCJB	R
	IND	Delhi	100	AIR	R
	BGD	Dhaka	250	R Bangladesh	R
	GUM	Agana	100		R
	AUS	Shepparton	100	R Australia	R
	CHN	Xian	150	RFI	O
11 915	URS	Orenburg	240	Domestic/External	R
	D	Julich	100	DW	R
	D	Wertachtal	500	DW	R
	D/USA	Holzkirchen	250	RFE/RL	R
	POR	Sines	250	RCI	R
	LBR	Careysburg	250	VoA	R
	SEY	Mahe	75	FEBA	R
	USA	Greenville	250	VoA	R
	PRU	Lima	40		R

Frequency [kHz]	Country	Station Site	Power [kW]	Programme/ Network	O or R
11 915	B	Pt Alegre	7.5	R Gaucha	R
(cont'd)	PRG	Concepcion	100		R
	CHN	Xian	150	REE	R
	PHL	Palauig	100	R Veritas Asia	R
	USA	Okeechobee	100	WYFR/VoFC	O
	TWN	Taipei	250	VoFC	O
11 920	URS	Kazan	20/150	Domestic/External	R
	UKR	Lvov	240	Domestic/External	R
	E	Arganda	100	REE	R
	MRC	Tangier	50	VoA	R
	CTI	Abidjan	500	R Abidjan	R
	AFS	Meyerton	250	R RSA	R
	IND	Delhi	50	AIR	R
	PHL	Tinang	250	VoA	R
	SNG/G	Kranji	100/250	BBC	R
	NOR	Fredrikstad	350	R Norway/Danmarks R	R
	URS	Kazan	240	R Havana Cuba	O
	MRC	Tangier	50	RTM Rabat	O
11 925	NOR	Fredrikstad	350	R Norway/Danmarks R	R
	S	Horby	350	R Sweden	R
	URS	Voroney	250	Domestic/External	R
	D/USA	Biblis	100	RFE/RL	R
	G	Woofferton	300	VoA	R
	G	Rampisham	500	BBC	R
	HNG	Jaszbereny	250	R Budapest	R
	AUT	Vienna	300	RCI	R
	TUR	Ankara	250	TRT	R
	SYR	Adra	500	R Damascus	R
	MLT	Cyclops	250	Vo Mediterranean	R
	AFS	Meyerton	500	R RSA	R
	EQA	Quito	100	HCJB	R
	B	Sao Paulo	10	R Banderirantes	R
	PAK	Karachi	50	R Pakistan	R
	IND	Delhi	50	AIR	R
	IND	Aligarh	250	AIR	R
	CHN	Beijing	50	Domestic/External	R
	PHL	Tinang	250	VoA	R
11 930	F	Allouis	100/500	RFI	R
	SEY	Mahe	75/100	FEBA	O
	USA	Cypress Creek	500	Christian Science Mon	R
	USA	Greenville	250	VoA	R
	CUB	Havana	100/250	R Havana Cuba	R
	ATN	Bonaire	100	TWR	R
	URS	Sverdlovsk	240	Domestic/External	R

Frequency [kHz]	Country	Station Site	Power [kW]	Programme/ Network	O or R
11 930	CLN	Ekala	35	SLBC	R
(cont'd)	PHL	Tinang	250	VoA	R
	AUS	Brandon	10	R Australia	O
	URS	Moscow	100	R Havana Cuba	O
11 935	D/USA	Holzkirchen	250	RFE/RL	R
	HOL	Flevo	500	R Netherlands	R
	G	Daventry	300	RCI	R
	E	Playa de Pals	250	RFE/RL	R
	POR	Lisbon	250	RFE/RL	R
	IRQ	Salah el Deen	500	R Baghdad	R
	ARS	Riyadh	350	BSKSA	R
	USA	Greenville	500	VoA	R
	B	Curitiba	7.5	R Clube Paranaense	R
	IND	Bangalore	500	AIR	R
	IND	Delhi	100	AIR	R
	J	Tokyo Yamata	100	R Japan	R
	INS	Bandjarmasin	100		R
	ALB	Lushnje	100	R Tirana	O
11 938	CBG	Phnom-Penh	50	VoPO Cambodia	O
11 940	ROU	Bucharest	120/250	R Romania	R
	JOR	Al Karanah	500	R Jordan	R
	UAE	Dubai	300	UAE R	R
	LSO/G	Lancers	100	BBC	R
	CAN	Sackville	250	RCI	R
	PRG	Encarnacion	5		R
	URS	Sverdlovsk	100	Domestic/External	R
	PAK	Islamabad	100	R Pakistan	R
	SNG	Singapore	50	SBC	R
11 945	URS	Moscow	20	Domestic	R
	D	Julich	100	DW	R
	GRC	Kavalla	250	VoA	R
	E	Noblejas	350	REE	R
	CYP/G	Limassol	100/250	BBC	R
	CAN	Sackville	250	RCI	R
	USA	Delano	250	VoA	R
	PRG	Encarnacion	5	R Encarnacion	R
	CLN	Perkara	250	DW	R
	KRE	Kujang	200/400	R Pyongyang	R
	KOR	Kimjae	100/250	R Korea	R
	CHN	Baoding	240	R Beijing	R
	CHN	Xian	150	R Beijing	R
	HKG/G	Tsang Tsui	250	BBC	R
	G	Rampisham	500	BBC	O
	UAE	Dubai	300	UAE R	O

Frequency [kHz]	Country	Station Site	Power [kW]	Programme/ Network	O or R
11 950	D	Wertachtal	500	DW	R
	POR	Sines	250	DW	R
	ARS	Diriyya	50	BSKSA	R
	AFS	Meyerton	250	R RSA	R
	CUB	Havana	250	R Havana Cuba	R
	URS	Alma Ata	100	Domestic/External	R
	CHN	Lhasa	15	Domestic/External	R
	PHL	Palauig	100	R Veritas Asia	O
	B	Rio de Janeiro	7.5	R Mec	O
11 955	G	Rampisham	500	BBC	R
	G	Daventry	100	BBC	R
	UKR	Ivanofranovsk	50	Domestic/External	R
	SUI	Schwarzenburg	150	SRI	R
	F	Allouis	500	RFI	R
	TUR	Ankara	250	TRT	R
	OMA/G	Masirah	100	BBC	R
	CYP/G	Limassol	300	BBC	R
	JOR	Al Karanah	500	R Jordan	R
	UAE	Dubai	300	UAE R	R
	LBR	Monrovia	50	ELWA	R
	AGL	Luanda	100	R N Angola	R
	CAN	Sackville	250	RCI	R
	URG	Montevideo	10		R
	CHN	Xian	150	RCI	R
	PHL	Tinang	250	VoA	R
	SNG/G	Kranji	125/250	BBC	R
	MDG	Talata Volondry	300	R Netherlands	O
11 960	D/USA	Wertachtal	500	RFE/RL	R
	BEL	Wavre	100	BRT	R
	GRC	Rhodes	50	VoA	R
	IRQ	Salah el Deen	500	R Baghdad	R
	ISR	Jerusalem	50/300	Kol Israel	R
	UAE	Abu Dhabi	500	UAE R	R
	MLI	Bamako	50	RTV Malienne	R
	LBR	Monrovia	50	ELWA	R
	USA	Rancho Simi	50		R
	CUB	Havana	250	R Havana Cuba	R
	EQA	Quito	250	HCJB	R
	IND	Bangalore	500	AIR	R
	CHN	Beijing	50	Domestic	R
	ATG	Antigua	250	DW	O
	URS	Moscow	100	Lao National R	O
	ALB	Lushnje	100	R Tirana	O
	G	Woofferton	250	VoA	O

Frequency [kHz]	Country	Station Site	Power [kW]	Programme/ Network	O or R
11 965	URS	Kaunas	150	Domestic/External	R
	F	Allouis	100/500	RFI	R
	UAE	Abu Dhabi	500	UAE R	R
	GUI	Conakry	100		R
	RRW	Kigali	250	DW	R
	GUF	Montsinery	500	RFI	R
	B	Sao Paulo	7.5	R Record	R
	PAK	Karachi	50	R Pakistan	R
	CLN	Perkara	250	DW	R
	KOR	Kimjae	100	R Korea	R
	PHL	Tinang	250	VoA	R
	INS	Jayapura	100		R
	ATG	Antigua	250	DW	O
11 970	POL	Warsaw	100	R Polonia	R
	D	Nauen	500	DW	R
	ROU	Bucharest	120/250	R Romania	R
	F	Allouis	100	RFI	R
	E	Playa de Pals	250	RFE/RL	R
	POR	Lisbon	50/250	RFE/RL	R
	IRQ	Salah el Deen	500	R Baghdad	R
	CUB	Havana	100	R Havana Cuba	R
	GUF	Montsinery	500	RFI	R
	NPL	Kathmandu	100	R Nepal	R
	CHN	Beijing	50	Domestic	R
	URS	Sverdlovsk	200	Domestic/External	O
	IND	Delhi	100	AIR	O
11 975	URS	Tashkent	100	Domestic/External	O
	EGY	Abu Zaabal	100	R Cairo	O
	KRE	Pyongyang	200	R Pyongyang	O
11 980	URS	Armavir	500	Domestic/External	O
	UKR	Vinnitsa	100	Domestic/External	O
	EGY	Abis	250	R Cairo	O
11 985	BEL	Wavre	100	BRT	O
	ALB	Lushnje	100	R Tirana	O
	URS	Tashkent	100	Domestic/External	O
	UAE	Abu Dhabi	500	UAE R	O
11 990	KWT	Sulaibiyah	500	R Kuwait	O
	TCH	Rimavska Sobota	250	R Prague Intl	O
11 995	URS	Kazan	100	Domestic/External	O
	URS	Moscow	240	Domestic/External	O
	F	Allouis	100	RFI	O
	GUF	Montsinery	500	RFI	O
	PHL	Bocaue	50	FEBC	O

Frequency [kHz]	Country	Station Site	Power [kW]	Programme/ Network	O or R
12 000	URS	Frunze	500	Domestic/External	O
	URS	Moscow	100	Domestic/External	O
	URS	Vladivostock	100	Domestic/External	O
	MNG	Ulan Bator	25	R Ulan Bator	O
	AUS	Carnarvon	250/300	R Australia	O
12 005	URS	Irkutsk	500	Domestic/External	O
	URS	Novosibirsk	500	Domestic/External	O
	TUN	Sfax	100	RTV Tunisienne	O
12 008	E	San Fernando	1	EBC Cadiz	O
12 010	URS	Moscow	240	Domestic/External	O
	URS	Petropavlokam	100	Domestic/External	O
	AUT	Moosbrunn	100	R Austria Intl	O
12 015	URS	Tashkent	100	Domestic/External	O
	URS	Yerevan	100	Domestic/External	O
	GAB	Moyabi	500	RFI	O
	MNG	Ulan Bator	250	R Ulan Bator	O
	CHN	Beijing	120	R Beijing	O
12 020	URS	Moscow	250	Domestic/External	O
	MCO	Monte Carlo	500	TWR	O
	VTN	Hanoi	120	Vo Vietnam	O
12 025	URS	Leningrad	100	Domestic/External	O
	IRQ	Salah el Deen	500	R Baghdad	O
	MRA	Saipan	100	KFBS	O
	GAB	Moyabi	500	RFI	O
	MNG	Ulan Bator	250	R Ulan Bator	O
12 030	URS	Kazan	250	Domestic/External	O
	URS	Moscow	240/500	Domestic/External	O
	BGD	Dhaka	250	R Bangladesh	O
	SUI	Beromunster	250	SRI	O
12 035	URS	Novosibirsk	100	Domestic/External	O
	E	Noblejas	350	REE	O
	GAB	Moyabi	500	SRI	O
	SUI	Schwarzenburg	150	SRI	O
	VTN	Hanoi	15	R Hanoi	O
12 040	G	Daventry	300	BBC	O
	G	Rampisham	500	BBC	O
	URS	Frunze	500	Domestic/External	O
	URS	Sverdlovsk	100	Domestic/External	O
	VTN	Hanoi	15	Vo Vietnam	O
12 045	URS	Kazan	100	Domestic/External	O
	URS	Leningrad	100	Domestic/External	O

Frequency [kHz]	Country	Station Site	Power [kW]	Programme/ Network	O or R
12 050	URS	Armavir	240	Domestic/External	O
	EGY	Abis	250	R Cairo	O
	EGY	Abu Zaabal	100	R Cairo	O
	URS	Petropavlovsk	100	Domestic/External	O
	MNG	Ulan Bator	250	R Ulan Bator	O
12 055	URS	Armavir	100	Domestic/External	O
	CHN	Beijing	100	R Beijing	O
12 060	URS	Frunze	500	Domestic/External	O
	UKR	Simferopol	500	Domestic/External	O
	UKR	Vinnitsa	500	Domcstic/External	O
12 065	URS	Armavir	50	Domestic/External	O
	URS	Petropavlovsk	240	Domestic/External	O
12 070	URS	Khabarovsk	100	Domestic/External	O
	URS	Vladivostock	100	Domestic/External	O
12 077	ISR	Jerusalem	300	Kol Israel	O
12 085	SYR	Adra	500	R Damascus	O
12 095	G	Daventry	300	BBC	O
	G	Skelton	250	BBC	O
12 105	GRC	Athens	100/250	Voice of Greece	O
	GRC	Kavalla	250	Voice of Greece	O
12 120	CHN	Beijing	50	CPBS	O
12 140	FJI	Suva	0.15	South Pacific Univ	O
12 200	CHN	Beijing	50	CPBS	O
12 230	EGY	Abis	250	Vo Unity	O
12 307	PRU	Callao	1	OBC Peru	O
12 450	CHN	Beijing	15	R Beijing	O
13 595	USA	Scotts Corners	500	Christian Science Mon	O
13 600	IRQ	Salah el Deen	500	R Baghdad	O
13 605	AUS	Darwin	250	R Australia	O
	AUS	Carnarvon	300	R Australia	O
	URS	Petropavlovsk	100	Domestic/External	O
	UAE	Abu Dhabi	500	UAE R	O
13 610	D	Leipzig	100	DW	O
	D	Nauen	50	DW	O
	KWT	Sulaibiyah	500	R Kuwait	O
13 615	URS	Irkutsk	250	Domestic/External	O

Frequency [kHz]	Country	Station Site	Power [kW]	Programme/ Network	O or R
13 620	KWT	Sulaibiyah	500	R Kuwait	O
	BGD	Dhaka	250	R Bangladesh	O
13 625	URS	Novosibirsk	100	Domestic/External	O
	MRA	Aginan Point	100	Christian Science Mon	O
13 635	SUI	Sottens	500	SRI	O
13 645	URS	Yerevan	100	Domestic/External	O
	IRQ	Salah el Deen	500	R Baghdad	O
13 650	URS	Yerevan	100	Domestic/External	O
	CAN	Sackville	100/250	RCI	O
	KRE	Pyongyang	200	R Pyongyang	O
13 655	JOR	Al Karanah	500	R Jordan	O
13 660	G	Rampisham	500	BBC	O
	IRQ	Salah el Deen	500	R Baghdad	O
13 665	URS	Petropavlovsk	100	Domestic/External	O
	PAK	Karachi	50	R Pakistan	O
13 670	CAN	Sackville	100	RCI	O
	KOR	Kimjae	250	R Korea	O
13 675	BEL	Wavre	180	BRT	O
	UAE	Dubai	300/500	UAE R	O
13 680	URS	Moscow	100	Domestic/External	O
	URS	Simferopol	240	Domestic/External	O
13 685	SUI	Sottens	500	SRI	O
	GUF	Montsinery	500	R Beijing	O
13 690	D	K Wusterhausen	50	DW	O
	URS	Moscow	100	Domestic/External	O
13 695	USA	Van Nuys	50	KVOH	O
	USA	Okeechobee	100	WYFR	O
13 700	URS	Moscow	100	Domestic/External	O
	HOL	Flevo	500	R Netherlands	O
13 705	URS	Moscow	20/100	Domestic/External	O
	AUS	Shepparton	100	R Australia	O
	AUS	Carnarvon	300	R Australia	O
13 710	URS	Moscow	100	Domestic/External	O
13 715	URS	Tashkent	100	Domestic/External	O
	TCH	Litomysl	100	R Prague Intl	O
13 720	URS	Simferopol	240	Domestic/External	O
	GUM	Agat	100	AWR	O

Frequency [kHz]	Country	Station Site	Power [kW]	Programme/ Network	O or R
13 720	CAN	Sackville	250	RCI	O
(cont'd)	USA	New Orleans	100	WRNO	O
13 730	AUT	Moosbrunn	100/500	R Austria Intl	O
13 735	URS	Kazan	50	Domestic/External	O
	URS	Moscow	250	Domestic/External	O
	USA	Bethany	250	VoA	O
	USA	Delano	250	VoA	O
13 745	G	Rampisham	500	BBC	O
	AUS	Carnarvon	300	R Australia	O
	AUS	Shepparton	100	R Australia	O
13 750	ISR	Jerusalem	50	Kol Israel	O
13 760	D	Wertachtal	500	DW	O
	USA	Noblesville	100	WHRI	O
	USA	Cypress Creek	500	Christian Science Mon	O
13 675	URS	Vladivostock	100	Domestic/External	O
13 770	D	K Wusterhausen	100	DW	O
	HOL	Flevo	500	R Netherlands	O
	USA	Scotts Corners	500	Christian Science Mon	O
13 775	URS	Moscow	100	Domestic/External	O
	URS	Novosibirsk	100	Domestic/External	O
	USA	Greenville	250	VoA	O
	KRE	Pyongyang	200	R Pyongyang	O
13 780	D	Julich	100	DW	O
	D	Wertachtal	500	DW	O
	MLT	Cyclops	250	DW	O
	MNG	Ulan Bator	250	R Ulan Bator	O
13 785	UKR	Kiev	20	Domestic	O
13 790	D	Julich	100	DW	O
	D	Wertachtal	500	DW	O
13 795	UKR	Kiev	20	Domestic	O
13 830	ISL	Reykjavik	10	IBS	O
14 918	KIR	Bairiki	0.50	R Kiribati	O
15 020	IND	Delhi	250	AIR	O
15 030	CHN	Beijing	50	CPBS	O
15 050	IND	Aligarh	250	AIR	O
15 060	ARS	Riyadh	350	BSKSA	O

Frequency [kHz]	Country	Station Site	Power [kW]	Programme/ Network	O or R
15 070	G	Daventry	100	BBC	O
	G	Rampisham	500	BBC	O
	G	Skelton	250	BBC	O
15 084	IRN	Kamalabad	350	VoIRI	O
15 090	CVA	S M Galeria	100	Vatican R	O
15 095	SYR	Adra	500	R Damascus	O
	ISR	Jerusalem	300	Kol Israel	O
15 100	UAE	Abu Dhabi	500	UAE R	O
	PHL	Bocaue	50	FEBC	O
	EGY	Abis	250	Iran's Flag of Freedom	O
15 105	D	Wertachtal	500	DW	R
	YUG	Bijeljina	500	R Yugoslavia	R
	CVA	S M Galeria	100	Vatican R	R
	MLT	Cyclops	250	DW	R
	MRC	Tangier	50	RTVM Rabat	R
	ISR	Jerusalem	100	Kol Israel	R
	ASC	Ascension	250	BBC	R
	USA	Noblesville	100	WHRI	R
	ATG	Antigua	250	DW	O
	PAK	Islamabad	100	R Pakistan	R
	IND	Delhi	100	AIR	R
	CLN	Perkara	250	DW	R
	CHN	Xian	150	R Beijing	R
	CHN	Baoding	240	R Beijing	R
15 110	BLR	Orcha	100	Domestic/External	R
	URS	Serpukhov	20	Domestic	R
	TCH	Litomysl	120	R Prague	R
	E	Noblejas	350	REE	R
	IRQ	Salah el Deen	500	R Baghdad	R
	MLI	Bamako	50		R
	MEX	Mexico	100		R
	CHL	Santiago	100		R
	URS	Sverdlovsk	240	Domestic/External	R
	IND	Bangalore	500	AIR	R
	CHN	Beijing	120	Vo Dem Cambodia	R
	PHL	Palauig	250	R Veritas Asia	R
15 115	FNL	Pori	500	R Finland	R
	BLR	Minsk	20	Domestic	R
	G	Rampisham	500	BBC	R
	POR	Lisbon	250	RFE/RL	R
	EGY	Abu Zaabal	100	R Cairo	R
	EQA	Quito	100	HCJB	R

Frequency [kHz]	Country	Station Site	Power [kW]	Programme/ Network	O or R
15 115	CHL	Santiago	100		R
(cont'd)	PAK	Karachi	50	R Pakistan	R
	KRE	Kujang	200	R Pyongyang	R
	MRA	Aginan Point	100		R
	ALB	Lushnje	100	R Tirana	O
15 120	POL	Warsaw	100	R Polonia	R
	CVA	S M Galeria	100/250	Vatican R	R
	NIG	Ikorodu	500		R
	GAB	Moyabi	250	Africa No 1	R
	USA	Greenville	250	VoA	R
	MEX	Mexico	100		R
	ATN	Bonaire	300	R Netherlands	R
	URS	Sverdlovsk	20	Domestic	R
	IND	Aligarh	250	AIR	R
	CLN	Ekala	35	SLBC	R
	AFS	Meyerton	250	R RSA	O
	PHL	Palauig	100	R Veritas Asia	O
15 125	ISL	Reykjavik	10	IBS	R
	E	Noblejas	350	REE	R
	OMA/G	Masirah	100	BBC	R
	GAB	Moyabi	250	Africa No 1	R
	SWZ	Manzini	100	TWR	R
	MEX	Mexico	10		R
	IND	Bombay	100	AIR	R
	CHN	Xian	300	R Beijing	R
	CHN	Beijing	120	Domestic/External	R
	GUM	Agat	100		R
	PHL	Poro	50	VoA	R
	TWN	Taipei	250	BCC Taipei	O
15 130	UKR	Simferopol	50/240	Domestic/External	R
	E	Playa de Pals	250	RFE/RL	R
	IRQ	Salah el Deen	500	R Baghdad	R
	MLI	Bamako	50	R Beijing	R
	USA	Okeechobee	50/100	WYFR/VoFC	R
	URS	Sverdlovsk	200	Domestic/External	R
	URS	Vladivostock	240	Domestic/External	R
	URS	Tchita	500	Domestic/External	R
	AUS	Shepparton	100	R Australia	R
15 135	ISL	Reykjavik	10	IBS	R
	D	Wertachtal	500	DW	R
	F	Allouis	100/500	RFI	R
	SWZ	Manzini	100	TWR	R
	B	Sao Paulo	4.5	R Record	R
	CHL	Santiago	100		R

Frequency [kHz]	Country	Station Site	Power [kW]	Programme/ Network	O or R
15 135	IND	Delhi	100	AIR	R
(cont'd)	CHN	Kunming	120	Domestic/External	R
	PHL	Palauig	250	VoA	R
15 140	POR	S Gabriel	100	RDP	R
	ARS	Jeddah	50	BSKSA	R
	CAN	Sackville	250	RCI	R
	CHL	Santiago	25/100	R Nacional Chile	R
	URS	Dushanbe	100	Domestic/External	R
	IND	Delhi	50	AIR	R
	KRE	Kanggye	200/400	R Pyongyang	R
	SNG/G	Kranji	100	BBC	R
15 145	URS	Murmansk	20	Domestic	R
	D	Nauen	500	DW	R
	D/USA	Biblis	100	RFE/RL	R
	GRC	Athens	100	ERT	R
	GRC	Kavalla	250	VoA	R
	POR	Lisbon	250	RFE/RL	R
	USA	Okeechobee	100	WYFR	R
	USA	Red Lion	50	WINB	R
	NOR	Kvitsoy	500	R Norway/Danmarks R	O
15 150	URS	Moscow	500	Domestic/External	R
	IRQ	Salah el Deen	500	R Baghdad	R
	IRQ	Babel	500	R Baghdad	R
	SWZ	Manzini	100	TWR	R
	CAN	Sackville	250	RCI	R
	PRU	Lima	15		R
	CHL	Santiago	25		R
	BGD	Dhaka	250	R Bangladesh	R
	KRE	Pyongyang	200/400	R Pyongyang	R
	KOR	Kimjae	250	R Korea	R
	PHL	Tinang	250	VoA	R
	INS	Jakarta	250		R
	NZL	Rangatiki	100	R New Zealand	R
	MDG	Talata Volondry	300	R Netherlands	O
15 155	TCH	Velkekostolany	120	R Prague	R
	F	Allouis	100	RFI	R
	EGY	Abu Zaabal	100	R Cairo	R
	GAB	Moyabi	250	Africa No 1	R
	CUB	Havana	100	R Havana Cuba	R
	EQA	Quito	100	HCJB	R
	IND	Delhi	100	AIR	R
	IND	Aligarh	250	AIR	R
	KOR	Kimjae	250	R Korea	R
	PHL	Tinang	250	VoA	R

Frequency [kHz]	Country	Station Site	Power [kW]	Programme/ Network	O or R
15 160	NOR	Fredrikstad	350	R Norway/Danmarks R	R
	HNG	Jaszbereny	250	R Budapest	R
	HNG	Diosd	100	R Budapest	R
	HNG	Szekesferhervar	20	R Budapest	R
	BUL	Sofia	250	R Sofia	R
	TUR	Ankara	250	TRT	R
	ALG	Bouchaoui	100		R
	ASC	Ascension	250	BBC	R
	USA	Bethany	250	VOA/Vo OEA	R
	MEX	Mexico	10	R XEW 900	R
	EQA	Quito	100	HCJB	R
	BGD	Dhaka	100	R Bangladesh	R
	URS	Niko	500	Domestic/External	R
	KRE	Kujang	200	R Pyongyang	R
	PHL	Tinang	250	VoA	R
	AUS	Shepparton	100	R Australia	R
15 165	ISL	Reykjavik	10	IBS	R
	NOR	Kvitsoy	500	R Norway/Danmarks R	R
	NOR	Sveio	500	R Norway/Danmarks R	R
	NOR	Fredrikstad	350	R Norway/Danmarks R	R
	YUG	Bijeljina	500	R Yugoslavia	R
	CYP/G	Limassol	100	BBC	R
	IND	Delhi	50	AIR	R
	IND	Bombay	100	AIR	R
	CHN	Xian	150	Domestic/External	R
	CHN	Jinhua	500	R Beijing	R
	PHL	Tinang	250	VoA	R
15 170	ISL	Reykjavik	10	IBS	R
	POR	Lisbon	50/250	RFE/RL	R
	IRQ	Salah el Deen	500	R Baghdad	R
	ARS	Jeddah	50	BSKSA	R
	USA	Okeechobee	50/100	WYFR	R
	URS	Irkutsk	50	Domestic/External	R
	AUS	Darwin	250	R Australia	R
	MNG	Ulan Bator	50	R Moscow	O
	SWZ	Manzini	100	TWR	O
	OCE	Papeete	20	RFO Tahiti	O
15 175	URS	Kalinin	100	Domestic/External	R
	URS	Jigulevsk	20	Domestic	R
	UKR	Lvov	20	Domestic	R
	EGY	Abu Zaabal	100	R Cairo	R
	EGY	Abis	250	R Cairo	R
	CHL	Santiago	100		R
	IND	Aligarh	250	AIR	R

Frequency [kHz]	Country	Station Site	Power [kW]	Programme/ Network	O or R
15 175	NOR	Fredrikstad	350	R Norway/Danmarks R	O
(cont'd)	NOR	Kvitsoy	500	R Norway/Danmarks R	O
	ALB	Lushnje	100	R Tirana	O
15 180	URS	Leningrad	100	Domestic/External	R
	G	Skelton	250	BBC	R
	F	Allouis	100	RFI	R
	CVA	S M Galeria	250	Vatican R	R
	E	Noblejas	350	REE	R
	GAB	Moyabi	250	Africa No 1	R
	CHL	Santiago	100		R
	URS	Koms	100	Domestic/External	R
	KRE	Kujang	200/400	R Pyongyang	R
	KOR	Kimjae	250	R Korea	R
	CHN	Xian	150	Domestic/External	R
	PHL	Poro	50	VoA	R
	URS	Baku	20	Domestic	O
15 185	ISL	Reykjavik	10	IBS	R
	FNL	Pori	500	R Finland	R
	URS	Jigulevsk	100	Domestic/External	R
	D	Wertachtal	500	DW	R
	D	Julich	100	DW	R
	MLT	Cyclops	250	DW	R
	NIG	Ikorodu	500		R
	USA	Greenville	250	VoA	R
	USA	Red Lion	50	WINB	R
	IND	Bangalore	500	AIR	R
	CLN	Perkara	250	DW	R
	PHL	Tinang	250	VoA	R
	PHL	Poro	50	VoA	R
15 190	URS	Tula	240	Domestic/External	R
	BEL	Wavre	100	BRT	R
	F	Allouis	100	RFI	R
	GAB	Moyabi	250	Africa No 1	R
	GAB/J	Moyabi	500	R Japan	R
	COG	Brazzaville	50	Vo Rev Congolaise	R
	ASC	Ascension	250	BBC	R
	PAK	Islamabad	100	R Pakistan	O
	ATN	Bonaire	300	R Netherlands	O
	URS	Moscow	100	Lao National R	O
15 195	ISL	Reykjavik	10	ABS	R
	F	Allouis	100	RFI	R
	CVA	S M GAleria	250/500	Vatican R	R
	CYP/G	Limassol	250	BBC	R
	MRC	Tangier	100	VoA	R

Frequency [kHz]	Country	Station Site	Power [kW]	Programme/ Network	O or R
15 195	SEY	Mahe	100		R
(cont'd)	USA	Greenville	250	VoA	R
	BGD	Dhaka	250	R Bangladesh	R
	J	Tokyo Yamata	100/300	R Japan	R
	CHN	Baoding	120/240	R Beijing	R
	NOR	Sveio	500	R Norway/Danmarks R	R
	D/USA	Munich	100	VoA	O
15 200	BLR	Minsk	20	Domestic	R
	URS	Kalatch	240	Domestic/External	R
	URS	Jigulevsk	240	Domestic/External	R
	F	Allouis	100/500	RFI	R
	ISR	Jerusalem	50/300	Kol Israel	R
	GUF	Montsinery	500	RFI	R
	URS	Dushanbe	100	Domestic/External	R
	PAK	Islamabad	250	R Pakistan	R
	NPL	Kathmandu	100	R Nepal	R
	GUM	Agana	100	KTWR	R
	SNG	Singapore	50	SBC	R
	BGD	Dhaka	250	R Bangladesh	O
	SEY	Mahe	100	FEBA	O
	PHL	Palauig	100	R Veritas Asia	O
15 205	URS	Yerevan	100	Domestic/External	R
	G	Woofferton	300	VoA	R
	GRC	Kavalla	250	VoA	R
	CYP/G	Limassol	250	BBC	R
	ALG	Bouchaqui	50		R
	MRC	Tangier	35	VoA	R
	SEY	Mahe	100		R
	USA	Greenville	250	VoA	R
	SWZ	Manzini	100	TWR	O
15 210	EGY	Abis	250	R Cairo	R
	SWZ	Manzini	100	TWR	R
	PRG	Asuncion	100		R
	PAK	Islamabad	10	R Pakistan	R
	URS	Irkutsk	500	Domestic/External	R
	CHN	Xian	120	R Beijing	R
	PHL	Tinang	250	VoA	R
	GAB	Moyabi	500	R Japan	O
	CVA	S M Galeria	100/250	Vatican R	O
15 215	URS	Kazan	20	Domestic	R
	URS	Petrozavodsk	20	Domestic	R
	URS	Simferopol	20	Domestic	R
	POR	Lisbon	250	RFE/RL	R
	ALG	Bouchaoui	100	R Algiers	R

Frequency [kHz]	Country	Station Site	Power [kW]	Programme/ Network	O or R
15 215	USA	Okeechobee	100	WYFR/VoFC	R
(cont'd)	B	S Luiz	2.5	R Timbira	R
	KOR	Kimjae	250	R Korea	R
	PHL	Tinang	250	VoA	R
	PHL	Poro	50	VoA	R
	J	Yamata	300	RFI	O
15 220	NOR	Fredrikstad	350	R Norway/Danmarks R	R
	NOR	Kvitsoy	500	R Norway/Danmarks R	R
	NOR	Sveio	500	R Norway/Danmarks R	R
	URS	Jigulevsk	240	Domestic/External	R
	URS	Armavir	240	Domestic/External	R
	HNG	Diosd	100	R Budapest	R
	HNG	Szekesfehervar	20	R Budapest	R
	CYP/G	Limassol	100/250	BBC	R
	IRQ	Salah el Deen	500	R Baghdad	R
	EGY	Abu Zaabal	100	R Cairo	R
	EGY	Abis	250	R Cairo	R
	AFS	Meyerton	250	R RSA	R
	CUB	Havana	50	R Havana Cuba	R
	EQA	Quito	100	HCJB	R
	ATG	Antigua	250	BBC	O
15 225	ISL	Reykjavik	10	IBS	R
	NOR	Kvitsoy	500	R Norway/Danmarks R	R
	G	Woofferton	250	VoA	R
	G	Daventry	100	BBC	R
	UKR	Vinnitsa	250	Domestic/External	R
	POR	S Gabriel	100	RDP	R
	SYR	Adra	500	R Damascus	R
	CYP/G	Limassol	250	BBC	R
	TUN	Sfax	100		R
	USA	Greenville	250	VoA	R
	GUM	Agat	100	AWR	R
	D/USA	Munich	100	VoA	O
15 230	S	Horby	350	R Sweden	R
	CYP/G	Limassol	250	BBC	R
	ISR	Jerusalem	50	Kol Israel	R
	CUB	Havana	100	R Havana/R Moscow	R
	B	Brasilia	250	R Bras	R
	URG	Melo	5		R
	URS	Alma Ata	240	Domestic/External	R
	IND	Delhi	100	AIR	R
	J	Tokyo Yamata	100/300	R Japan	R
	KRE	Kujang	200	R Pyongyang	R
	NOR	Kvitsoy	500	R Norway/Danmarks R	O

Frequency [kHz]	Country	Station Site	Power [kW]	Programme/ Network	O or R
15 235	NOR	Sveio	500	R Norway/Danmarks R	R
	G	Woofferton	250/300	VoA	R
	G	Rampisham	500	BBC	R
	OMA/G	Masirah	100	BBC	O
	LBY	Tripoli	500	Tripoli R	R
	UGA	Kampala	250		R
	IND	Delhi	100	AIR	R
	CHN	Beijing	120	Domestic/External	R
	PHL	Tinang	250	VoA	R
15 240	URS	Riazan	20	Domestic	R
	URS	Armavir	20	Domestic	R
	D	K Wusterhausen	100	DW	R
	D	Nauen	500	DW	R
	E	Noblejas	350	REE	R
	IRQ	Salah el Deen	500	R Baghdad	R
	CUB	Havana	100	R Havana Cuba	R
	CHL	Santiago	100		R
	GUM	Agana	100		R
	AUS	Shepparton	100	R Australia	R
	PHL	Palauig	100	R Veritas Asia	O
15 245	FNL	Pori	500	R Finland	R
	I	Rome	100	RAI	R
	POR	Sines	250	DW	R
	OMA/G	Masirah	100	BBC	R
	CYP/G	Limassol	250	BBC	R
	MRC	Tangier	35	VoA	R
	ARS	Riyadh	350	BSKSA	R
	ZAI	Kinshasa	100	Voix du Zaire	R
	USA	Greenville	250/500	VoA	R
	KRE	Kujang	200	R Pyongyang	R
	CHN	Beijing	250	Domestic	R
15 250	ROU	Bucharest	250	R Romania	R
	POR	S Gabriel	250	RDP	R
	UGA	Kampala	250		R
	SEY	Mahe	100	FEBA	R
	EQA	Quito	250	HCJB	R
	PAK	Islamabad	250	R Pakistan	R
	IND	Delhi	100	AIR	R
	CLN	Colombo	35	VoA	R
	PHL	Tinang	250	VoA	R
	PHL	Palauig	250	VoA	R
	NOR	Kvitsoy	500	R Norway/Danmarks R	R
15 255	URS	Volgograd	20	Domestic	R
	URS	Petrozavodsk	20	Domestic	R

Frequency [kHz]	Country	Station Site	Power [kW]	Programme/ Network	O or R
15 255 *(cont'd)*	UKR	Ivan	20	Domestic	R
	ROU	Bucharest	250	R Romania	R
	POR	Lisbon	50	RFE/RL	R
	EGY	Abu Zaabal	100	R Cairo	R
	BGD	Dhaka	250	R Bangladesh	R
15 260	URS	Kazan	200	R Afghanistan	R
	UKR	Kiev	100	Domestic/External	R
	UKR	Kiev	20	Domestic	R
	ASC	Ascension	250	BBC	R
	CAN	Sackville	250	RCI	R
	IRN	Kamalabad	350	VoIRI	R
	J/USA	Tokyo	10	Far East Network	R
	CHN	Xian	150	Domestic/External	R
15 265	URS	Serpukhov	250	Domestic/External	R
	TUR	Ankara	250	TRT	R
	QAT	Al Khaisah	100	R Qatar	R
	SYR	Adra	500	R Damascus	R
	GAB	Moyabi	250	Africa No 1	R
	USA	Greenville	500	VoA	R
	B	Brasilia	250	R Bras	R
	URS	Frunze	250	Domestic/External	R
	IND	Bangalore	500	AIR	R
	GUM	Agana	100		R
	PHL	Palauig	250	VoA	R
	D	Nauen	100	DW	O
	D	Julich	100	DW	O
15 270	BLR	Minsk	20	Domestic	R
	URS	Moscow	20	Domestic	R
	MRC	Tangier	35	VoA	R
	RRW	Kigali	250	DW	R
	AFS	Meyerton	250	R RSA	R
	CUB	Havana	100	R Havana Cuba	R
	EQA	Quito	20/500	HCJB	R
	URS	Alma Ata	20	Domestic	R
	IND	Aligarh	250	AIR	R
	J	Tokyo Yamata	100/300	R Japan	R
	CHN	Beijing	50	Domestic/External	R
	PHL	Palauig	250	VoA	R
	PAK	Karachi	50	R Pakistan	O
	TWN	Panchiay	50	VoFC	O
	TWN	Taipei	250	VoFC	O
15 275	POL	Warsaw	100	R Polonia	R
	D	Julich	100	DW	R

Frequency [kHz]	Country	Station Site	Power [kW]	Programme/ Network	O or R
15 275	D	Wertachtal	500	DW	R
(cont'd)	ARS	Riyadh	350	BSKSA	R
	SEY	Mahe	100	FEBA	R
	URG	Montevideo	10		R
	IND	Aligarh	250	AIR	R
	CHN	Beijing	120	RFI	R
	MRA	Aginan Point	100	Christian Science Mon	R
	ATG	Antigua	250	DW	O
15 280	URS	Volgograd	20	Domestic	R
	URS	Kazan	240	Domestic/External	R
	D/USA	Wertachtal	500	VoA	R
	HOL	Flevo	500	R Netherlands	R
	E	Noblejas	350	REE	R
	USA	Redwood City	50	KGEI	R
	IND	Bombay	100	AIR	R
	BGD	Dhaka	250	R Bangladesh	R
	KOR	Kimjae	100/250	R Korea	R
	HKG/G	Tsang Tsui	250	BBC	R
	SNG/G	Kranji	100	BBC	R
15 285	UKR	Kharkov	20	Domestic	R
	POR	S Gabriel	100	RDP	R
	QAT	Al Khaisah	100	R Qatar	R
	EGY	Abu Zaabal	100	R Cairo	R
	GHA	Ejura	250		R
	GHA	Tema	100		R
	CUB	Havana	50	R Havana Cuba	R
	CHN	Beijing	120	RFI	R
	MRA	Aginan Point	100	Christian Science Mon	R
	PHL	Palauig	100	R Veritas Asia	O
15 290	ISL	Reykjavik	10	IBS	R
	E	Playa de Pals	500	RFE/RL	R
	POR	Lisbon	50	RFE/RL	R
	ARG	S Fernando	1	R N Buenos Aires	R
	CHL	Xian	300	R Beijing	R
	PHL	Tinang	250	VoA	R
15 295	ISL	Reykjavik	10	IBS	R
	MOZ	Maputo	100		R
	EQA	Quito	100	HCJB	R
	USA	Red Lion	50	WINB	R
	URS	Tashkent	200	Domestic/External	R
	PAK	Islamabad	100	R Pakistan	R
	URS	Moscow	100	R Afghanistan	O
	MLA	Kuala Lumpur	250	Vo Malaysia	O

Frequency [kHz]	Country	Station Site	Power [kW]	Programme/ Network	O or R
15 300	F	Allouis	100/500	RFI	R
	UAE	Dubai	500	UAE R	R
	GAB	Moyabi	250	RFI	R
	USA	Scotts Corners	500	WCSN	R
	CUB	Havana	50	R Havana Cuba	R
	GUF	Montsinery	500	RFI	R
	J	Tokyo Yamata	100	R Japan	R
15 305	URS	Voronej	240	Domestic/External	R
	URS	Starobelsk	500	Domestic/External	R
	TUR	Ankara	500	TRT	R
	UAE	Abu Dhabi	500	UAE R	R
	IND	Delhi	100	AIR	R
	MNG	Ulan Bator	250	R Ulan Bator	R
	KRE	Kujang	200	R Pyongyang	R
	PHL	Palauig	250	R Veritas Asia	R
	PHL	Poro	35	VoA	R
	NOR	Fredrikstad	350	R Norway/Danmarks R	O
15 310	NOR	Fredrikstad	350	R Norway/Danmarks R	R
	NOR	Sveio	500	R Norway/Danmarks R	R
	BUL	Sofia	250	R Sofia	R
	OMA/G	Masirah	100	BBC	R
	CYP/G	Limassol	100	BBC	R
	IRQ	Salah el Deen	500	R Baghdad	R
	GUI	Conakry	100	R N Guinee	R
	GUM	Agat	100	AWR	R
15 315	BLR	Minsk	20	Domestic	R
	UKR	Ivan	20	Domestic	R
	F	Allouis	100/500	RFI	R
	UAE	Abu Dhabi	500	UAE R	R
	LBR	Careysburg	250	VoA	R
	GAB	Moyabi	250	RFI	R
	CAN	Sackville	250	RCI	R
	ATN	Bonaire	300	R Netherlands	R
	URS	Kras	50	Domestic/External	R
	URS	Alma Ata	20	Domestic	R
	BGD	Dhaka	250	R Bangladesh	R
	USA	Delano	250	BBC	O
15 320	BLR	Orcha	100	Domestic/External	R
	D	Wertachtal	500	DW	R
	IRQ	Salah el Deen	500	R Baghdad	R
	UAE	Dubai	300	UAE R	R
	LBR	Careysburg	250	VoA	R
	CHL	Santiago	100		R
	IND	Delhi	100	AIR	R

Frequency [kHz]	Country	Station Site	Power [kW]	Programme/ Network	O or R
15 320	BGD	Dhaka	100	R Bangladesh	R
(cont'd)	CHN	Xian	150	Domestic/External	R
	MRA	Marpi	100	KFBS	R
	AUS	Shepparton	100	R Australia	R
15 325	FNL	Pori	1000	R Finland	R
	YUG	Bijelina	500	R Yugoslavia	R
	E	Noblejas	350	REE	R
	POR	Sines	250	RCI	R
	SEY	Mahe	100	FEBA	R
	CAN	Sackville	250	RCI	R
	GUF	Montsinery	500	R Japan	R
	B	Sao Paulo	1	R Gazeta	R
	PAK	Islamabad	250	R Pakistan	R
	J	Tokyo Yamata	300	R Japan	R
	PHL	Tinang	250	VoA	R
15 330	URS	Armavir	500	Domestic/External	R
	BUL	Sofia	250	R Sofia	R
	I	Rome	100	RAI	R
	SYR	Adra	500	R Damascus	R
	MRC	Tangier	50	RTVM Rabat	R
	LBR	Careysburg	250	VoA	R
	SEY	Mahe	100	FEBA	R
	ATN	Bonaire	300	R Netherlands	R
	CHN	Beijing	120	R Beijing	R
	PHL	Tinang	250	VoA	R
	URS	Moscow	100	R Havana Cuba	O
15 335	ROU	Bucharest	250	R Romania	R
	MRC	Tangier	100	RTVM Rabat	R
	EGY	Abis	250	R Cairo	R
	ARS	Riyadh	350	BSKSA	R
	IND	Madras	100	AIR	R
	IND	Aligarh	250	AIR	R
	IND	Bangalore	500	AIR	R
	KOR	Kimjae	250	R Korea	R
	CLM	Bogota	25	R N Colombia	O
15 340	D/USA	Lampertheim	100	RFE/RL	R
	ROU	Bucharest	250	R Romania	R
	CUB	Havana	50	R Havana Cuba	R
	URS	Sverdlovsk	240	RFE/RL	R
	BGD	Dhaka	100	R Bangladesh	R
	KRE	Kujang	200	R Pyongyang	R
	I	Rome	100	RAI	O
15 345	URS	Moscow	240	Domestic/External	R
	KWT	Sulaibiyah	500	R Kuwait	R

Frequency [kHz]	Country	Station Site	Power [kW]	Programme/ Network	O or R
15 345	ARS	Riyadh	350	BSKSA	R
(cont'd)	ATN	Bonaire	100	TWR	R
	ARG	Gral Pacheco	100	RAE Buenos Aires	O
	TWN	Panchiau	25	VoFC	O
	USA	Okeechobee	100	WYFR	O
15 350	URS	Serpukhov	240	Domestic/External	R
	URS	Petrozavodsk	20	Domestic	R
	URS	Armavir	100	R Havana Cuba	R
	D	Nauen	500	DW	R
	LUX	Junglinster	10	R Luxembourg	R
	ZAI	Kinshasa	100		R
	GUF	Montsinery	500	R Japan	R
	BGD	Dhaka	250	R Bangladesh	R
	CHN	Beijing	50	Domestic/External	R
	PHL	Bocaue	50	VoA	R
	URS	Moscow	100	R Afghanistan	O
	IRQ	Salah el Deen	500	R Baghdad	O
	USA	Greenville	500	VoA	O
15 355	POR	Lisbon	250	RFE/RL	R
	IRQ	Abu Ghraib	250	R Baghdad	R
	USA	Redwood City	50		R
	ATN	Bonaire	100	TWR	R
	URG	Montevideo	10		R
	KOR	Hwasung	100	R Korea	R
	PHL	Palauig	100	VoA	R
	GAB	Moyabi	500	R Japan	O
	USA	Okeechobee	100	WYFR	O
15 360	URS	Moscow	20	Domestic	R
	URS	Leningrad	20	Domestic	R
	F	Allouis	100/500	RFI	R
	MRC	Tangier	50	RTVM Rabat	R
	GAB	Moyabi	500	Africa No 1	R
	GAB/J	Moyabi	350/500	R Japan	R
	URS	Kenga	100	Domestic/External	R
	URS	Tashkent	200	Domestic/External	R
	URS	Alma Ata	20	Domestic	R
	IND	Aligarh	250	AIR	R
	IND	Bombay	100	AIR	R
	CLN	Perkara	250	DW	R
	KOR	Kimjae	250	R Korea	R
	SNG/G	Kranji	250	BBC	R
	NOR	Fredrikstad	350	R Norway/Danmarks R	O
15 365	ROU	Bucharest	250	R Romania	R
	F	Allouis	100	RFI	R

Frequency [kHz]	Country	Station Site	Power [kW]	Programme/ Network	O or R
15 365	E	Noblejas	350	REE	R
(cont'd)	AFS	Meyerton	250	R RSA	R
	ATN	Bonaire	300	R Netherlands	R
	GUF	Montsinery	500	RFI	R
	IND	Aligarh	250	AIR	R
	IND	Delhi	100	AIR	R
	AUS	Darwin	250	R Australia	R
15 370	D/USA	Holzkirchen	250	RFE/RL	R
	ROU	Bucharest	250	R Romania	R
	BUL	Sofia	250	R Sofia	R
	POR	Lisbon	250	RFE/RL	R
	SEY	Mahe	100	FEBA	R
	KRE	Kujang	200	R Pyongyang	R
	TWN	Pa-Li	50	VoFC	O
15 375	ISL	Reykjavik	10	IBS	R
	URS	Moscow	240	Domestic/External	R
	E	Noblejas	350	REE	R
	EGY	Abu Zaabal	100	R Cairo	R
	URS	Kenga	100	Domestic/External	R
	KOR	Kimjae	250	R Korea	R
	MRA	Marpi	100	KFBS	R
15 380	ROU	Bucharest	250	R Romania	R
	E	Playa de Pals	250	RFE/RL	R
	E	Noblejas	350	REE	R
	POR	Lisbon	250	RFE/RL	R
	ATN	Bonaire	50	TWR	R
	PAK	Islamabad	100	R Pakistan	R
	CHN	Beijing	50	Domestic/External	R
	SNG/G	Kranji	250	BBC	R
	AUS	Carnarvon	250	R Australia	R
15 385	URS	Moscow	20	Domestic	R
	UKR	Kiev	20	Domestic	R
	BUL	Sofia	250/500	R Sofia	R
	I	Rome	100	RAI	R
	URS	Novo	240	Domestic/External	R
	MRA	Aginan Point	100	KFBS	R
15 390	S	Horby	350	R Sweden	R
	D	Julich	100	DW	R
	G	Rampisham	500	BBC	R
	ROU	Bucharest	250	R Romania	R
	ASC	Ascension	250	BBC	R
	CHN	Beijing	50	Domestic/External	R
	J	Tokyo Yamata	300	R Japan	O

Frequency [kHz]	Country	Station Site	Power [kW]	Programme/ Network	O or R
15 395	URS	Armavir	100	Domestic/External	R
	URS	Serpukhov	250	Domestic/External	R
	E	Noblejas	350	REE	R
	QAT	Al Khaisah	250	R Qatar	R
	OMA	Thumrait	100	R Oman	R
	URS	Tashkent	100	Domestic/External	R
	CLN	Colombo	35	VoA	R
	KOR	Kimjae	250	R Korea	R
	PHL	Tinang	250	VoA	R
15 400	FNL	Pori	500	R Finland	R
	IRQ	Abu Ghraib	250	R Baghdad	R
	UAE	Dubai	500	UAE R	R
	ASC	Ascension	250	BBC	R
	USA	Greenville	250	VoA	R
	CUB	Havana	100	R Havana Cuba	R
	CHN	Baoding	120	Domestic/External	R
	CLN	Perkara	250	SLBC	R
	PHL	Palauig	100/250	R Veritas Asia	O
15 405	ROU	Bucharest	250	R Romania	R
	TUR	Ankara	250	TRT	R
	CVA	S M Galeria	100/250/ 500	Vatican R	R
	JOR	Al Karanah	500	R Jordan	R
	URS	Tashkent	500	Domestic/External	R
	URS	Petropavlo Kam	100	Domestic/External	R
	MRA	Aginan Point	100	Christian Science Mon	R
	ALB	Lushnje	100	R Tirana	O
	D/USA	Wertachtal	500	VoA	O
15 410	UKR	Lvov	120	Domestic/External	R
	AUT	Vienna	100	R Austria Intl	R
	GRC	Athens	100	ERT	R
	SYR	Adra	500	R Damascus	R
	RRW	Kigali	250	DW	R
	USA	Greenville	250	VoA	R
	PAK	Karachi	50	R Pakistan	R
	CLN	Perkara	250	DW	R
	PHL	Tinang	250	VoA	R
	PHL	Bocaue	50	VoA	R
	ATG	Antigua	250	DW	O
15 415	LBY	Tripoli	500	Tripoli R	R
	ISR	Jerusalem	300	Kol Israel	R
	B	Riberiao Preto	1	R Clube Riberiao Preto	R
	KRE	Kujang	200	R Pyongyang	R

Frequency [kHz]	Country	Station Site	Power [kW]	Programme/ Network	O or R
15 420	BLR	Minsk	20	Domestic	R
	CYP/G	Limassol	100/250	BBC	R
	EGY	Abu Zabaal	100	R Cairo	R
	SEY/G	Mahe	250	BBC	R
	USA	New Orelans	100	WRNO	R
	URS	Frunze	500	Domestic/External	R
	IND	Delhi	100	AIR	R
	CHN	Baoding	120	Domestic/External	R
	CHN	Xian	150	Domestic/External	R
	GUM	Agana	100	TWR	R
	ASC	Ascension	250	BBC	O
	URS	Moscow	100	Lao National R	O
15 425	D	Julich	100	DW	R
	F	Allouis	100	RFI	R
	MLT	Cyclops	250	DW	R
	ISR	Jerusalem	50	Kol Israel	R
	CAN	Sackville	250	RCI	R
	CUB	Havana	250	R Havana Cuba	R
	CLN	Ekala	35	SLBC	R
	URS	Petropavlokam	100	Domestic/External	R
	PHL	Poro	50	VoA	R
	AUS	Perth	50	ABC Perth	R
15 430	G	Skelton	250	BBC	R
	AUT	Vienna	500	R Austria Intl	R
	SUI	Schwarzenburg	150	SRI	R
	ARS	Riyadh	350	BSKSA	R
	SEY	Mahe	75	FEBA	R
	MEX	Mexico	50	R Mexico Int	R
	PAK	Islamabad	250	R Pakistan	R
15 435	URS	Kazan	100	Domestic/External	R
	URS	Yerevan	100	Domestic/External	R
	D	Wertachtal	500	DW	R
	D	Julich	100	DW	R
	G	Rampisham	500	BBC	R
	F	Allouis	100/500	RFI	R
	GRC	Kavalla	250	VoA	R
	CYP/G	Limassol	250	BBC	R
	LBY	Tripoli	500	Tripoli R	R
	JOR	Al Karanah	500	R Jordan	R
	UAE	Dubai	500	UAE R	R
	ARS	Jeddah	50	BSKSA	R
	TZA	Dar es Salaam	100		R
	CUB	Havana	100	R Havana Cuba	R
	GUF	Montsinery	500	RFI	R

Frequency [kHz]	Country	Station Site	Power [kW]	Programme/ Network	O or R
15 435	CLN	Perkara	250	DW	R
(cont'd)	CHN	Beijing	120	Domestic/External	R
	MRA	Aginan Point	100	Christian Science Mon	R
15 440	URS	Tbilisi	100	Domestic/External	R
	URS	Petropavlokam	20	Domèstic	R
	D	K Wusterhausen	100	DW	R
	USA	Okeechobee	100	WYFR	R
	GUF	Montsinery	500	RFI	R
	CHN	Kunming	120	Domestic/External	R
	OMA	Seeb	100	Oman R	O
15 445	D/USA	Lampertheim	100	RFE/RL	R
	ROU	Bucharest	250	R Romania	R
	POR	Lisbon	250	RFE/RL	R
	IRQ	Salah el Deen	500	R Baghdad	R
	LBR	Careysburg	250	VoA	R
	ATN	Bonaire	100	TWR	R
	PAK	Islamabad	250	R Pakistan	R
	PHL	Bocaue	50	VoA	R
	PHL	Palauig	100	VoA	R
	B	Brasilia	250	R N da Amazonia	O
	URS	Simferopol	240	Domestic/External	O
15 460	URS	Leningrad	100	Domestic/External	O
	F	Allouis	100	RFI	O
	PHL	Bocaue	50	FEBC	O
15 465	URS	Leningrad	100	Domestic/External	O
	AUS	Shepparton	100	R Australia	O
15 470	POR	Sines	250	DW	O
	URS	Moscow	100	Domestic/External	O
	URS	Armavir	100	Domestic/External	O
	URS	Irkutsk	250	Domestic/External	O
15 475	URS	Moscow	100	Domestic/External	O
	UKR	Simferopol	500	Domestic/External	O
	GAB	Moyabi	250	Africa No 1	O
	B	San Gabriel	1	R Nacional	O
15 480	URS	Frunze	500	Domestic/External	O
	URS	Irkutsk	100	Domestic/External	O
	PHL	Bocaue	50	FEBC	O
15 485	URS	Yerevan	500	Domestic/External	O
	F	Allouis	100	RFI	O
	ISR	Jerusalem	50	Kol Israel	O
	GUM	Agana	100	KTWR	O

Frequency [kHz]	Country	Station Site	Power [kW]	Programme/ Network	O or R
15 485	NZL	Taupo	100	R New Zealand Intl	O
(cont'd)	TUR	Ankara	500	TRT	O
15 490	URS	Armavir	500	Domestic/External	O
	URS	Frunze	500	Domestic/External	O
	URS	Moscow	100	Domestic/External	O
	KWT	Sulaibiyah	500	R Kuwait	O
15 495	URS	Moscow	100	Domestic/External	O
15 500	URS	Yerevan	50	Domestic	O
	URS	Vladivostock	100	Domestic/External	O
	CHN	Beijing	50	CPBS	O
15 505	KWT	Sulaibiyah	500	R Kuwait	O
15 510	URS	Alma Ata	100	Domestic/External	O
	UKR	Vinnitsa	500	Domestic/External	O
	URS	Yerevan	50	Domestic/External	O
15 515	BEL	Wavre	100	BRT	O
	PAK	Karachi	100	R Pakistan	O
15 520	URS	Kazan	100	Domestic/External	O
	URS	Moscow	100	R Afghanistan	O
	URS	Frunze	500	Domestic/External	O
	BGD	Dhaka	50	R Bangladesh	O
15 525	UKR	Kiev	100	Domestic/External	O
	URS	Novosibirsk	100	Domestic/External	O
	SUI	Schwarzenburg	150	SRI	O
15 530	UKR	Vinnitsa	500	Domestic/External	O
	URS	Kazan	100	Domestic/External	O
	F	Allouis	500	RFI	O
	PHL	Iba	100	FEBC	O
	AUS	Shepparton	100	R Australia	O
	AUS	Darwin	250	R Australia	O
15 535	UKR	Khabarovsk	100	Domestic/External	O
	UKR	Kiev	100	Domestic/External	O
	URS	Novosibirsk	50	Domestic/External	O
15 540	URS	Kazan	100	Domestic/External	O
	BEL	Wavre	100	RTBF	O
15 545	URS	Moscow	500	Domestic/External	O
	URS	Novosibirsk	100	Domestic/External	O
	D	Wertachtal	500	DW	O
15 550	URS	Moscow	100	Domestic/External	O
	URS	Khabarovsk	100	Domestic/External	O
	CHN	Beijing	50	CPBS	O

Frequency [kHz]	Country	Station Site	Power [kW]	Programme/ Network	O or R
15 560	URS	Moscow	100	Domestic/External	O
	URS	Irkutsk	500	Domestic/External	O
	HOL	Flevo	500	R Netherlands	O
	MDG	Talata Volondry	300	R Netherlands	O
	ATN	Bonaire	300	R Netherlands	O
	AUS	Shepparton	100	R Australia	O
15 565	EGY	Abis	250	Iran's Flag of Freedom	O
	USA	Okeechobee	100	WYFR	O
15 570	MDG	Talata Volondry	300	R Netherlands	O
	SUI	Schwarzenburg	150	SRI	O
15 575	CYP/G	Limassol	250	BBC	O
	KOR	Kimjae	250	R Korea	O
15 580	URS	Irkutsk	500	Domestic/External	O
	USA	Greenville	250	VoA	O
15 585	URS	Armavir	240	Domestic/External	O
	URS	Yerevan	500	Domestic/External	O
15 590	CYP/G	Limassol	250	BBC	O
	URS	Tashkent	100	Domestic/External	O
	USA	Salt Lake City	100	KUSW	O
15 595	URS	Novosibirsk	500	Domestic/External	O
	URS	Moscow	100	Domestic/External	O
	D	Wertachtal	500	DW	O
15 600	URS	Moscow	20	Domestic/External	O
	LBR	Monrovia	250	VoA	O
15 605	PAK	Islamabad	250	R Pakistan	O
15 610	USA	Cypress Creek	500	Christian Science Mon	O
	MRA	Aginan Point	100	Christian Science Mon	O
	GUM	Agat	100	AWR	O
15 615	ISR	Jerusalem	100	Kol Israel	O
15 625	GRC	Athens	100	ERT	O
15 640	ISR	Jerusalem	300	Kol Israel	O
15 650	GRC	Athens	100	ERT	O
	ISR	Jerusalem	300	Kol Israel	O
	EGY	Abis	250	R Irana	O
15 670	CHN	Beijing	50	CPBS	O
15 685	EGY	Abis	250	Vo Unity	O
15 690	USA	Nashville	100	WWCR	O

Frequency [kHz]	Country	Station Site	Power [kW]	Programme/ Network	O or R
15 710	CHN	Beijing	50	CPBS	O
15 770	ISL	Reykjavik	10	IBS	O
15 880	CHN	Beijing	50	CPBS	O
16 230	ALB	Lushnje	100	R Tirana	O
17 387	IND	Delhi	100	AIR	O
17 440	ISL	Reykjavik	10	IBS	O
17 493	ISL	Reykjavik	10	IBS	O
17 535	GRC	Athens	100	ERT	O
17 545	ISR	Jerusalem	50	Kol Israel	O
17 550	BEL	Wavre	180	BRT	O
17 555	MRA	Aginan Point	100	Christian Science Mon	O
	PAK	Islamabad	100	R Pakistan	O
	USA	Cypress Creek	500	Christian Science Mon	O
17 560	URS	Tashkent	100	Domestic/External	O
	URS	Kazan	240	Domestic/External	O
17 565	URS	Moscow	500	Domestic/External	O
	PAK	Islamabad	250	R Pakistan	O
17 570	URS	Armavir	100	Domestic/External	O
	UKR	Khabarovsk	100	Domestic/External	O
	SUI	Schwarzenburg	150	SRI	O
17 575	HOL	Flevo	500	R Netherlands	O
	ISR	Jerusalem	300	Kol Israel	O
	MDG	Talata Volondry	300	R Netherlands	O
17 580	URS	Moscow	100	R Afghanistan	O
	URS	Frunze	500	Domestic/External	O
17 590	URS	Moscow	100	R Afghanistan	O
	URS	Vladivostock	240	Domestic/External	O
	URS	Moscow	240	Domestic/External	O
17 595	EGY	Abis	250	R Cairo	O
	MRC	Tangier	50	RTVM Rabat	O
17 600	URS	Dushanbe	240	Domestic/External	O
	URS	Moscow	240	Domestic/External	O
17 605	URS	Petropavlovsk	100	Domestic/External	O
	ATN	Bonaire	300	R Netherlands	O
	CHN	Beijing	50	CPBS	O

Frequency [kHz]	Country	Station Site	Power [kW]	Programme/ Network	O or R
17 610	URS	Tashkent	100	Domestic/External	O
	URS	Alma Ata	100	Domestic/External	O
	TUN	Sfax	100	RTV Tunisienne	O
17 612	USA	Okeechobee	100	WYFR	O
17 615	URS	Moscow	500	Domestic/External	O
	URS	Kazan	240	Domestic/External	O
17 620	URS	Novosibirsk	500	Domestic/External	R
	F	Allouis	100/500	RFI	O
	GUF	Montsinery	500	RFI	O
17 625	URS	Armavir	100	Domestic/External	O
	UKR	Vinnitsa	500	Domestic/External	O
17 630	URS	Moscow	250	Domestic/External	O
	ISR	Jerusalem	300	Kol Israel	O
	AUS	Shepparton	100	R Australia	O
	AUS	Darwin	250	R Australia	O
	AUS	Carnarvon	300	R Australia	O
17 635	URS	Moscow	250	Domestic/External	O
	CHN	Beijing	50	CPBS	O
17 640	G	Daventry	100	BBC	O
	G	Woofferton	300	BBC	O
	USA	Okeechobee	100	WYFR	O
	USA	Greenville	500	VoA	O
17 645	URS	Leningrad	100	Domestic/External	O
	UKR	Khabarovsk	100	Domestic/External	O
17 650	URS	Armavir	500	Domestic/External	O
	F	Allouis	100/500	RFI	O
	CHN	Beijing	120	R Beijing	O
17 655	URS	Moscow	100	R Afghanistan	O
	URS	Armavir	500	Domestic/External	O
17 660	URS	Leningrad	100	Domestic/External	O
17 665	UKR	Khabarovsk	240	Domestic/External	O
17 670	UKR	Vinnitsa	500	Domestic/External	O
	URS	Moscow	100	Domestic/External	O
	EGY	Abu Zaabal	100	R Cairo	O
	SUI	Schwarzenburg	150	SRI	O
17 675	URS	Irkutsk	100	Domestic/External	O
	URS	Moscow	100	Domestic/External	O
	BEL	Wavre	180	RTBF	O
	NZL	Taupo	100	RNZI	O

Frequency [kHz]	Country	Station Site	Power [kW]	Programme/ Network	O or R
17 680	UKR	Simferopol	240	Domestic/External	O
	URS	Yerevan	500	Domestic/External	O
	CHN	Beijing	120	R Beijing	O
17 685	URS	Yerevan	500	Domestic/External	O
	ISR	Jerusalem	300	Kol Israel	O
17 690	UKR	Khabarovsk	240	Domestic/External	O
	URS	Yerevan	100	Domestic/External	O
	EGY	Abis	240	R Cairo	O
17 695	G	Daventry	300	BBC	O
	G	Skelton	250	BBC	O
	URS	Khabarovsk	100	Domestic/External	O
	F	Allouis	500	RFI	O
	URS	Vladivostock	100	Domestic/External	O
17 700	BLR	Minsk	100	Domestic/External	O
	URS	Yerevan	100	Domestic/External	O
	CHN	Beijing	50	CPBS	O
17 705	G	Rampisham	500	BBC	O
	G	Skelton	250	BBC	O
	LBR	Careysburg	250	VoA	O
	GAB	Moyabi	250	RFI	O
	J	Tokyo Yamata	300	RFI	O
	IND	Delhi	50	AIR	O
21 450	PHL	Palauig	100	R Veritas Asia	O
	URS	Yerevan	100	Domestic/External	O
21 455	POR	Lisbon	250	RFE/RL	R
	PAK	Islamabad	250	R Pakistan	R
21 460	S	Horby	350	R Sweden	R
	URS	Armavir	500	Domestic/External	R
	BEL	Wavre	250	RTBF	R
	E	Noblejas	350	REE	R
	PAK	Karachi	50	R Pakistan	R
21 465	D	Leipzig	100	DW	R
	UKR	Vinnitsa	500	Domestic/External	O
21 470	CYP/G	Limassol	300	BBC	R
	ASC	Ascension	250	BBC	R
	EQA	Quito	500	HCJB	R
	URS	Petro	100	Domestic/External	R
21 475	E	Noblejas	350	REE	R
	AUT	Vienna	300	Austrian R	O
	USA	Bethany	250	VoA	R

Frequency [kHz]	Country	Station Site	Power [kW]	Programme/ Network	O or R
21 475	PAK	Karachi	50	R Pakistan	R
(cont'd)	PHL	Tinang	250	VoA	R
21 480	HOL	Flevo	500	R Netherlands	R
	ROU	Bucharest	250	R Romania	R
	PAK	Islamabad	100	R Pakistan	R
	BGD	Dhaka	100	R Bangladesh	R
	EQA	Quito	100	HCJB	O
	URS	Petropavlovsk	100	Domestic/External	O
21 485	CVA	S M Galeria	250/500	Vatican R	R
	LBR	Careysburg	15/50	VoA	R
	MDG	Talata	300	R Netherlands	O
	USA	Greenville	500	VoA	O
21 490	AUT	Vienna	100/300	Austrian R	R
	ASC	Ascension	250	BBC/VoA	R
	PAK	Islamabad	100/250	R Pakistan	R
	URS	Irkutsk	250	Domestic/External	O
21 495	E	Noblejas	350	REE	R
	POR	S Gabriel	100	RDP	R
	ISR	Jerusalem	300	Kol Israel	R
	ARS	Riyadh	500	BSKSA	O
21 500	S	Karlsborg	350	R Sweden	R
	HOL	Flevo	500	R Netherlands	R
	IRN	Sirjan	500	VoIRI	R
	USA	Okeechobee	100	WYFR/VoFC	O
	J	Tokyo Yamata	300/500	R Japan	O
	GAB	Moyabi	500	R Japan	O
21 505	TCH	Litomysl	120	R Prague	R
	ARS	Riyadh	350	BSKSA	R
	URS	Frunze	100	Domestic/External	R
21 510	D/USA	Holzkirchen	250	RFE/RL; R F Afghanistan	R
	BEL	Wavre	100	BRT	R
	POR	Lisbon	250	RFE/RL	R
	ARS	Riyadh	350	BSKSA	R
	PAK	Islamabad	100	R Pakistan	R
21 515	CVA	S M Galeria	500	Vatican R	R
	UAE	Abu Dhabi	500	UAE R	R
	I	Rome	100	RAI	R
	ATN	Bonaire	300	R Netherlands	R
	URS	Frunze	50	Domestic/External	O

Frequency [kHz]	Country	Station Site	Power [kW]	Programme/ Network	O or R
21 520	HOL	Flevo	500	R Netherlands	R
	GRC	Kavalla	250	VoA	R
	GAB	Moyabi	250	RFI	R
	PAK	Islamabad	250	R Pakistan	O
21 525	QAT	Al Khaisah	250	R Qatar	R
	USA	Okeechobee	100	WYFR	R
	PAK	Islamabad	250	R Pakistan	R
	AUS	Carnarvon	250	R Australia	R
	URS	Vladivostock	100	Domestic/External	O
21 530	UKR	Lvov	240	Domestic/External	R
	POR	Lisbon	250	RFE/RL; R Free Afghanistan	R
	POR	S Gabriel	100	RDP	R
	HOL	Flevo	500	R Netherlands	O
	BGD	Dhaka	250	R Bangladesh	R
	URS	Petropavlo Kam	100	Domestic/External	R
	PAK	Islamabad	250	R Pakistan	O
	F	Allouis	500	RFI	O
21 535	QAT	Al Khaisah	100	R Qatar	R
	I	Rome	50	RAI	O
	D/USA	Wertachtal	500	VoA	O
21 540	D	Nauen	500	DW	R
	ATN	Bonaire	300	R Netherlands	R
	D/USA	Wertachtal	500	VoA	O
21 545	GHA	Tema	100		R
	CAN	Sackville	250	RCI	R
	IND	Delhi	250	AIR	R
	PHL	Poro	50	VoA	R
	URS	Moscow	100	Domestic/External	O
21 550	FNL	Pori	500	R Finland	R
	ROU	Bucharest	250	R Romania	R
	URS	Leningrad	100	Domestic/External	O
21 555	YUG	Bijeljina	500	R Yugoslavia	R
	E	Noblejas	350	REE	R
	QAT	Al Khaisah	100	R Qatar	R
	URS	Leningrad	100	Domestic/External	O
21 560	D	Julich	100	DW	R
	I	Rome	100	AIR	R
	MLT	Cyclops	250	DW	R
	GAB	Moyabi	250	Africa No 1	R
	CLN	Perkara	250	DW	R
	PHL	Palauig	250	R Veritas Asia	O

Frequency [kHz]	Country	Station Site	Power [kW]	Programme/ Network	O or R
21 565	URS	Leningrad	240	Domestic/External	R
	URS	Irkutsk	500	Domestic/External	R
	QAT	Doha	250	Qatar BC	O
21 566	CTR	Ciudad Colon	2/5	R for Peace Int	O
21 570	S	Horby	350	R Sweden	R
	E	Noblejas	350	REE	R
	LBY	Tripoli	500	Tripoli R	R
	BGD	Dhaka	250	R Bangladesh	R
	GRC	Kavalla	250	VoA	O
	D/USA	Wertachtal	500	VoA	O
21 575	E	Noblejas	350	REE	R
	PAK	Karachi	50/250	R Pakistan	R
	URS	Moscow	500	Domestic/External	O
21 580	BEL	Wavre	100	BRT	R
	F	Allouis	500	R France Int	R
	IRQ	Salah el Deen	500	R Baghdad	R
	USA	Greenville	250	VoA	R
	GUF	Montsinery	500	R France int	R
	PAK	Islamabad	250	R Pakistan	R
21 585	PHL	Tinang	250	VoA	R
	URS	Dushanbe	240	Domestic/External	O
	PHL	Tinang	250	VoA	O
	URS	Irkutsk	500	Domestic/External	O
21 590	G	Rampisham	500	BBC	O
	G	Daventry	100	BBC	O
21 595	F	Allouis	100	R France Intl	R
	E	Noblejas	350	REE	R
	PAK	Islamabad	100	R Pakistan	R
21 600	D	Julich	100	DW	R
	D	Wertachtal	500	DW	R
	PRU	Lima	50		R
	CLN	Perkara	250	DW	R
	URS	Kazan	100	R Afghanistan	O
21 605	UAE	Dubai	300	UAE R	R
21 610	NOR	Kvitsoy	500	R Norway/Danmarks R	R
	S	Horby	350	R Sweden	O
	GRC	Kavalla	250	VoA	R
	USA	Greenville	250	VoA	R
	PAK	Islamabad	100	R Pakistan	R
	J	Tokyo Yamata	100	R Japan	R

Frequency [kHz]	Country	Station Site	Power [kW]	Programme/ Network	O or R
21 615	I	Rome	100	RAI	R
	HOL	Flevo	500	R Netherlands	O
	USA	Okeechobee	100	WYFR	R
	URS	Tashkent	100	Domestic/External	R
21 620	F	Allouis	100	RFI	R
	GUF	Montsinery	500	RFI	R
21 625	D/USA	Wertachtal	500	VoA	R
	ISR	Jerusalem	300	Kol Israel	R
	URS	Omsk	250	Domestic/External	R
	PAK	Karachi	50	R Pakistan	R
21 630	SUI	Schwarzenburg	150	SRI	R
	MLT	Cyclops	250	DW	R
	ATN	Bonaire	300	R Netherlands	R
	CLN	Perkara	250	DW	R
	URS	Starobelsk	100	Domestic/External	O
21 635	F	Allouis	100	RFI	R
	UAE	Abu Dhabi	500	UAE R	R
	GAB/J	Moyabi	500	R Japan	R
	URS	Dushanbe	240	Domestic/External	R
	YUG	Bijeljina	500	R Yugoslavia	O
21 640	G	Rampisham	500	BBC	R
	ARS	Riyadh	350	BSKSA	R
	GAB/J	Moyabi	500	R Japan	R
	ASC	Ascension	250	BBC	R
	USA	Scotts Corners	500	WCSN	R
	CLN	Perkara	250	DW	R
21 645	F	Allouis	500	RFI	R
	GUF	Montsinery	500	RFI	R
	URS	Moscow	100	Domestic/External	O
21 650	D	Julich	100	DW	R
	D	Wertachtal	500	DW	R
	CVA	S M Galeria	500	Vatican R	R
	MLT	Cyclops	250	DW	R
	CLN	Perkara	250	DW	R
21 655	URS	Armavir	100	Domestic/External	R
	S	Horby	350	R Sweden	O
21 660	ASC	Ascension	250	BBC	R
	IND	Aligarh	250	AIR	R
	ISR	Jerusalem	300	Kol Israel	O
21 665	ROU	Bucharest	250	R Romania	R
	POR	Lisbon	50/250	RFE/RL	R
	URS	Moscow	100	Domestic/External	O

Frequency [kHz]	Country	Station Site	Power [kW]	Programme/ Network	O or R
21 670	ARS	Riyadh	350	BSKSA	R
	IND	Delhi	250	AIR	R
	URS	Armavir	100	R Havana Cuba	O
	URS	Moscow	100	Domestic/External	O
	PAK	Islamabad	250	R Pakistan	O
21 675	ISR	Jerusalem	300	Kol Israel	R
	KWT	Sulaibiyah	500	R Kuwait	R
	UAE	Dubai	300	UAE R	R
	CAN	Sackville	250	RCI	O
21 680	URS	Armavir	100	Domestic/External	R
	D	Julich	100	DW	R
	D	Wertachtal	500	DW	R
	POR	Sines	250	DW	R
	HOL	Flevo	500	R Netherlands	O
21 685	F	Allouis	500	RFI	R
	ATN	Bonaire	300	R Netherlands	R
	GUF	Montsinery	500	RFI	R
	ATN	Bonaire	300	R Netherlands	O
21 690	S	Horby	350	R Sweden	R
	I	Rome	50/100	RAI	R
	GAB/J	Moyabi	500	R Japan	R
	URS	Vladivostock	500	Domestic/External	R
21 695	SUI	Schwarzenburg	150	SRI	R
	NOR	Kvitsoy	500	R Norway/Danmarks R	O
21 700	E	Noblejas	350	REE	R
	POR	S Gabriel	100	RDP	R
	UAE	Dubai	300	UAE R	R
	GAB/J	Moyabi	500	R Japan	R
	PAK	Karachi	50	R Pakistan	R
21 705	NOR	Kvitsoy	500	R Norway/Danmarks R	R
	NOR	Sveio	500	R Norway/Danmarks R	R
	URS	Armavir	240	Domestic/External	R
	TCH	Rimavska	250	R Prague	R
21 710	NOR	Kvitsoy	500	R Norway/Danmarks R	R
	ISR	Jerusalem	50	Kol Israel	R
	BGD	Dhaka	250	R Bangladesh	R
	ATN	Bonaire	300	R Netherlands	O
21 715	HKG/G	Tsang Tsui	250	BBC	R
	SNG/G	Kranji	100	BBC	R
	URS	Armavir	100	Domestic/External	O
	YUG	Bijeljina	500	R Yugoslavia	O

Frequency [kHz]	Country	Station Site	Power [kW]	Programme/ Network	O or R
21 720	POR	Lisbon	250	RFE/RL	R
	GHA	Ejura	250		R
	USA	Okeechobee	100	VoFC/WYFR	O
21 725	URS	Tbilisi	100	Domestic/External	R
	UAE	Abu Dhabi	500	UAE R	O
21 730	NOR	Kvitsoy	500	R Norway/Danmarks R	R
	F	Allouis	100	RFI	R
	PAK	Islamabad	250	R Pakistan	O
21 735	NOR	Kvitsoy	500	R Norway/Danmarks R	R
	G	Rampisham	500	BBC	R
	UAE	Abu Dhabi	500	UAE R	R
	USA	Okeechobee	100	WYFR	R
	PAK	Karachi	50	R Pakistan	R
	IND	Delhi	250	AIR	R
21 740	GAB	Moyabi	250	Africa No 1	R
	PAK	Islamabad	100	R Pakistan	R
	AUS	Shepparton	50	R Australia	R
	URS	Yerevan	100	Domestic/External	O
21 745	MDG	Talata	300	R Netherlands	O
	ISR	Tel Aviv	300	Kol Israel	O
	PAK	Islamabad	250	R Pakistan	O
	POR	Sines	250	RFE/RL	O
	USA	Bethany	250	VoA	O
21 750	URS	Leningrad	100	Domestic/External	O
21 755	UKR	Vinnitsa	500	Domestic/External	O
21 760	ISR	Tel Aviv	50/300	Kol Israel	O
21 765	GUF	Montsinery	500	RFI	O
	URS	Leningrad	100	Domestic/External	O
21 770	F	Allouis	500	RFI	O
	SUI	Schwarzenburg	150	SRI	O
21 775	AUS	Carnarvon	250	R Australia	O
21 780	ISR	Tel Aviv	300	Kol Israel	O
	USA	Scotts Corners	500	WCSN	O
	USA	Cypress Creek	500	WCSN	O
21 790	ISR	Jerusalem	300	Kol Israel	O
	URS	Irkutsk	250	Domestic/External	O
21 810	BEL	Wavre	250	BRT	O
	GUF	Montsinery	500	RFI	O
	GAB	Moyabi	250	RFI	O

Frequency [kHz]	Country	Station Site	Power [kW]	Programme/ Network	O or R
21 815	BEL	Wavre	250	BRT	O
21 820	URS	Moscow	240	Domestic/External	O
21 825	AUS	Darwin	250	R Australia	O
	URS	Moscow	100	Domestic/External	O
21 830	GAB	Moyabi	250	RFI	O
	URS	Tashkent	100	Domestic/External	O
21 840	USA	Noblesville	100	WHRI	O
	URS	Moscow	100	Domestic/External	O
25 645	BEL	Wavre	250	BRT	R
25 680	SUI	Schwarzenburg	150	SRI	R
	URS	Armavir	100	Domestic/External	O
25 690	UAE	Abu Dhabi	500	UAE R	O
25 730	NOR	Kvitsoy	500	R Norway/Danmarks R	R
	NOR	Fredrikstad	350	R Norway/Danmarks R	R
25 740	D	Julich	100	DW	R
25 750	G	Daventry	50	BBC	R
25 780	URS	Armavir	100	Domestic/External	O
25 795	YUG	Bijeljina	500	R Yugoslavia	O
25 820	F	Allouis	100	RFI	R
25 870	G	Daventry	300	BBC	O
25 890	UAE	Abu Dhabi	500	UAE R	O
25 940	HOL	Flevo	500	R Netherlands	O
25 950	EQA	Quito	10	HCJB - ssb txmns	O
25 970	HOL	Flevo	500	R Netherlands	R

Section 7

EUROPEAN, MIDDLE EASTERN AND NORTH AFRICAN LONG WAVE RADIO STATIONS

Frequency [kHz]	Country	Station Site	Power [kW]	Programme/ Network
153	ROU	Brasov	1200	Bucharest 1
	ALG	Bechar	1000	Arabic Network
	D	Donebach	500	DLF
	NOR	Tromsoe	10	P1
	URS	Engelsk	150	Moscow 1 & 2
162	F	Allouis	2000	France Inter
	TUR	Agri	1000	TRT 1
	URS	Tashkent	150	Moscow 1
171	MRC	Nador	1200	Medi 1
	URS	Kaliningrad	1000	Moscow 1
180	D	Oranienburg	750	DS Kultur
	D	Saarlouis-Felsburg	2000	Europe No 1
	TUR	Ankara	1200	TRT 2
	URS	Alma Ata	250	Kazakh R/Moscow 1
189	S	Motala	300	P1
	I	Caltaniessetta	10	Radio Due
	URS	Tbilisi	500	First/Moscow 2
198	G	Droitwich	500	R4 UK
	G	Burghead	50	R4
	G	Westerglen	50	R4
	ALG	Ouargla	1000	Arabic Network
	URS	Leningrad	150	Moscow 2
	TUR	Etimesgut	120	TRT 1
	POL	Warsaw	200	Warsaw 4
207	MRC	Azilal	800	Arabic Network
	D	Aholming	500/250	DLF
	UKR	Kiev	500	First/Second
	ISL	Vatnsendi	100	First
216	MCO	Roumoules	1400	R Monte Carlo
	NOR	Oslo	200	P1
	URS	Baku	500	First
225	POL	Warsaw	2000	Warsaw 1
234	LUX	Junglinster	2000	RTL
	URS	Kishinev	1000	Moscow First

Frequency [kHz]	Country	Station Site	Power [kW]	Programme/ Network
243	DNK	Kalundborg	300	P1
	TUR	Erzurum	200	TRT 1
252	ALG	Tipazi	1500/750	French Network
	FNL	Lahti	200	First Programme
	IRL	Kilmessan	500	Atlantic 252
261	URS	Moscow	2000	Moscow 1/2
	BUL	Plovdiv	500	Programme 1
	D	Burg	200	R Volga/R Moscow
270	TCH	Ceskoslovensko	1500	Ceskoslovensko
	URS	Novosibirsk	150	Moscow 1
279	BLR	Minsk	100	Moscow 1 & 2
	URS	Ashkhabad	150	First/Moscow 1 & 2

Section 8

EUROPEAN, NEAR AND MIDDLE EASTERN AND NORTH AFRICAN MEDIUM WAVE RADIO STATIONS

Frequency [kHz]	Country	Station Site	Power [kW]	Programme/ Network
522	D	Hof Saale	0.2	Bayern 1
	CVA	Citta del Vaticano	5	Vatican R
531	ALG	Ain Beida	600/300	Arabic Network
	SUI	Beromunster	500	DRS-1
	D	Leipzig	100	Sacschenrundfunk
	E	Oviedo	10	RNE5
	URS	Cheboksary	30	Moscow 2
540	HNG	Solt	2000	Kossuth
	MRC	Sidi Bennour	600	Arabic
	BEL	Wavre-Overijse	150/50	BRT 2
	IRL	Conamara	2	R Na Gaeltachta
	KWT	Sulaibiyah	1500	R Kuwait Main Prog
549	ALG	Les Trembles	600/300	Arabic Network
	D	Bayreuth	200	DLF
	D	Nordkirchen	100	DLF
	URS	Leningrad	100	Moscow 2
	YUG	Pristina	100	R Lubljana
	ARS	Duba	2000	Arabic 1/2
558	TUR	Denizli	600	TRT 1
	SUI	Monte Ceneri-Cima	300	Italian First Prog
	ROU	Targu Jiu	200	2nd Prog/Regional
	FNL	Helsinki	100	First Programme
	E	Valencia	20	RNE5
	D	Neubrandenburg	20	NDR2
	POR	Faro	10	Antena 1
	G	Lots Road	0.3	Spectrum R
	CYP	Paphos	10	CBC1
567	SYR	Samas-Adra	1000	Arabic Network
	IRL		500	Tullamore RTE R1
	D	Berlin	1	Sender Freise Berlin
	I	Bologna	20	R Uno
	POR	Valenca do Minho	10	Antena 1
	E	Marbella	5	RNE5
	URS	Volgograd	250	Moscow 1/2

Frequency [kHz]	Country	Station Site	Power [kW]	Programme/ Network
576	URS	Riga	500	First
	D	Stuttgart	300	SDR 1
	D	Schwerin	250	RA
	ISR	Tel Aviv	200	Network A
	BUL	Vidin	100	Programme 2
	POR	Braga	10	R Renascenca
585	AUT	Vienna	600/240	ORF1
	TUN	Gafsa	350	Arabic Network
	E	Madrid	200	RNE1
	F	Paris	10	France Inter
	G	Dumfries	2	BBC R Solway
	ARS	Riyadh	1200	Arabic Programme
594	D	Frankfurt	400	Hessischer RF
	BUL	Pleven	250	Programme 1
	MRC	Oujda	100	Arabic/Regional
	POR	Muge	100	R Renascenca
	ARS	Duba	2000	Arabic Programme
	URS	Ijevsk	150	Moscow 2
603	F	Lyon-Tramoyes	300	R France Lyon
	ROU	Botosani	50	Bucharest 1
	D	Koenigswusterhausen	30	RA
	CYP	Nicosia	20	CBC2
	E	Seville	20	RNE5
	TUN	Sousse	10	Regional
	G	Newcastle	2	BBC R4
	G	Maidstone	0.5	Coast Classics [Invicta]
	G	Gloucester	0.1	BBC R Gloucestershire
612	YUG	Sarajevo	600	Sarajevo 1
	MRC	Sebaa-Aiou	300	R Medi 1
	IRL	Athlone	100	RTE R2
	URS	Petrozavodsk	100	Moscow 2
	D	Kiel	10	NDR
	E	Lerida	10	RNE1
621	EGY	Batra	1000	Nile Valley R
	BEL	Wavre	300	RTBF 1
	E	Santa Cruz Tenerife	100	RNE1
	URS	Syktyvkar	20	

Frequency [kHz]	Country	Station Site	Power [kW]	Programme/ Network
630	TUN	Djedeida	600	Arabic Network
	ROU	Timisoara	400	Bucharest 1
	TUR	Cukurova	300	TRT 1
	NOR	Vigra	100	P1
	D	Dannenberg	80	NDR
	POR	Montemorvelho	50	Antena 1
	G	Redruth	2	BBC R Cornwall
	G	Luton	0.3	BBC R Bedfordshire
	URS	Saratov	50	Moscow 2
639	TCH	Prague	1500	Prague Programme
	CYP	Zakaki	500	BBC World Service
	E	La Coruna	100	RNE1
	IRN	Bonab	400	VoIRI
648	G	Orfordness	500	BBC World Service
	UKR	Simferopol	150	Moscow 1/First
	ALB	Rrogozhina	15	Regional Prog
	E	Palma de Mallorca	10	RNE1
	YUG	Murska Sobota	10	R Ljubljana
	LBY	Tobruk	300	Tripoli R
657	D	Burg	500	Jugendradio DT64
	D	Neubrandenburg	20	
	I	Naples	120	R Uno
	E	Madrid	20	RNE5
	G	Wrexham	2	BBC R Clwyd
	G	Bodmin	0.5	BBC R Cornwall
666	SYR	Damas-Sabboura	600	Arabic Network
	URS	Vilnius	500	R Vilnius
	D	Bodeseesender	300/180	SWF
	POR	Lisbon	135	Antena 1
	E	Barcelona	20	R Miramar
	G	Fulford	0.8	BBC R York
	G	Exeter	0.5	Devonair
675	F	Marseille	600	France Inter
	HOL	Lopik	120	Hilversum 3
	LBY	Benghazi	100	Tripoli R
	UKR	Ujgorod	50	First
684	YUG	Belgrade	2000	R Beograd 1
	E	Seville	250	RNE1
	D	Hof-Saale	40	RIAS
693	CYP	Nicosia	20	CBC 1
	D	Berlin	250	BR
	G	Droitwich	150	BBC R 5 [+ 10 stns]

Frequency [kHz]	Country	Station Site	Power [kW]	Programme/ Network
693	I	Potenza	20	R Due
(cont'd)	ALB	Pogradec	10	
	POR	Viseu	10	Antena 1
	YUG	Negotin	10/5	R
	ALG	Ain-el-Hamam	5	
702	TCH	Banska Bystrica	400	Bratislava Programme
	MCO	Monte Carlo	300	R Monte Carlo 2
	MRC	Sebaa-Aioun	140	Network C
	NOR	Finnmark	20	P1
	D	Flensburg	5	WDR
	E	Zamora	5	RNE1
711	F	Rennes	300	R Bleue/R France Armorique/RFI
	EGY	Abu Zaabal	100	People's Comm Prog
	LBY	Ghadames	50	
	ROU	Sighet	30	Bucharest 2
	YUG	Nis	20	R Beograd 1/2
	D	Heidelberg	5	SDR
	MRC	Laayoune	600	Arabic/Regional
720	CYP	Zakaki	500	BBC World Serivce
	D	Langenberg	200	WDR 2
	TUN	Sfax	200	Sfax Regional Prog
	D	Munich	150	RFE
	POR	Azurara	100	Antena 1
	G	Lisnagarvey	10	BBC R 4
	G	London	0.5	BBC R 4
	G	Londonderry	0.25	BBC R 4
	ROU	Predeal	2	Bucharest 2
	IRN	Taybad	400	VoIRI
	E	Santa Cruz Tenerife	20	RNE5
729	GRC	Athens	150	ERT 1
	E	Oviedo	50	RNE1
	IRL	Cork	10	RTE R1
	D	Leipzig	5	S1
	D	Putbus	5	RMV/NDR2
	G	Manningtree	0.2	BBC Essex
738	ISR	Tel Aviv	1200	Network D
	POL	Poznan	300	Warsaw 4
	E	Barcelona	250	RNE1
	YUG	Zagreb	25	Regional
	F	Paris	5	RFI
	G	Worcester	0.04	BBC Hereford & Worcester
	URS	Moscow	5	Moscow 1

Frequency [kHz]	Country	Station Site	Power [kW]	Programme/ Network
747	BUL	Petrich	500	Programme 1
	HOL	Flevoland	400	Hilversum 1
	SYR	Sarakeb	100	Arabic Network
	E	Cadiz	10	RNE5
756	D	Braunschweig	800/200	DLF
	ROU	Lugoj	400	Bucharest 2
	POR	Lisbon	5	R Comercial
	G	Redruth	2	BBC R 4
	G	Carlisle	1	BBC R Cumbria
	G	Shrewsbury	1	BBC R Shropshire
765	SUI	Sottens	600	R Suisse Romande 1
	TUR	Gaziantep	600	TRT 1
	URS	Medvejiegorsk	150	Moscow 1
	GRC	Ioannina	20	ERT 4
	G	Chelmsford	0.5	BBC Essex
	ARS	Damman	1000	
774	URS	Voronej	150	Moscow 2
	BUL	Sofia Stolnik	60	Programme 1
	E	Caceres	60	RNE1
	YUG	Zagreb	50/10	R Zagreb
	D	Bonn	5	WDR
	G	Enniskillen	1	BBC R 4
	G	Plymouth	1	BBC R 4
	G	Leeds	0.5	BBC R Leeds
	G	Canterbury	0.7	BBC R Kent
	G	Gloucester	0.2	IBA Severn Sound
783	D	Burg	1000	RA
	SYR	Tartus	600	Arabic Network
	POR	Porto Miramar	50	R Porto
	YUG	Zagreb	10	R Zagreb 2
	ARS	Damman	100	
792	GRC	Kavalla	500	VoA
	F	Limoges	300	France Culture
	TCH	Prague	30	Prague Programme
	E	Seville	20	R Sevilla
	G	Londonderry	1	BBC R Foyle
	G	Bedford	0.2	Supergold [Chiltern R]
	URS	Astrakhan	50	
801	JOR	Ajlun	2000	Arabic Network
	URS	Leningrad	1000/500	Moscow 1
	D	Munich	450/420	Bayern 1

Frequency [kHz]	Country	Station Site	Power [kW]	Programme/ Network
801	E	Castellon	5	RNE1
(cont'd)	G	Barnstaple	2	BBC R Devon
810	YUG	Skopje	1000	R Skopje 1
	G	Burghead	100	BBC R Scotland
	G	Westerglen	100	BBC R Scotland
	G	Redmoss	5	BBC R Scotland
	E	Madrid	20	R Madrid
	D	Berlin	5	DLF
	URS	Vyru	5	First/Second
	URS	Volgograd	150	Moscow 2
819	AND	Andorra	900	Sud R
	EGY	Batra	450	Arabic Programme
	POL	Warsaw	300	Warsaw 4
	I	Trieste	25	R Uno
	MRC	Rabat	25	Arabic Network
	G	Hereford	0.04	BBC Hereford & Worcester
828	BUL	Shumen	500	Programme 2
	MRC	Oujda	100	French Network
	D	Hannover	100/5	NDR
	D	Freiburg	1	SWF
	E	Barcelona	20	R Barcelona
	G	Bournemouth	0.3	2CR
	G	Sedgley	0.2	BBC R WM
	G	Luton	0.18	Supergold [Chiltern R]
	G	Leeds	0.18	R Aire
	URS	Gorkii	150	
837	F	Nancy	200	R France Nancy
	UKR	Kharkov	150	Second
	E	Seville	10	R Popular Seville
	YUG	Zagreb	10	R Zagreb
	G	Leicester	0.45	BBC R Leicester
	G	Barrow	1	BBC R Furness/ Cumbria
	E	Las Palmas	10	R Popular de Ibiza
846	I	Rome	540	R Due
	URS	Moscow	60	Moscow 1
855	ROU	Bucharest	1500	Bucharest 2
	E	Murcia	125	RNE1
	D	Berlin	100	RIAS
	G	Plymouth	1	BBC R Devon

Frequency [kHz]	Country	Station Site	Power [kW]	Programme/ Network
855	G	Norwich	1	BBC R Norfolk
(cont'd)	G	Preston	0.5	BBC R Lancashire
864	EGY	Santah	500	Holy Koran R
	F	Paris	300	R France Paris
	BUL	Blagoevgrad	30	Programme 2
	TCH	Olomouc	20	Prague Programme
	YUG	Zagreb	10	R Zagreb
	ALB	Kelcyra	1	Regional Prog
	ARS	Damman	500	
873	D	Frankfurt	150	AFN
	URS	Leningrad	150	Moscow 2 & 3
	E	Zaragoza	20	R Zaragoza
	HNG	Budapest	20	2nd Programme
	G	Enniskillen	1	BBC R Ulster
	G	King's Lynn	0.25	BBC R Norfolk
882	YUG	Titograd	300/100	R Titograd
	D	Wachenbrunn	250	Thuringen Eins
	G	Washford	100	BBC R Wales [+3 stns]
	E	Alicante	2	R Popular de Alicante
	ARS	Damman	100	
	URS	Stavropol	500	
891	ALG	Algiers	600/300	Arabic Network
	TUR	Antalya	600	TRT 1
	UKR	Ujgorod	150	Moscow 2
	HOL	Hulsberg	20	Hilversum 5
	D	Berlin	5	DS Kultur
900	ARS	Guriat	1000	
	I	Milan	600	R Uno
	TCH	Karlovy Vary	30	Prague Prog
909	G	Moorside Edge	200	BBC R 5 [+10 stns]
	ROU	Cluj	50	Bucharest 2
	E	Palma de Mallorca	10	R Cadena Espana
	ALB	Korce	15	
918	YUG	Ljubljana	600/100	R Ljubljana 1
	E	Madrid	20	R Intercontinental
	URS	Mezen	100	
927	BEL	Wolvertem	300	BRT1
	TUR	Izmir	200	TRT1
	POR	Evora	1	Regional Programme
	ALG	Timimoun	5	Arabic Programme

Frequency [kHz]	Country	Station Site	Power [kW]	Programme/ Network
936	UKR	Lvov	500	First/Foreign
	D	Bremen	100	R Bremen
	I	Venice	20	R Due
	E	Lerida	1	
	G	Chippenham	0.2	GWR/Brunel R
945	F	Toulouse	300	R France Toulouse
	URS	Rostov	300	Moscow 2
	YUG	Sarajevo	100	R Sarajevo 2
	BUL	Pleven	30	Programme 2
	GRC	Larissa	5	ERT 4
	G	Derby	0.2	R Trent
	TCH	Liberac	6	Prague Programme
954	TUR	Trabzon	300	TRT1
	TCH	Brno	200	Prague Programme
	BUL	Shumen	30	Programme 1
	E	Madrid	20	R Espana
	GRC	Iraklion	20	Regional Programme
	G	Torbay	0.4	Devonair
	G	Hereford	0.4	R Wyvern
963	FNL	Pori	600	First Prog/R Finland
	TUN	Djedeida	200	Intl Network
	BUL	Sofia	150	Programme 1
	POR	Seixal	10	R Renascenca
972	UKR	Nikolaev	500	Moscow 2/Foreign
	D	Hamburg	300	NDR
	E	Monforte de Lemos	2	RNE1
981	ALG	Algiers	600/300	French Network
	GRC	Megara	200	ERT 4
	I	Trieste	10	Slovene
	TCH	Ceske Budejovice	7	Prague Programme
	POR	Coimbra	10	R Renascenca
990	D	Berlin	300	RIAS
	ALB	Kukes	15	Regional Programme
	E	Bilbao	10	R Bilbao
	I	Potenza	10	R Uno
	G	Exeter	1	BBC R Devon
	G	Aberdeen	1	BBC R Aberdeen
	G	Tywyn	1	BBC R 5
	G	Wolverhampton	0.1	Beacon R
	G	Doncaster	0.3	Hallam R
	G	London	1	Spectrum R
	G	Redmoss	1	BBC R Scotland

Frequency [kHz]	Country	Station Site	Power [kW]	Programme/ Network
999	URS	Kishinev	500	First/Foreign
	I	Turin	50	R Due
	E	Madrid	20	R Popular Madrid
	D	Hoyerswerda	20	Sorbischer Rundfunk
	D	Schwerin	20	RMV/NDR2
	MLT	Delimara	5	R Malta 1
	G	Fareham	1	BBC R Solent
	G	Nottingham	0.2	R Trent
	G	Preston	0.8	Red Rose R
1 008	HOL	Flevoland	400	Radio 5
	YUG	Aleksinac	400/120	R Beograd2/3
	BLR	Mozyr	50	Second/Moscow 2
	GRC	Kerkyra	50	ERT 1/2/Regional
	E	Las Palmas	10	R Cadena Espana
1 017	TUR	Istanbul	1200	TRT 1
	D	Wolfsheim	600	SWF
	BUL	Kardjali	30	Programme 1
	D	Seelow	5	RA
1 026	AUT	Linz Kronstorf	100	ORF 1/3
	BLR	Brest	5	Moscow 2/Second
	G	Belfast	1	Downtown R
	G	St Helier	1	BBC R Jersey
	G	Cambridge	0.5	BBC R Cambridgeshire
	E	Reus	2	R Reus
	E	Gijon	2	
1 035	IRQ	Babel	1000	Arabic Prog
	URS	Tallin	500	First/Foreign
	POR	Lisbon	135	R Comercial
	I	Milan	50	R Due
	G	Sheffield	1	BBC R Sheffield
	G	Gillingham	0.5	BBC R Kent
	G	Aberdeen	0.78	North Sound
	G	Ayr	0.32	West Sound
1 044	MRC	Sebaa Aioun	300	Arabic/Regional
	D	Burg	250	S1
	GRC	Macedonia	150	ERT 1/2/Regional
	CYP	Limassol	10	CBC 1
	E	San Sebastian	10	R San Sebastian
1 053	ROU	Iasi	1000	Bucharest 2
	MRC	Tangier	600	Arabic/Regional

Frequency [kHz]	Country	Station Site	Power [kW]	Programme/ Network
1 053	G	Droitwich	150	BBC R 1 [+13 stns]
(cont'd)	LBY	Tripoli	50	Tripoli R
1 062	DNK	Kalundborg	250	P3
	POR	Azurara	100	R Comercial
	I	Cagliari	25	R Uno
	YUG	Svetozarevo	10	Belgrad 1
	TUR	Diyabakir	300	TRT1
1 071	SYR	Tartus	60	French Network
	TCH	Prague	60/30	Interprogramme
	URS	Riga	60	Second
	F	Lille	40	France Inter
	YUG	Karaotok	40	R Sarajevo 1
1 080	POL	Katowice	1500	Warsaw 4
	GRC	Orestias	20	ERT 4/Regional
	E	La Coruna	3	
	E	Granada	5	R Granada
	E	Mallorca	2	R Mallorca
1 089	URS	Krasnodar	300	Moscow 2
	ALB	Durres	150	National/Foreign
	G	Brookmans Park	150	BBC R 1 [+9 stns]
	D	Dresden	20	T1
	ALG	Adrar	5	Arabic Network
1098	TCH	Bratislava	750	Bratislava
	CYP	Yeni Iskele	100	R Bayrak
	E	Lugo	5	RNE5
	URS	Alma Ata	150	
	E	Santa Cruz de Palma	2	R Cadena Espana
1 107	EGY	Batra	600	Nile Valley
	URS	Kaunas	150	R Vilnius
	YUG	Novi Sad	150	R Novi Sad 1
	D	Munich	40	AFN
	I	Rome	6	R Tre
	G	Northampton	0.5	BBC R Northampton
	G	Wallasey	0.5	BBC R 1
	G	Inverness	1	Moray Firth R
1 116	IRQ	Rutba	300	Arabic Programme
	I	Bari	150	R Due
	URS	Kaliningrad	30	Moscow 1
	HNG	Miskolc	120	Kossuth R
	D	Karl Marx Stadt	5	S1
	G	Derby	1.2	BBC R Derby
	G	St Peter Port	0.5	BBC R Guernsey

Frequency [kHz]	Country	Station Site	Power [kW]	Programme/ Network
1 125	YUG	Zagreb	300/100	R Zagreb
	BEL	La Louviere	20	RTBF 2
	URS	Leningrad	20	Moscow 3 & 4
	G	Llandrindod Wells	1	BBC R Wales
	E	Castellon	10	RNE5
1 134	YUG	Zagreb	1200	R Zagreb
	E	Bilbao	10	R Popular de Bilbao
	E	Figueras	2	R P Figueras
	KWT	Sulaibiyah	750	
1 143	URS	Kaliningrad	150	Moscow 2/Foreign
	YUG	Zagreb	100	R Zagreb
	D	Stuttgart	10	AFN
	I	Sassari	10	R Due
1 152	ROU	Cluj	950	Bucharest 2
	G	London	5.5	London Talkback R
	G	Glasgow	2	R Clyde
	G	Birmingham	0.8	BRMB R
	G	Manchester	0.35	Piccadilly 1152
	G	Plymouth	0.5	Plymouth Sound
	G	Newcastle-on-Tyne	1	Metro R [Gt Northern]
	G	Great Yarmouth	0.8	R Broadland
1 161	BUL	Stara Zagora	500	Programme 1
	F	Strasbourg	200	France Inter
	EGY	Tanta	60	Regional Programme
	G	Bexhill	1	BBC R Sussex
	G	Bedford	0.8	BBC R Bedfordshire
	G	Swindon	0.2	GWR/Brunel R
	G	Dundee	0.5	R Tay
	G	Hull	0.35	Viking R
1 170	BLR	Moghilev	1000	Moscow 2
	YUG	Beli Kriz	300/100	R Ljubljana 2
	D	Brenburg	20	Sachsenradio
	POR	Vila Read	10	R Comercial
	G	Swansea	0.8	Swansea Sound
	G	Stockton-on-Tees	0.5	TFM R [Gt Northern]
	G	Stoke-on-Trent	0.2	Signal R
	G	Ipswich	0.28	R Orwell
	G	Portsmouth	0.12	Ocean Sound
	URS	Maikop	500	

Frequency [kHz]	Country	Station Site	Power [kW]	Programme/ Network
1 179	S	Soelvesborg	600	R Sweden
	ROU	Bacau	200	Bucharest 1
	GRC	Thessaloniki	50	Regional Programme
	E	Murcia	5	R Murcia
1 188	HNG	Szolnok	135	Programme 2
	I	San Remo	6	R Due
	BEL	Kuurne	5	BRT 2
	D	Wachenbrunn	20	Sorbischer Rundfunk
	MRC	Casablanca	1	French Network
1 197	D	Munich	300	VoA
	BLR	Minsk	50	Moscow 2
	MRC	Agadir	20	French Network
	G	Enniskillen	1	BBC R 3 [+3 stns]
	YUG	Bijeljina	1	
1 206	POL	Wroclaw	200	Warsaw 4
	F	Bordeaux	100	R France Bordeaux
	ISR	Haifa	50	Network B
1 215	ALB	Lushnje	500	Foreign Services
	G	Moorside Edge	100	BBC R 3 [+16 stns]
	URS	Kaliningrad	500	
	YUG	Djurdevac	1	R Ljubljana
1 224	BUL	Vidin	500	Programme 1
	IRQ	Nasiriya	300	
	E	Santander	2	R Pop de Santander
1 233	CYP	Cape Greco	600	R Monte Carlo
	TCH	Prague	400	Ceskoslovensko
	MRC	Tangier	200	F Medi 1
	BEL	Liege	5	RTBF 2
1 242	F	Marseille	150	R France Marseille
	UKR	Kiev	150	Kiev 2
	YUG	Ohrid	10	R Skopje 1
	G	Gillingham	0.32	Coast Classics [Invicta]
	G	Isle of Wight	0.5	Isle of Wight R
1 251	HNG	Siofok	500	Programme 2
	LBY	Tipoli	500	Tripoli R
	HOL	Hulsberg	10	Hilversum 1
	POR	Porto	10	R Renascenca
	G	Bury St Edmunds	0.5	Saxon R

Frequency [kHz]	Country	Station Site	Power [kW]	Programme/ Network
1 260	GRC	Rhodes	500	VoA
	E	Valencia	20	R Valencia
	POL	Szczecin	10	Warsaw 4
	ALB	Fier	1	Regional Programme
	G	Bristol	0.8	GWR
	G	Wrexham	0.32	Marcher Sound
	G	Leicester	0.2	Leicester Sound
	G	Scarborough	0.5	BBC R York
1 269	D	Neumueunster	600	DLF
	YUG	Novi Sad	600	R Novi Sad 2
	E	Leon	2	R Popular de Leon
1 278	F	Strasbourg	300	R France Strasbourg
	UKR	Odessa	150	Moscow 3 & 2
	IRL	Cork	10	RTE 2
	GRC	Florina	20	RTE R2
	G	Bradford	0.43	Pennine R
1 287	TCH	Ceskoslovensko	300	R Prague
	ISR	Tel Aviv	100	Israel Defence R
	POR	Portalegre	1	Antena 1
	ALG	El Golea	5	Arabic Network
1 296	G	Orfordness	500	BBC World Service
	BUL	Kardjali	150	Programme 2
	URS	Baku	150	
1 305	POL	Rzeszow	100	Warsaw 4
	ISR	Haifa	20	Israel Defence R
	ALB	Gjirokaster	15	Regional Programme
	BEL	Marche	10	RTBF 2
	I	Pisa	2	R Tre
	G	Barnsley	0.3	R Hallam
	G	Newport	0.2	Red Dragon R
1 314	NOR	Kvitsoy	1200	P1
	ROU	Timisoara	30	Bucharest 1/2
	GRC	Tripolis	20	ERT 4/Regional
	I	Ancona	6	R Due
	UAE	Abu Dhabi	1000	
1 323	D	Wachenbrunn	1000/150	RMR
	CYP	Zyyi	200	BBC World Service
	YUG	Bitola	10	Skopje
	G	Taunton	1	BBC R Bristol
	G	Brighton	0.5	Southern Sound
1 332	I	Rome	300	R Uno
	TCH	Moravske	50	Prague/Regional

Frequency [kHz]	Country	Station Site	Power [kW]	Programme/ Network
1 332	URS	Vyru	30	First
(cont'd)	ROU	Galatzi	15	Programme 1
	G	Peterborough	0.5	Hereward R
	G	Lacock	0.4	BBC Wiltshire Sound
	IRN	Teheran	100	VoIRI
1 341	HNG	Budapest	300	Programme 2
	G	Lisnagarvey	100	BBC R Ulster
	YUG	Zajecar	10	Regional
	D	Marneukirchen	1	S1
	E	Tarrasa	2	R Popular de Tarrasa
1 350	F	Nancy	100	France Inter
	URS	Madona	50	First
	HNG	Pecs	10	Programme 2
	YUG	Studio B 1	10	Regional Programme
	GRC	Pyrgos	4	ERT 4/Regional Prog
	MTN	Nouakchott	50	ORTM
1 359	D	Berlin	250/100	Antenne Brandenburg
	ALB	Tirana	50	R Tirana
	URS	Moscow	15	Moscow 2, 3 & 4
	E	Melilla	5	RNE 1
	G	Chelmsford	0.3	Breeze AM [Essex R]
	G	Coventry	0.1	Mercia Sound
	G	Cardiff	0.25	Red Dragon R
	G	Bournemouth	0.25	BBC R Solent
	IRQ	Kirkuk	120	Kurdish Programme
1 368	POL	Krakow	60	Warsaw 4
	I	Venice	20	R Tre
	G	Isle of Man	10	Manx R
	G	Lincoln	2	BBC R Lincolnshire
	G	Crawley	0.5	BBC R Sussex
	ISR	Shivta	20	Israel Defence R
	G	Swindon	0.1	BBC Wiltshire Sound
1 377	F	Lille	300	R France Lille
	UKR	Lutsk	50	Second
	POR	Canidelo	10	Antena 1
	YUG	Prizren	10	Regional Programme
	D	Klingenthal	1	Sachsenradio
1 386	URS	Kaliningrad	150	Moscow 1/External
	GRC	Athens	50	ERT 2
	IRN	Ahwaz	400	First Frogramme
1 395	ALB	Lusnje	1000	R Tirana
	E	Leon	5	RNE 5

Frequency [kHz]	Country	Station Site	Power [kW]	Programme/ Network
1 404	GRC	Komotini	50	Regional
	UKR	Dniepropetrovsk	30	Second
	F	Ajaccio	20	R France Ajaccio
	LBY	Tripoli	20	Holy Koran Prog
	ROU	Baia Mare	15	Bucharest 1
1 413	YUG	Pristina	1000	R Pristina
	D	Heidenheim	0.2	SDR
	G	Hounslow	0.13	Sunrise R
	OMA	Masirah	750	BBC World Service
1 422	D	Saarbrucken	1200/600	SR1
	URS	Valmeira	50	First
	ALG	Algiers	50/25	Kabyl & French
1 431	UKR	Krivoi Rog	500	First
	D	Dresden	250	S1
	I	Foggia	2	R Due
	G	Southend	0.4	Essex R
	G	Reading	0.2	R 210
1 440	LUX	Marnach	1200	R Luxembourg
	YUG	Svetozarevo	20/10	R Beograd 2/3
	ARS	Damman	1600	
1 449	I	Squinzano	50	R Due
	URS	Kishinev	50	Moscow 2
	LBY	Miurata	20	Tripoli R
	D	Berlin	5	SFB
	G	Redmoss	2	BBC R 4
	G	Peterborough	0.1	BBC R Cambridgeshire
	URS	Mezen	100	
1 458	ALB	Lushnje	500	R Tirana
	ROU	Constantza	50	Bucharest 2
	G	Brookmans Park	50	BBC GLR
	G	Birmingham	7	BBC R WM
	G	Manchester	5	BBC R Manchester
	G	Newcastle-on-Tyne	2	BBC R Newcastle
	G	Torbay	1	BBC R Devon
	G	Whitehaven	0.5	BBC R Cumbria
	YUG	Kraljevo	10	
	D	Weida	5	Thuringen Eins
	URS	Medvejiegorsk	5	
1 467	MCO	Monte Carlo	1000/400	R Monte Carlo/TWR
	UKR	Kiev	300	Moscow 1
	YUG	Zrenjanin	2	R Ljubljana

Frequency [kHz]	Country	Station Site	Power [kW]	Programme/ Network
1 476	AUT	Vienna Bisamberg	600	ORF 1/2/3
	UKR	Lvov	120	
	G	Guildford	0.5	County Sound
	E	Bilbao	10	RNE 5
1 485	I	Bolzano	2	R Due
	G	Hull	1.5	BBC R Humberside
	G	Wallasey	2	BBC R Merseyside
	G	Bournemouth	2	BBC R 1
	G	Carlisle	1	BBC R 4
	G	Shoreham	1	BBC R Sussex
	G	Oxford	0.5	BBC R Oxford
	D	Augsburg	1	AFN
	POL	Gizycko	1	Warsaw 4
	E	Gerona	2	R Gerona
	E	Santander	2	R Santander
1 494	URS	Leningrad	1000	First
	F	Bastia	20	R France Bastia
	CTI	Abidjan	20	
1 503	POL	Stargard	300	Warsaw 4
	G	Stoke-on-Trent	1	BBC R Stoke
	E	Burgos	10	RNE 5
1 512	BEL	Wolvertem	600	BRT2/BRT Intl
	GRC	Chania	50	Regional prog
	URS	Sotchi	30	Moscow 3
	I	Palermo	2	R Tre
	ARS	Jeddah	1200	Call of Islam
1 521	TCH	Kosice	600	Hvezda
	G	Reigate	0.74	R Mercury
	G	Nottingham	0.5	BBC R Nottingham
	E	Oveido	5	R Asturias
	ARS	Duba	2000	
1 530	CVA	Vatican City	450	Vatican R
	ROU	Mahmudia	15	Bucharest 1
	UKR	Jitomir	5	Moscow 2
	G	Halifax	1	Pennine R
	G	Southend-on-Sea	0.1	BBC R Essex
	G	Worcester	0.5	R Wyvern
	G	Kettering & Corby	0.1	KCBC
1 539	D	Mainflingen	450	DLF
	URS	Borovitchi	5	Second
	E	Valladolid	5	R Valladolid

Frequency [kHz]	Country	Station Site	Power [kW]	Programme/ Network
1 548	UKR	Vinnitsa	50	First
	G	London	27.5	Capital Gold
	G	Bristol	5	BBC R Bristol
	G	Stockton-on-Tees	1	BBC R Cleveland
	G	Liverpool	1.2	R City
	G	Sheffield	0.3	R Hallam
	G	Edinburgh	2	R Forth
1 557	MLT	Cyclops	600	DW/R Medi
	F	Nice	300	R France Nice
	URS	Kaunas	75	Second
	G	Northampton	0.76	Chiltern R
	G	Lancaster	0.25	BBC R Lancashire
	G	Southampton	0.5	Ocean Sound
	G	Tendring	0.1	Tendring R
1 566	TUN	Sfaz Sidi Mansour	1200	Arabic Network
	SUI	Monte Ceneri	300	DRS 1
	UKR	Odessa	5	Moscow 3
	URS	Tartu	5	
	YUG	Smarje	2	R Ljubljana
	POR	Covilha	1	Antena 1
1 575	D	Burg	250	DS Kultur
	I	Genova	50	R Uno
	POR	Canidelo	10	R Comercial
	E	Cordoba	5	R Cordoba
	UAE	Sharjah	50	
1 584	POL	Ostoda	1	Warsaw 4
	D	Cottbus	1	R Mecklenburg
	G	Mansfield	1	BBC R Nottingham
	G	Woofferton	0.3	BBC R Shropshire
	G	Perth	0.2	R Tay
	E	Pamplona	2	
	G	Heathrow	0.1	Airport Info R
	G	Gatwick	0.1	Airport Info R
1 593	D	Langenburg	800	WDR
	ROU	Baneasa	14	Bucharest 1
1 602	I	Bolzano	2	R Tre
	POL	Gorzow Wielk	1	Warsaw 4
	D	Bautzen	1	R Mecklenburg
	G	Rusthall	0.25	BBC R Kent
	E	Lugo	2	R Lugo
1 611	CVA	Vatican City	5	Vatican R

Section 9

CANADIAN MEDIUM WAVE RADIO STATIONS

Frequency [kHz]	Station Site	Province	Power [kW]	Call Sign
530	Fort Erie	ON	0.25	CJFT
540	Grand Falls	NF	10	CBT
	Windsor	ON	2.5	CBEF
	New Carlisle	PQ	10	CBGA
	Ottawa	ON	50	CJSB
	Sault Ste. Marie	ON	15	CKCY
	Watrous	SK	50	CBK
550	Kamloops	BC	25	CFJC
	Prince George	BC	10	CKPG
	Fredricton	NB	50	CFNB
	Sudbury	ON	10	CHNO
	Trois Rivieres	PQ	10	CHLN
560	Fort St John	BC	1	CKNL
	Prince Rupert	BC	1	CHTK
	Marystown	NF	10	CHVO
	Kirkland Lake	ON	5	CJKL
	Owen Sound	ON	5	CFOS
	Sept Iles	PQ	10	CKCN
570	Cranbrook	BC	10	CKEK
	Williams Lake	BC	1	CKWL
	Edmundston	NB	5	CJEM
	Corner Brook	NF	1	CFCB
	Kitchener	ON	10	CHYM
	Swift Current	SK	10	CKSW
	Whitehorse	YT	5	CFWH
580	Edmonton	AB	10	CKUA
	Salmon Arm	BC	10	CKXR
	Winnipeg	MB	50	CKY
	Antigonish	NS	10	CJFX
	Kapuskasing	ON	10	CKAP
	Ottawa	ON	50	CFRA
	Thunder Bay	ON	5	CKPR
	Hauterive	PQ	10	CHLC
590	Terrace	BC	1	CFTK
	Flin Flon	MB	10	CFAR
	Sussex	NB	1	CJCW
	St John's	NF	25	VOCM

Frequency [kHz]	Station Site	Province	Power [kW]	Call Sign
590	Toronto	ON	50	CKEY
(cont'd)	Jonquiere	PQ	10	CKRS
600	Vancouver	BC	10	CHRX
	St Anthony	NF	10	CBNA
	Truro	NS	10	CKCL
	North Bay	ON	10	CFCH
	Montreal	PQ	10	CFCF
	Saskatoon	SK	10	CFQC
610	Peace River	AB	10	CKYL
	Kamloops	BC	25	CHNL
	Trail	BC	10	CJAT
	Thompson	MB	1	CHTM
	Grand Bank	NF	10	CKXJ
	St Catherines	ON	10	CKTB
	Mont Laurier	PQ	1	CFLO
	New Carlisle	PQ	10	CHNC
	Whitehorse	YT	1	CKRW
620	Prince George	BC	10	CJCI
	Grand Falls	NF	10	CKCM
	Timmins	ON	10	CFCL
	Riviere Portneuf	PQ	1	CFRP
	Regina	SK	10	CKCK
630	Edmonton	AB	50	CHED
	Kelowna	BC	5	CKOV
	Winnipeg	MB	10	CKRC
	Chatham	ON	10	CFCO
	Smiths Falls	ON	10	CJET
	Charlottetown	PEI	10	CFCY
	Sherbrooke	PQ	10	CHLT
640	St John's	NF	10	CBN
	Fort Frances	ON	1	CFOB
	Toronto	ON	50	CHOG
650	Richmond	BC	10	CISL
	Saskatoon	SK	10	CKOM
	Gander	NF	5	CKGA
660	Calgary	AB	50	CFFR
670	Musgravetown	NF	10	CKXB
680	Edmonton	AB	10	CHFA
	Winnipeg	MB	50	CJOB
	Grand Falls	NF	10	CKXG
	Dartmouth	NS	50	CDFR
	Toronto	ON	25	CFTR

Frequency [kHz]	Station Site	Province	Power [kW]	Call Sign
690	Vancouver	BC	50	CBU
	Montreal	PQ	50	CBF
	Gravelborg	SK	5	CBKF-1
700	Red Deer	AB	50	CKRD
	St John	NB	10	CHSJ
710	Clarenville	NF	10	CKVO
	Leamington	ON	10	CHYR
	Niagara Falls	ON	5	CJRN
	Port Cartier	PQ	1	CIPC
	Ville Marie	PQ	10	CKVM
720	Charlottetown	PEI	10	CHTN
730	Vancouver	BC	50	CKLG
	Dauphin	MB	10	CKDM
	Blind River	ON	1	CJNR
	Leamington	ON	1	CHYR-7
	Montreal	ON	50	CKAC
740	Edmonton	AB	50	CBX
	Toronto	ON	50	CBL
	Marystown	NF	10	CHCM
750	Bonavista	NF	10	CBGY
	Timmins	ON	10	CKGB
	Saskatoon	SK	10	CJWW
760	Burns Lake	BC	1	CFLD
	Castlegar	BC	20	CKQR
770	Calgary	AB	50	CHQR
780	Penticton	BC	20	CKOK
	Dartmouth	NS	50	CFDR
790	Camrose	AB	50	CFCW
	Newcastle	NB	5	CFAN
	Port au Choix	NF	1	CFNW
	Brampton	ON	5	CIAO
	Sudbury	ON	50	CIGM
	Baie Comeau	PQ	1	CKBH
800	Langley	BC	10	CKST
	Penticton	BC	10	CKOK
	St John's	NF	5	VOWR
	Belleville	ON	10	CJBQ
	Windsor	ON	50	CKLW
	Montreal	PQ	50	CJAD

Frequency [kHz]	Station Site	Province	Power [kW]	Call Sign
800	Quebec	PQ	50	CHRC
(cont'd)	Moose Jaw	SK	10	CHAB
810	Winnipeg	MB	10	CKJS
	Caraquet	NB	10	CJVA
820	Hamilton	ON	50	CHAM
830	Brockville	ON	5	CFJR
840	100 Mile House	BC	1	CKBX
	North Bay	ON	10	CHUR
	Grand Prairie	AB	25	CJXX
850	Abbotsford	BC	10	CFVR
	Montreal	PQ	50	CKVL
	Athabasca	AB	1	CKBA
860	Prince Rupert	BC	10	CFPR
	Inuvik	NWT	1	CHAK
	Nelson	BC	1	CKKC
	Toronto	ON	50	CJBC
	Saskatoon	SK	10	CBKF-2
870	Invermere	BC	1	CKIR
	Smithers	BC	1	CFBV
880	Edmonton	AB	50	CHQT
	Brandon	MB	25	CKLQ
890	Dawson Creek	BC	10	CJDC
900	Victoria	BC	10	CJVI
	Amherst	NS	1	CKDH
	Hamilton	ON	50	CHML
	Sudbury	ON	10	CFBR
	Rimouski	PQ	10	CJBR
	Saint Jerome	PQ	1	CJER
	Sherbrooke	PQ	10	CKTS
	Val d'Or	PQ	10	CKVD
	Prince Albert	SK	10	CKBI
910	Drumheller	AB	50	CKDQ
	Lindsay	ON	10	CKLY
	Roberval	PQ	10	CHRL
920	Quesnel	BC	10	CKCQ
	Portage la Prairie	MB	10	CFRY
	Woodstock	NB	10	CJCJ
	Halifax	NS	25	CJCH
	Ottawa	ON	50	CBO

Frequency [kHz]	Station Site	Province	Power [kW]	Call Sign
920	Sault Sainte Marie	ON	10	CKCY
(cont'd)	Wingham	ON	10	CKNX
	Levis	PQ	10	CFLS
930	Edmonton	AB	50	CJCA
	St John	NB	50	CFBC
	St John's	NF	50	CJYQ
	Espanola	ON	10	CKNS
940	Vernon	BC	10	CJIB
	Montreal	PQ	50	CBM
	Yorkton	SK	10	CJGX
950	Altona	MB	10	CFAM
	Campbellton	NB	10	CKNB
	Sydney	NS	10	CHER
	Barrie	ON	10	CKBB
960	Calgary	AB	50	CFAC
	Halifax	NS	10	CHNS
	Cambridge	ON	1	CIAM
	Kingston	ON	10	CFFX
970	Edson	AB	10	CJYR
	Harbour Grace	NF	1	CFIQ
	Hull	PQ	10	CKCH
980	New Westminster	BC	50	CKNW
	London	ON	10	CFPL
	Peterborough	ON	10	CHEX
	Quebec	PQ	50	CBV
	Regina	SA	10	CKRM
990	Winnipeg	MB	50	CBW
	Corner Brook	NF	10	CBY
	Montreal	PQ	50	CHTX
1 000	Bridgewater	NS	10	CKBW
	Rimouski	PQ	10	CFLP
1 010	Calgary	AB	50	CBR
	Gander	NF	1	CKXD
	Toronto	ON	50	CFRB
1 020	High Prairie	AB	1	CKVH
1 040	Vancouver	BC	50	CKXY
	St Jean	PQ	10	CFZZ
1 050	Grande Prairie	AB	10	CFGP
	Vernon	BC	10	CICF

Frequency [kHz]	Station Site	Province	Power [kW]	Call Sign
1 050	Winnipeg	MB	10	CKSB
(cont'd)	Sault Sainte Marie	ON	10	CIRS
	Toronto	ON	50	CHUM
	North Battleford	SK	10	CJNB
1 060	Calgary	AB	50	CFCN
	Quebec	PQ	50	CJRP
1 070	Victoria	BC	5	CFAX
	Moncton	NB	50	CBA
	Sarnia	ON	10	CHOK
1 080	Lloydminster	AB	50	CKSA
1 090	Lethbridge	AB	10	CHEC
	Kitchener	ON	10	CKKW
1 110	Sarnia	ON	10	CKJD
1 130	Vancouver	BC	50	CKWX
1 140	Calgary	AB	50	CISS
	Sydney	NS	10	CBI
	Trois Rivieres	PQ	10	CJTR
1 150	Kelowna	BC	10	CKIQ
	Brandon	MB	50	CKX
	Hamilton	ON	50	CKOC
	Ottawa	ON	50	CJRC
	Gaspe	PQ	5	CHGM
1 170	Red Deer	AB	50	CKGY
1 190	Weyburn	SK	10	CFSL
1 200	Victoria	BC	50	CKDA
	Ottawa	ON	50	CFGO
	St Albert	AB	25	CHMG
	Tilsonburgh	ON	10	CKOT
1 210	Slave Lake	AB	1	CKWA
	Kindersley	SK	1	CFYM
1 220	Lethbridge	AB	10	CJOC
	Boissevain	MB	10	CJRB
	Moncton	NB	25	CKCW
	Cornwall	ON	1	CJSS
	Kenora	ON	1	CJRL
	St Catherines	ON	10	CHSC
	Amqui	PQ	10	CFVM
	Shawinigan	PQ	10	CKSM

Frequency [kHz]	Station Site	Province	Power [kW]	Call Sign
1 230	Thunder Bay	ON	4	CJLB
	Dolbeau	PQ	10	CHVD
1 240	Yellowknife	NWT	4	CJCD
1 250	Steinbach	MB	10	CHSM
	Oakville	ON	10	CHWO
	Ottawa	ON	50	CBOF
	Matane	PQ	10	CBGA
1 260	Edmonton	AB	50	CFRN
	Fredericton	NB	10	CIHI
1 270	Medicine Hat	AB	10	CHAT
	Chilliwack	BC	10	CHWK
	Sydney	NS	10	CJCB
	Trenton	ON	1	CJTN
	Alma	PQ	10	CFGT
1 280	High River	AB	10	CHRB
	Powell River	BC	1	CHQB
	Montreal	PQ	50	CJMS
	Quebec	PQ	50	CKCV
	Estevan	SK	10	CJSL
1 290	Winnipeg	MB	10	CIFX
	London	ON	10	CJBK
	Matane	PQ	10	CHRM
1 300	Regina	SK	10	CJME
1 310	St Paul	AB	10	CHLW
	Ottawa	ON	50	CIWW
	La Pocatiere	PQ	10	CHGB
1 320	Vancouver	BC	50	CHQM
	New Glasgow	NS	25	CKEC
	Mississauga	ON	20	CJMR
1 330	Thetford Mines	PQ	10	CKLD
	Rosetown	SK	10	CJYM
1 340	Cornerbrook	NF	10	CKXX
	Yellowknife	NWT	2.5	CFYK
	Yarmouth	NS	4	CJLS
	Happy Valley	NF	1	CKHV
1 350	Nanaimo	BC	10	CKEG
	Middleton	NS	1	CKAD
	Oshawa	ON	10	CKAR
	Pembroke	ON	1	CHRO

Frequency [kHz]	Station Site	Province	Power [kW]	Call Sign
1 350	Joilette	PQ	10	CJLM
(cont'd)	St Pamphile	PQ	1	CHAL
1 360	Bathurst	NB	10	CKBC
	Ste Marie de Beauce	PQ	10	CJVL
1 370	Westlock	AB	10	CFOK
	Parksville	BC	1	CHPQ
	Valleyfield	PQ	10	CFLV
	Ville Degelis	PQ	1	CFVD
1 380	Brantford	ON	10	CKPC
	Kingston	ON	10	CKLC
	Victoriaville	PQ	10	CFDA
1 390	Medicine Hat	AB	10	CJCY
	Nelson	BC	1	CKKC
	Ajax	ON	10	CHOO
1 400	Gander	NF	4	CBG
	Riviere du Loup	PQ	20	CJFP
	Rouyn	PQ	10	CKRN
1 410	Vancouver	BC	50	CFUN
	Port Hawkesbury	NS	10	CIGO
	London	ON	10	CKSL
	Montreal	PQ	10	CFMB
1 420	Digby	NS	1	CKDY
	Peterborough	ON	10	CKPT
	Chicoutimi	PQ	10	CJMT
	Plessisville	PQ	1	CKTL
	Melfort	SA	10	CJVR
1 430	Grande Prairie	AB	10	CJXX
	Toronto	ON	50	CJCL
1 440	Wetaskiwin	AB	10	CJOI
	Courtenay	BC	1	CFCP
1 450	Granby	PQ	20	CHEF
1 460	Medicine Hat	AB	10	CJMH
	Guelph	ON	10	CJOY
	St George de Beauce	PQ	10	CKRB
1 470	Vancouver	BC	50	CJVB
	Welland	ON	10	CHOW
1 480	Newmarket	ON	10	CKAN
	Edmonton	AB	10	CKER
	Drummondville	PQ	10	CHRD

Frequency [kHz]	Station Site	Province	Power [kW]	Call Sign
1 500	Duncan	BC	10	CKAY
1 510	Tilsonburg	ON	10	CKOT
	Sherbrooke	PQ	50	CJRS
1 540	Toronto	ON	50	CHIN
1 550	Windsor	ON	10	CBE
1 570	Taber	AB	10	CFEZ
	Nanaimo	BC	10	CHUB
	Orillia	ON	10	CFOR
	St Thomas	ON	10	CHLO
	Montreal	PQ	50	CKLM
	Winkler	MB	10	CKMW
1 580	Chicoutimi	PQ	50	CBJ
1 600	Simcoe	ON	10	CHNR

Section 10

UNITED STATES OF AMERICA MEDIUM WAVE RADIO STATIONS

Frequency [kHz]	Station Site	State	Power [kW]	Call Sign
540	Columbus	GA	5	WSTH
	Fort Dodge	IA	5	KWMT
	Monroe	LA	5	KNOE
	Las Vegas	NM	5	KNMX
	Wendell	NC	5	WETC
	Hesperia	CA	25	KKJZ
	Salinas	CA	10	KPUP
	Pine Hills	FL	50	WGTO
	Canonsberg	PA	7.5	WWCS
550	Anchorage	AK	5	KENI
	Phoenix	AZ	5	KOY
	Bakersfield	CA	5	KCWR
	Craig	CO	5	KRAI
	Gainesville	GA	5	WDUN
	Salina	KS	5	KFRM
	St Louis	MO	5	KUSA
	Butte	MT	5	KBOW
	Buffalo	NY	5	WGR
	Bismarck	ND	5	KYFR
	Cincinnati	OH	5	WKRC
	Corvallis	OR	5	KOAC
	Bloomsburg	PA	1	WJMW
	Midland	TX	5	KCRS
	San Antonia	TX	5	KTSA
	Waterbury	VT	5	WDEV
	Harrisonburg	VA	5	WSVA
	Blaine	WA	5	KARI
	Wassau	WI	5	WSAU
560	Dotham	AL	5	WOOF
	Kodiak	AK	1	KVOK
	Yuma	AZ	1	KBLU
	San Francisco	CA	5	KSFO
	Denver	CO	5	KLZ
	Miami	FL	5	WQAM
	Chicago	IL	5	WIND
	Portland	ME	5	WGAN
	Frostburg	MD	5	WFRB
	Springfield	MA	5	WHYN

Frequency [kHz]	Station Site	State	Power [kW]	Call Sign
560	Monroe	MI	5	WHND
(cont'd)	Duluth	MN	5	WEBC
	Springfield	MO	5	KWTO
	Great Falls	MT	5	KMON
	Philadelphia	PA	5	WEAZ
	Columbia	SC	5	WVOC
	Memphis	TN	5	WHBQ
	Beaumont	TX	5	KLVI
	Wenatchee	WA	5	KPQ
	Beckley	WV	5	WJLS
570	Gadsden	AL	5	WAAX
	Alturas	CA	5	KCNO
	Los Angeles	CA	5	KLAC
	Pinellas Park	FL	5	WTKN
	Waycross	GA	5	WACL
	Paducah	KY	1	WKYX
	Bethesda	MD	5	WGMS
	Biloxi	MS	5	WVMI
	Las Cruces	NM	5	KGRT
	New York	NY	5	WMCA
	Syracuse	NY	5	WSYR
	Asheville	NC	5	WWNC
	Youngstown	OH	5	WKBN
	Yankton	SD	5	WNAX
	Dallas	TX	5	KKWM
	Salt Lake City	UT	5	KISN
	Seattle	WA	5	KVI
580	Petersburg	AK	5	KRSA
	Tucson	AZ	5	KSAZ
	Fresno	CA	5	KMJ
	Montrose	CO	5	KUBC
	Orlando	FL	5	WDBO
	Augusta	GA	5	WGAC
	Nampa	ID	5	KFXD
	Urbana	IL	5	WILL
	Manhattan	KS	5	KKSU
	Topeka	KS	5	WIBW
	Alexandria	LA	5	KALB
	Worcester	MA	5	WTAG
	Traverse City	MI	5	WTCM
	Ashland	OR	1	KCMX
	Harrisburg	PA	5	WHP
	Charleston	WV	5	WCHS
	LaCrosse	WI	5	WKTY
	Lubbock	TX	5	KRLB

Frequency [kHz]	Station Site	State	Power [kW]	Call Sign
590	Anchorage	AK	5	KHAR
	Hot Springs	AR	5	KBHS
	San Bernardino	CA	1	KRSO
	South Lake Tahoe	CA	2.5	KTHO
	Pueblo	CO	1	KCSJ
	Panama City	FL	2.5	WGNE
	Atlanta	GA	5	WKHX
	Idaho Falls	ID	5	KID
	Wood River	IL	1	WCEO
	Lexington	KY	5	WVLK
	Boston	MA	5	WEEI
	Ironwood	MI	5	WJMS
	Kalamazoo	MI	5	WKZO
	Omaha	NE	5	WOW
	Albany	NY	5	WROW
	Wilson	NC	5	WGTM
	Eugene	OR	5	KUGN
	Scranton	PA	5	WARM
	Uniontown	PA	1	WMBS
	Austin	TX	5	KLBJ
	Cedar City	UT	5	KSUB
	Lynchburg	VA	5	WLVA
	Spokane	WA	5	KAQQ
600	Flagstaff	AZ	5	KCLS
	Redding	CA	5	KHTE
	San Diego	CA	5	KKLQ
	Fort Collins	CO	5	KIIX
	Jacksonville	FL	5	WOKV
	Cedar Rapids	IA	5	WMT
	Paintsville	KY	5	WKLW
	Caribou	ME	5	WFST
	Baltimore	MD	5	WCAO
	Kalispell	MT	5	KGEZ
	Winston-Salem	NC	5	WSJS
	Jameston	ND	5	KSJB
	Memphis	TN	5	WREC
	El Paso	TX	5	KROD
	Tyler	TX	5	KTBB
610	Birmingham	AL	5	WZZK
	San Francisco	CA	5	KFRC
	Vail	CO	5	KSKE
	Miami	FL	10	WIOD
	Russellville	KY	2.5	WRUS
	Duluth	MN	5	KDAL
	Kansas City	MO	5	WDAF

Frequency [kHz]	Station Site	State	Power [kW]	Call Sign
610	Havre	MT	1	KOJM
(cont'd)	Manchester	NH	5	WGIR
	Albuquerque	NM	5	KZSS
	Charlotte	NC	5	WROQ
	Columbus	OH	5	WTVN
	Medford	OR	5	KYJC
	Philadelphia	PA	5	WIP
	Houston	TX	5	KILT
	Logan	UT	5	KVNU
	Roanoke	VA	5	WSLC
	Tri-Cities	WA	5	KONA
620	Homer	AK	5	KGTL
	Lexington	AL	5	WKNI
	Phoenix	AZ	5	KTAR
	Hanford	CA	1	KIGS
	Grand Junction	CO	5	KSTR
	St Petersburg	FL	10	WSUN
	Wallace	ID	1	KWAL
	Sioux City	IA	1	KMNS
	Bangor	ME	5	WZON
	Jackson	MS	5	WJDS
	Newark	NJ	5	WSKQ
	Syracuse	NY	5	WHEN
	Durham	NC	5	WDNC
	Portland	OR	5	KGW
	Knoxville	TN	5	WRJZ
	Wichita Falls	TX	5	KWFT
	Burlington	VT	5	WVMT
	Milwaukee	WI	5	WTMJ
630	Juneau	AK	5	KJNO
	Nenana	AK	5	KIAM
	Monterey	CA	1	KXDC
	Denver	CO	5	KHOW
	Washington	DC	5	WMAL
	Savannah	GA	5	WBMQ
	Boise	ID	5	KIDO
	Lexington	KY	5	WLAP
	St Paul	MN	5	KDWB
	St Louis	MO	5	KXOK
	Reno	NV	5	KOH
	Wilmington	NC	1	WMFD
	Coquille	OR	5	KWRO
	East Providence	RI	5	WPRO
	San Antonio	TX	5	KSLR
	Seattle	WA	39	KCIS

Frequency [kHz]	Station Site	State	Power [kW]	Call Sign
640	Bethel	AK	10	KYUK
	Los Angeles	CA	50	KFI
	Royal Palm Beach	FL	10	WLVJ
	Atlanta	GA	50	WGST
	Ames	IA	5	WOI
	Thibodeaux	LA	5	KTIB
	Westfield	MA	50	WNNZ
	Belgrade	MT	10	KGVW
	Mt Holly	NJ	5	WWJZ
	Fayetteville	NC	10	WFNC
	Akron	OH	5	WHLO
	Moore	OK	1	WWLS
	Blountsville	TN	5	WJTZ
	Collierville	TN	10	WCRV
	Zeeland	MI	1	WBMX
650	Anchorage	AK	50	KYAK
	Christmas	FL	10	WORL
	Clinton	MA	10	WBSO
	Hibbing	MN	10	WKKQ
	Emporium	PA	5	WLEM
	Nashville	TN	50	WSM
	Rancho Cordova	CA	25	KMCE
	Manti	UT	10	KMTI
	Cheyenne	WY	8.6	KUUY
660	Fairhope	AL	22	WBLX
	Fairbanks	AK	10	KFAR
	Window Rock	AZ	50	KTNN
	Orcutt	CA	10	KGDP
	Saulk Rapids	MN	10	WVAL
	New York	NY	50	WFAN
	Greenville	SC	50	WESC
	Dallas	TX	10	KSKY
	Mount Vernon	WA	10	KAPS
	Willston	ND	5	KQSR
670	Dillingham	AK	10	KDLG
	Glenwood	AR	5	KWXI
	Simi Valley	CA	1	KWNK
	Commerce City	CO	5	KMVP
	Miami	FL	50	WWFE
	Boise	ID	50	KBOI
	Chicago	IL	50	WMAQ
	Lewiston	PA	6	WIEZ
	Claremont	VA	20	WARO
	York	AL	5	WYLS

Frequency [kHz]	Station Site	State	Power [kW]	Call Sign
680	Barrow	AK	10	KBRW
	San Francisco	CA	50	KNBR
	North Atlanta	GA	50	WCNN
	Baltimore	MD	10	WCBM
	Boston	MA	50	WRKO
	Escanaba	MI	10	WDBC
	St Joseph	MO	5	KFEQ
	Raleigh	NC	50	WPTF
	Sylva	NC	1	WRGC
	Memphis	TN	10	WODZ
	San Antonio	TX	50	KKYX
	Omak	WA	5	KOMW
	Charlestown	WV	50	WCAW
	Helena	MT	5	KHKR
690	Birmingham	AL	50	WVOK
	Jacksonville	FL	50	WPDQ
	Coffeyville	KS	10	KGGF
	New Orleans	LA	10	WTIX
	El Paso	TX	10	KHEY
	Bristol	VA	10	WZAP
700	Anchorage	AK	1	KBYR
	Silt	CO	50	KRMW
	Cincinnati	OH	50	WLW
	Winston	OR	25	KGRV
	Tomball	TX	2.5	KSEV
	Salt Lake City	UT	50	KFAM
	Newport	WA	10	KJMY
710	Mobile	AL	1	WKRG
	Black Canyon City	AZ	50	KUET
	Carmichael	CA	10	KFIA
	Los Angeles	CA	50	KMPC
	Denver	CO	5	KNUS
	Miami	FL	50	WAQI
	Shreveport	LA	50	KEEL
	Kansas City	MO	10	WHB
	Ennis	MT	10	KKMT
	New York	NY	50	WOR
	Amarillo	TX	10	KGNC
	Christianburg	VA	5	WFNR
	Seattle	WA	10	KIRO
	Superior	WI	10	WDSM
	Monticello	ME	5	WREM
	Bismarck	ND	50	KBMR

Frequency [kHz]	Station Site	State	Power [kW]	Call Sign
720	Kotzebue	AK	10	KOTZ
	Hogansville	GA	10	WMXY
	Chicago	IL	50	WGN
	Richland	MS	5	WRBR
	Las Vegas	NV	50	KDWN
	Universal City	TX	10	KSAH
	Hernando	FL	10	WRZN
	Tuckahoe	VA	10	WGNZ
730	Thomasville	GA	5	WSTT
	Vancleve	KY	5	WMTC
	Springfield	MA	5	WACE
	Billings	MT	5	KURL
	Pittsburgh	PA	5	WPIT
	Alexandria	VA	5	WCPT
740	Montgomery	AL	50	WLWI
	Avalon	CA	10	KBRT
	San Francisco	CA	50	KCBS
	Colorado Springs	CO	3.3	KSSS
	Cortez	CO	1	KISZ
	Orlando	FL	5	WWNZ
	Carlsbad	NM	1	KATK
	Long Island	NY	25	WGSM
	Mount Airey	NC	10	WPAQ
	Tulsa	OK	50	KRMG
	Houston	TX	50	KTRH
	Texarkana	TX	1	KCMC
	Buckley	WA	5	KWNT
750	Anchorage	AK	50	KFQD
	Atlanta	GA	50	WSB
	Polson	MT	50	KERR
	Grand Island	NE	10	KMMJ
	Portsmouth	NH	1	WHEB
	Canton	NY	5	WYHV
	Portland	OR	50	KXL
	El Paso	TX	10	KAMA
	Price	UT	10	KOAL
	Carson City	NV	10	KKNK
	Lebanon	MO	5	KJEL
760	Sherwood	AR	10	KMTL
	San Diego	CA	50	KFMB
	Thornton	CO	5	KRZN
	Brandon	FL	5	WEND
	Leicester	MA	5	WVNE
	Detroit	MI	50	WJR

Frequency [kHz]	Station Site	State	Power [kW]	Call Sign
760 *(cont'd)*	Champlain	NY	25	WCHP
	San Antonio	TX	50	KSJL
	Saraland	AL	5	WAFK
	Overland Park	KS	6	KBCB
770	Athens	AL	10	WVNN
	Riverbank	CA	50	KPLA
	North Fort Myers	FL	10	WZRZ
	Lynn Haven	FL	5	WFBN
	Lafayette	LA	5	KJCB
	Minneapolis	MN	5	KUOM
	Northfield	MN	5	WCAL
	Miles City	MT	10	KATL
	Albuquerque	NM	50	KKOB
	New York	NY	50	WABC
	Rockingham	NC	5	WLWL
	Cedar Bluff	VA	5	WYRV
	Seattle	WA	50	KRPM
780	Lineville	AL	5	WZZX
	Nome	AK	10	KNOM
	Sedona	AZ	5	KAZM
	Siesta Key	FL	5	WJKB
	Chicago	IL	50	WBBM
	Ridgeland	MS	5	WLRM
	Norfolk	NE	1	WJAG
	Reno	NV	50	KROW
	Arlington	VA	5	WABS
	Baldvinsville	NY	7.5	WSEN
	Springville	UT	5	KRDA
790	Tuscaloosa	AL	5	WTSK
	Glenallen	AK	5	KCAM
	Tucson	AZ	5	KCEE
	Rogers	AR	5	KURM
	Clovis	CA	2.5	KOQO
	Eureka	CA	5	KFLI
	Los Angeles	CA	5	KABC
	Leesburg	FL	5	WLBE
	South Miami	FL	25	WNWS
	Atlanta	GA	5	WQXI
	Soda Springs	ID	5	KBRV
	Colby	KS	5	KXXX
	Louisville	KY	5	WWKY
	Saginaw	MI	5	WSGW
	Billings	MT	5	KGHL
	Watertown	NY	1	WTNY

Frequency [kHz]	Station Site	State	Power [kW]	Call Sign
790	Fargo	ND	5	KFGO
(cont'd)	Albany	OR	1	KWIL
	Allentown	PA	3.8	WAEB
	Providence	RI	5	WWAZ
	Johnson City	TN	5	WETB
	Memphis	TN	5	WMC
	Houston	TX	5	KKBQ
	Lubbock	TX	5	KFYO
	Norfolk	VA	5	WTAR
	Bellingham	WA	5	KGMI
	Spokane	WA	5	KJRB
	Eau Claire	WI	5	WEAQ
800	Juneau	AK	5	KINY
	Camden	NJ	5	WTMR
	Crewe	VA	5	WSVS
	Huntington	WV	5	WKEE
	Waupaca	WI	5	WDUX
810	Jacksonville	AL	50	WJXL
	San Francisco	CA	50	KGO
	Kansas City	MO	50	KCMO
	Magee	MS	50	WSJC
	Santa Fe	NM	5	KMIK
	Schenectady	NY	50	WGY
	St George	SC	5	WQIZ
	Sturgis	SD	5	KBHB
	Murfreesboro	TN	5	WMTS
	Ephrata	WA	41	KTBI
	Tomahawk	WI	10	WJJQ
	Jackson	KY	5	WEKG
820	Fairbanks	AK	50	KCBF
	Largo	FL	50	WRFA
	Chicago	IL	5	WXEZ
	Frederick	MD	5	WQSI
	Horseheads	NY	5	WIQT
	New York	NY	50	WNYC
	Charlotte	NC	10	WMPF
	Columbus	OH	5	WOSU
	Fort Worth	TX	50	WBAP
	Chester	VA	10	KGGM
	Seattle	WA	50	KGNW
830	Tucson	AZ	50	KFLT
	Grass Valley	CA	5	KNCO
	Orange	CA	2.5	KSRT
	Hialeah	FL	1	WRFM

Frequency [kHz]	Station Site	State	Power [kW]	Call Sign
830 *(cont'd)*	Norco	LA	5	WADU
	Minneapolis	MN	50	WCCO
	Kennett	MO	10	KBOA
	New York	NY	1	WNYC
	Eden	NC	1	WWMO
	Evansville	WY	10	KUYO
	Sand Point	AK	1	KSDP
	Lithia Springs	GA	50	WGBV
	Cherry Valley	MA	3	WCRN
840	Mobile	AL	10	WBHY
	Big Lake	AK	10	KABN
	Thomasville	GA	10	WHGH
	Louisville	KY	50	WHAS
	West Point	NE	5	KWPN
	Gardnerville	NV	10	KUIP
	North Las Vegas	NV	50	KVEG
	Columbia	SC	50	WCTG
	Pharr	TX	5	KIKN
	Earlysville	VA	8.2	WKTR
	Opportunity	WA	50	KHDL
	Plover	WI	5	WTLI
850	Birmingham	AL	50	WYDE
	Nome	AK	10	KICY
	Denver	CO	50	KOA
	Gainesville	FL	5	WRUF
	West Palm Beach	FL	5	WEAT
	Statesboro	GA	1	WPTB
	Boston	MA	50	WHDH
	Muskegon	MI	1	WKBZ
	Duluth	MN	10	WWJC
	Forest	MS	10	WQST
	Clayton	MO	5	KFUO
	Raleigh	NC	50	WKIX
	Cleveland	OH	10	WRMR
	Johnston	PA	10	WJAC
	Reading	PA	1	WEEU
	Knoxville	TN	50	WUTK
	Houston	TN	10	KEYH
	Norfolk	VA	5	WNIS
	Tacoma	WA	10	KTAC
860	Phoenix	AR	1	KVVA
	Modesto	CA	50	KTRB
	Atlanta	GA	5	WAEC
	Douglas	GA	5	WDMG

Frequency [kHz]	Station Site	State	Power [kW]	Call Sign
860 *(cont'd)*	Pittsburg	KS	10	KKOW
	Philadelphia	PA	10	WTEL
	San Antonio	TX	5	KONO
	Salt Lake City	UT	10	KLZX
	Oak Hill	WV	10	WOAY
870	McGrath	AK	10	KSKO
	Glendale	CA	10	KIEV
	New Orleans	LA	50	WWL
	East Lansing	MI	10	WKAR
	Park Rapids	MN	25	KPRM
	Laughlin	NV	10	KROL
	Ithaca	NY	5	WHCU
	Colonial Heights	TN	10	WPRQ
	Tri-Cities	WA	10	KORD
	Valley Head	AL	10	WQRX
	Gorham	ME	5	WKZN
	Baraboo	WI	5	WRPQ
880	Sheridan	AR	50	KGHT
	Gonzales	CA	5	KKMC
	Jefferson	GA	5	WBKZ
	Highland	IL	2.5	WINV
	Whitefish	MT	10	KJJR
	Lexington	NE	50	KRVN
	Tse Bonito	NM	10	KHAC
	Lovelock	NV	1	KLVK
	New York	NY	50	WCBS
	Columbus	OH	9	WRFD
	Dallas	OR	5	KWIP
	Phoenix	OR	1	KFMR
	Conroe	TX	10	KIKR
	Seattle	WA	50	KIXI
890	Homer	AK	10	KBBI
	Citrus Heights	CA	50	KPTO
	Stratmoor	CO	10	KCBB
	Chicago	IL	50	WLS
	Dedham	MA	10	WBMA
	Laurel	MS	10	WQIS
	Granite Falls	NC	25	WYCV
	Nicholson	PA	10	WFQA
	Pendleton	SC	25	WPGP
	Laredo	TX	10	KVOZ
	St George	UT	10	KDXU
900	Georgetown	DE	10	WJWL
	Savannah	GA	5	WEAS

Frequency [kHz]	Station Site	State	Power [kW]	Call Sign
900	Pikeville	KY	5	WLSI
(cont'd)	Minneapolis	MN	25	KTIS
910	Galena	AK	5	KIYU
	Phoenix	AZ	5	KFYI
	Blytheville	AR	5	KLCN
	Camden	AR	5	KAMD
	El Cajon	CA	5	KECR
	Oakland	CA	5	KNEW
	Oxnard	CA	5	KOXR
	Denver	CO	5	KPOF
	New Britain	CT	5	WNEZ
	Plant City	FL	1	WPLA
	Valdosta	GA	5	WFVR
	Mishawka	IN	1	WMSH
	Iowa City	IA	5	WSUI
	Baton Rouge	LA	1	WNDC
	Bangor	ME	5	WABI
	Flint	MI	5	WFDF
	Meridian	MS	5	WALT
	Roswell	NM	5	KBIM
	New City	NY	1	WRKL
	Jacksonville	NC	5	WLAS
	Minot	ND	5	KCJB
	Marietta	OH	5	WBRJ
	Miami	OK	1	KGLC
	Apollo	PA	5	WAVL
	York	PA	5	WSBA
	Spartanburg	SC	5	WORD
	Volga	SD	1	KJJQ
	Johnson City	TN	5	WJCW
	South Pittsburg	TN	5	WEPG
	McAllen	TX	5	KRIO
	Sherman	TX	1	KBLN
	Salt Lake City	UT	5	KALL
	Richmond	VA	5	WRNL
	Vancouver	WA	5	KKSN
	Hayward	WI	5	WHSM
920	Andalusia	AL	5	WWSF
	Soldotna	AK	5	KRSM
	Little Rock	AR	5	KARN
	Modesto	CA	2.5	KLOC
	Palm Springs	CA	5	KDES
	Lamar	CO	5	KLMR
	Melbourne	FL	1	WMEL
	Atlanta	GA	5	WAFS

Frequency [kHz]	Station Site	State	Power [kW]	Call Sign
920 *(cont'd)*	Shenandoah	IA	5	KYFR
	Whitesburg	KY	5	WTCW
	Bogalusa	LA	1	WBOX
	West Lafayette	IN	5	WBAA
	Lexington Park	MD	5	WPTX
	Faribault	MN	5	KDHL
	Wadena	MN	1	KWAD
	Las Vegas	NV	5	KORK
	Reno	NV	5	KQLO
	Trenton	NJ	1	WTTM
	Kingston	NY	5	WGHQ
	Lake Placid	NY	5	WIRD
	Burlington	NC	5	WBBB
	Lebanon	OR	1	KGAL
	Providence	RI	5	WHJJ
	Orangeburg	SC	5	WAZQ
	Rapid City	SD	5	KKLS
	Texas City	TX	5	KYST
	Vernal	UT	5	KVEL
	Olympia	WA	5	KQEU
	Spokane	WA	5	KXLY
	Fairmont	WV	5	WMMN
	Milwaukee	WI	5	WOKY
930	Rainbow City	AL	5	WJBY
	Monroeville	AL	5	WYNI
	Ketchikan	AK	5	KTKN
	Unalakleet	AK	2.5	KNSA
	Flagstaff	AZ	5	KAFF
	Los Angeles	CA	5	KKHJ
	Durango	CO	5	KIUP
	Jacksonville	FL	5	WRXJ
	Sarasota	FL	5	WKXY
	Bainbridge	GA	5	WMGR
	Pocatello	ID	5	KSEI
	Quincy	IL	5	WTAD
	Sandwich	IL	2.2	WAUR
	Bowling Green	KY	5	WKCT
	Frederick	MD	5	WFMD
	Battle Creek	MI	5	WBCK
	Jackson	MS	5	WSLI
	Poplar Bluff	MO	5	KWOC
	East Missoula	MT	5	KLCY
	Ogallala	NE	2.5	KOGA
	Rochester	NH	5	WZNN
	Paterson	NJ	5	WPAT
	Buffalo	NY	5	WBEN

Frequency [kHz]	Station Site	State	Power [kW]	Call Sign
930 *(cont'd)*	Charlotte	NC	5	WSOC
	Washington	NC	5	WRRF
	Elryia	OH	1	WEOL
	Oklahoma City	OK	5	WKY
	Grants Pass	OR	5	KAGI
	Bloomsburg	PA	1	WCNR
	Aberdeen	SD	5	KSDN
	Sevierville	TN	5	WSEV
	San Antonio	TX	5	KISS
	Lynchburg	VA	5	WLLL
	Yakima	WA	5	KZTA
	Huntington	WV	5	WRVC
	Auburndale	WI	5	WLBL
	Sheridan	WY	5	KROE
940	Tucson	AZ	5	KNST
	Fresno	CA	50	KFRE
	Miami	FL	50	WINZ
	Macon	GA	50	WMAZ
	Mount Vernon	IL	5	WMIX
	Des Moines	IA	10	KIOA
	New Orleans	LA	10	WYLD
	St Ignace	MI	5	WIDG
	Houston	MS	50	WCPC
	Valentine	NE	5	KVSH
	Burnsville	NC	5	WKYK
	Wartburg	TN	5	WECO
	Amarillo	TX	5	KIXZ
	Cedar City	UT	10	KBRE
	Grundy	VA	5	WNRG
	Smithfield	VA	10	WKGM
	Laurinburg	NC	5	WLNC
	Bend	OR	10	KGRL
950	Montgomery	AL	1	WSYA
	Juneau	AK	5	KAJD
	Seward	AK	1	KRXA
	Forrest City	AR	5	KXJK
	Fort Smith	AR	1	KFSA
	Auburn	CA	5	KAHI
	Denver	CO	5	KYGO
	Orlando	FL	5	WOMX
	Summerville	GA	5	WGTA
	Valdosta	GA	5	WGOV
	Lewiston	ID	5	KOZE
	Chicago	IL	1	WJPC
	Indianapolis	IN	5	WXLW

Frequency [kHz]	Station Site	State	Power [kW]	Call Sign
950	Oelwein	IA	5	KOEL
(cont'd)	Presque Isle	ME	5	WKZX
	Boston	MA	5	WROL
	Detroit	MI	5	WWJ
	St Louis Park	MN	1	KJJO
	Hattiesburg	MS	5	WBKH
	Jefferson City	MO	5	KLIK
	Helena	MT	5	KMTX
	Bayard	NM	5	KNFT
	Rochester	NY	1	WBBF
	Utica	NY	5	WIBX
	Philadelphia	PA	5	WPEN
	Spartanburg	SC	5	WSPA
	Watertown	SD	1	KWAT
	Houston	TX	5	KPRC
	Lubbock	TX	5	KSTQ
	Richmond	VA	5	WJDK
	Seattle	WA	5	KJR
	Charleston	WV	5	WQBE
	Kemmere	WY	5	KMER
960	Birmingham	AL	5	WERC
	Pritchard	AL	2.5	WLPR
	Phoenix	AZ	5	KOOL
	Apple Valley	CA	5	KQKL
	San Francisco	CA	5	KABL
	Marshall	AR	5	KCGS
	New Haven	CT	5	WELI
	Lake City	FL	1	WGRO
	Sebring	FL	5	WJCM
	Albany	GA	5	WJYZ
	Athens	GA	5	WRFC
	South Bend	IN	5	WSBT
	Shenandoah	IA	5	KMA
	Prestonburg	KY	5	WPRT
	Salisbury	MD	5	WLVW
	Fitchburg	MA	1	WFGL
	Rogers City	MI	5	WHAK
	Little Falls	MN	5	KLTF
	Cape Girardeau	MO	5	KZIM
	Baker	MT	5	KFLN
	Farmington	NM	5	KNDN
	Plattsburgh	NY	5	WEAV
	Kinston	NC	5	WRNS
	Enid	OK	1	KGWA
	Klamath Falls	OR	5	KLAD
	Carlisle	PA	5	WHYL

Frequency [kHz]	Station Site	State	Power [kW]	Call Sign
960	Sayre	PA	5	WATS
(cont'd)	San Angelo	TX	5	KGKL
	Provo	UT	5	KFMY
	Richland	WA	5	KALE
	Shawano	WI	5	WTCH
	Roanoke	VA	5	WFIR
970	Hamilton	AL	5	WERH
	Troy	AL	5	WTBF
	Fairbanks	AK	5	KIAK
	Show Low	AZ	5	KVWM
	Bakersfield	CA	1	KAFY
	Coachella	CA	5	KVIM
	Modesto	CA	1	KOOK
	Tampa	FL	5	WFLA
	Atlanta	GA	5	WNIV
	Harlan	KY	5	WFSR
	Vidalia	GA	5	WVOP
	Louisville	KY	5	WAVG
	Alexandria	LA	1	KSYL
	Portland	ME	5	WYNZ
	Ispheming	MI	5	WMVN
	Jackson	MI	1	WKHM
	Austin	MN	5	KQAQ
	Billings	MT	5	KCTR
	North Platte	NE	5	KJLT
	Paradise	NV	5	KNUU
	Hackensack	NJ	5	WWDJ
	Buffalo	NY	5	WEBR
	Canton	NC	5	WWIT
	Fargo	ND	5	WDAY
	Ashtabula	OH	5	WFUN
	Tulsa	OK	2.5	KCFO
	Portland	OR	5	KESI
	Pittsburgh	PA	5	WWSW
	Florence	SC	5	WJMX
	Del Valle	TX	1	KIXL
	Waynesboro	VA	5	WANV
	Spokane	WA	5	KTRW
	Madison	WI	5	WHA
980	Kenai	AK	1	KKEN
	Dardanelle	AR	5	KCAB
	Eureka	CA	5	KINS
	Los Angeles	CA	5	KFWB
	Washington	DC	5	WWRC
	Gainesville	FL	5	WLUS

Frequency [kHz]	Station Site	State	Power [kW]	Call Sign
980	Pensacola	FL	2.5	WFXP
(cont'd)	Pompano Beach	FL	5	WWNN
	Ammon	ID	5	KUPI
	Danville	IL	1	WITY
	Shreveport	LA	5	KOKA
	Lowell	MA	5	WCAP
	Richfield	MN	5	WAYL
	Perry	GA	5	WPGA
	McComb	MS	5	WAPF
	Kansas City	MO	5	KMBZ
	Fallon	NV	5	KVLV
	Clovis	NM	1	KICA
	Grants	NM	1	KMIN
	Troy	NY	5	WTRY
	Wilmington	NC	5	WAAV
	Dayton	OH	5	WONE
	Wilkes-Barre	PA	5	WILK
	Deadwood	SD	5	KDSJ
	Nashville	TN	5	WSIX
	Richfield	UT	5	KSVC
	Bristol	VA	5	WFHG
	Selah	WA	5	KUTI
	Manitovoc	WI	5	WCUB
990	Tucson	AZ	10	KTKT
	Pittsburg	CA	5	KKIS
	Santa Barbara	CA	5	KTUN
	Denver	CO	5	KRKS
	Miami	FL	5	WFBA
	Orlando	FL	50	WHOO
	Artesia	NM	1	KSVP
	Rochester	NY	5	WRMM
	Southern Pines	NC	10	WEEB
	Philadelphia	PA	50	WZZD
	Somerset	PA	10	WVSC
	Providence	RI	50	WALE
	Knoxville	TN	10	WIVK
	Memphis	TN	10	KWAM
	Beaumont	TX	1	KZZB
	Wichita Falls	TX	10	KGTM
	Narrows	VA	5	WNRV
1 000	Huntsville	AL	5	WTAK
	Montgomery	AL	5	WZTN
	Bullhead City	AZ	5	KRHS
	Hayden	CO	10	KKMX
	Remerton	GA	10	WMDE

Frequency [kHz]	Station Site	State	Power [kW]	Call Sign
1 000	Eagle	ID	10	KIDH
(cont'd)	Chicago	IL	50	WLUP
	Lexington	MS	5	WLTD
	Albuquerque	NM	10	KKIM
	Horseheads	NY	5	WLNL
	Oklahoma City	OK	5	KTOK
	Hemingway	SC	10	WKYB
	Sioux Falls	SD	10	KXRB
	Paris	TN	5	WMUF
	Seattle	WA	50	KOMO
1 010	Dora	AL	5	WPYK
	Phoenix	AR	7.5	KXEG
	Little Rock	AR	10	KBIS
	Delano	CA	5	KCHJ
	Thousand Palms	CA	5	KPSL
	San Francisco	CA	10	KIQI
	Brush	CO	5	KKGZ
	Crestview	FL	10	WCNU
	Jacksonville	FL	70	WXTL
	Seffner	FL	50	WQYK
	Decatur	GA	50	WGUN
	Meridian	MS	10	WMOX
	St Louis	MO	50	KXEN
	New York	NY	50	WINS
	Black Mountain	NC	50	WFGW
	Gallatin	TN	5	WHIN
	Amarillo	TX	5	KDJW
	Houston	TX	5	KLAT
	Waco	TX	10	KBBW
	Tooele	UT	50	KTLE
	Portsmouth	VA	5	WPMH
	Milwaukie	OR	8	KZRC
1 020	Eagle River	AK	10	KCFA
	Hollywood	CA	50	KTNQ
	Port Orange	FL	10	WART
	Ochlocknee	GA	10	WJEP
	Garyville	LA	50	WCKW
	Newport	NH	6.5	WNTK
	Roswell	NM	50	KCKN
	Watford City	ND	5	KKWC
	Pittsburgh	PA	50	KDKA
	Selah	WA	5	KYXE
	Moses Lake	WA	5	KWIQ
	Anderson	SC	10	WRIX

Frequency [kHz]	Station Site	State	Power [kW]	Call Sign
1 030	Fayetteville	AR	10	KFAY
	Cortaro	AZ	10	KEVT
	Folsom	CA	50	KKSA
	San Luis Obispo	CA	2.5	KJDJ
	Holcomb	KS	25	KBUF
	Boston	MA	50	WBZ
	Indian Head	MD	50	WNTL
	Sterling Heights	MI	5	WUFL
	Maplewood	MN	50	WMIN
	Mint Hill	NC	10	WNOW
	Wake Forest	NC	35	WFTK
	Memphis	TN	50	WXSS
	White Bluff	TN	10	WJKZ
	Corpus Christi	TX	50	KCTA
	Shelton	WA	10	KMAS
	Casper	WY	50	KTWO
	Point Pleasant	WV	10	WTGR
	Oveido	FL	25	WCAG
	Boulder City	NV	50	KGZA
	Reedsport	OR	10	KDUN
1 040	San Diego	CA	9.5	KIRS
	Monument	CO	5	KCBR
	Boynton Beach	FL	10	WYFX
	Des Moines	IA	50	WHO
	Lewisville	NC	9.1	WSGH
	North Ridgeville	OH	5	WJTB
	Everett	PA	10	WSKE
	Powell	TN	10	WQBB
	Flemington	NJ	4.7	WJHR
	Delmar	NY	5	WANQ
1 050	Tuba City	AZ	5	KTBA
	Jacksonville	FL	5	WROS
	Frazier Park	CA	10	KNOB
	San Mateo	CA	50	KOFY
	Augusta	GA	5	WFAM
	Ann Arbor	MI	5	WPZA
	Kinsey	MT	10	KMTA
	New York	NY	50	WEVD
	Conway	SC	5	WJXY
	Norfolk	VA	5	WCMS
	Dishman	WA	5	KFVR
	Seattle	WA	5	KBLE
	Parkersburg	WV	5	WADC
	Springfield	OR	5	KORE
	Pipestone	MN	8	KLOH

Frequency [kHz]	Station Site	State	Power [kW]	Call Sign
1 060	Tempe	AZ	5	KUKQ
	Chico	CA	10	KPAY
	Longmont	CO	10	KLMO
	Titusville	FL	10	WAMT
	Tallapoosa	GA	5	WKNG
	Caldwell	ID	10	KBGN
	New Orleans	LA	50	WNOE
	Natick	MA	25	WBIV
	Benton Harbor	MI	5	WHFB
	Las Vegas	NV	5	KKVV
	Canton	OH	5	WRCW
	Philadelphia	PA	50	KYW
	Pierre	SD	10	KGFX
	El Paso	TX	10	KFNA
	Gilmer	TX	10	KTLG
	Salt Lake City	UT	10	KRSP
1 070	Birmingham	AL	50	WAPI
	Los Angeles	CA	50	KNX
	Tallahassee	FL	10	WANM
	Indianapolis	IN	50	WIBC
	Wichita	KS	10	KFDI
	Monticello	MN	10	KMOM
	Hannibal	MO	5	KHMO
	Plentywood	MT	5	KATQ
	Plattsburgh	NY	5	WKDR
	Greenville	NC	10	WNCT
	Klamath Falls	OR	10	KWSA
	Sunbury	PA	10	WKOK
	Greenville	SC	50	WHYZ
	Lookout Mountain	TN	50	WFLI
	Memphis	TN	50	WDIA
	Alice	TX	1	KDSI
	Houston	TX	10	KKZR
	Charlottesville	VA	5	WINA
	Beckley	WV	10	WIWS
	Madison	WI	10	WTSO
1 080	Athens	AL	5	WKAC
	Anchorage	AK	10	KKSD
	Santa Cruz	CA	10	KSCO
	Hartford	CT	50	WTIC
	Coral Gables	FL	50	WVCG
	Kissimmee	FL	10	WFIV
	Marietta	GA	10	WFTD
	Coeur d'Alene	ID	10	KVNI
	Louisville	KY	10	WDJX

Frequency [kHz]	Station Site	State	Power [kW]	Call Sign
1 080 *(cont'd)*	Carthage	MS	5	WSSI
	Lenoir	NC	5	WKGX
	St Pauls	NC	50	WNCR
	Portland	OR	50	KWJJ
	Pittsburgh	PA	50	WEEP
	Dallas	TX	50	KRLD
	Price	UT	10	KRPX
	Hurricane	WV	5	WVKV
1 090	Little Rock	AR	50	KAAY
	Flomaton	AL	5	WRBK
	Fortuna	CA	10	KNCR
	Aurora	CO	50	KYBG
	Port Charlotte	FL	5	WKII
	Lake Tahoe	CA	5	KJRC
	Gonzales	LA	10	WSLG
	Baltimore	MD	50	WBAL
	Boston	MA	5	WILD
	Bozeman	MT	5	KBOZ
	Albuquerque	NM	50	KRZY
	Kingstree	SC	5	WKSP
	Kingsport	TN	10	WGOC
	Plainview	TX	5	KKYN
	Seattle	WA	50	KING
	Rice Lake	WI	5	WMYD
1 100	San Francisco	CA	50	KFAX
	Grand Junction	CO	50	KNZZ
	Woodbine	GA	10	WCGA
	Webb City	MO	5	KKLL
	Hempstead	NY	10	WHLY
	Cleveland	OH	50	WWWE
	Alamo Heights	TX	10	KDRY
	Las Vegas	NV	50	KDHB
	Umatilla	OR	10	KLWJ
	Wells River	VT	5	WYKR
1 110	Bay Minette	AL	10	WBCA
	Clinton	AR	5	KGFL
	Dermott	AR	10	KXSA
	Pasadena	CA	50	KRLA
	Roseville	CA	5	KRCX
	Tampa	FL	10	WTIS
	Chicago	IL	5	WMBI
	Pittsfield	MA	5	WUHN
	Petoskey	MI	10	WJML
	Omaha	NE	50	KFAB

Frequency [kHz]	Station Site	State	Power [kW]	Call Sign
1 110	Salem	NH	5	WNNW
(cont'd)	Humble City	NM	5	KYKK
	Charlotte	NC	50	WBT
	Atoka	OK	5	KEOR
	Bend	OR	25	KBND
	East Providence	RI	5	WHIM
	Norfolk	VA	50	WZAM
1 120	Gordon	GA	10	WYGO
	Washington	DC	5	WUST
	Concord	MA	5	WADN
	Clinton	MS	5	WTWZ
	St Louis	MO	50	KMOX
	Eugene	OR	50	KPNW
	Roy	UT	10	KANN
1 130	Dinuba	CA	5	KRDU
	San Diego	CA	50	KSDO
	Dillon	CO	5	KHTH
	Bartow	FL	2.5	WWBF
	Gainesville	GA	10	WLBA
	Moultrie	GA	10	WMGA
	Murray	KY	2.5	WSJP
	Shreveport	LA	50	KWKH
	Detroit	MI	50	WCXI
	Minnapolis	MN	50	WDGY
	Milan	NM	5	KOFK
	New York	NY	50	WNEW
	Lincoln	ND	50	KBMR
	Brownsville	PA	5	WASP
	Edna	TX	10	KTMR
	Milwaukee	WI	50	WISN
1 140	Hazel Green	AL	15	WIXC
	Soldotna	AK	10	KCSY
	Palm Springs	CA	10	KCMJ
	Sacramento	CA	50	KRAK
	Miami	FL	50	WQBA
	Boise	ID	10	KGEM
	Pekin	IL	5	WVEL
	Kentwood	MI	5	WKWM
	Senatobia	MS	5	WSAO
	Las Vegas	NV	10	KLUC
	Sioux Falls	SD	10	KSOO
	Concord	NH	10	WNHA
	Conroe	TX	5	KSSQ
	Richmond	VA	50	WRVA
	Greybull	WY	10	KZMQ

Frequency [kHz]	Station Site	State	Power [kW]	Call Sign
1 150	Tuscaloosa	AL	5	WZBQ
	Coolidge	AZ	5	KCKY
	Little Rock	AR	5	KLRG
	Los Angeles	CA	5	KIIS
	Morro Bay	CA	5	KBAI
	Santa Rosa	CA	5	KVRE
	Englewood	CO	5	KFRR
	Wilmington	DE	5	WDEL
	Daytona Beach	FL	1	WNDB
	Tampa	FL	5	WTMP
	Valdosta	GA	5	WJEM
	Marion	IL	5	WGGH
	Des Moines	IA	1	KWKY
	Salina	KS	5	KSAL
	Baton Rouge	LA	5	WJBO
	Boston	MA	5	WMEX
	Shelby	MT	5	KSEN
	Albuquerque	NM	5	KDEF
	Utica	NY	5	WRUN
	Goldsboro	NC	5	WGBR
	Lima	OH	1	WIMA
	McAlester	OK	1	KNED
	Klamath Falls	OR	5	KAGO
	Portland	OR	5	KKEY
	Huntingdon	PA	5	WHUN
	Orangeburg	SC	5	WORG
	Rapid City	SD	5	KIMM
	Chattanooga	TN	5	WGOW
	Morristown	TN	5	WCRK
	Seattle	WA	5	KEZX
	Welch	WV	5	WELC
	Kimberley	WI	5	WYNE
	Chippewa Falls	WI	5	WAYY
1 160	Mobile	AL	10	WKWA
	Chicago	IL	50	WJJD
	Callaghan	FL	50	WELX
	Woodville	FL	5	WTWF
	Hawesville	KY	2.5	WKCM
	Skowhegan	ME	10	WSKW
	Funkstown	MD	1	WPVG
	Fenton	MI	1	WACY
	Virginia City	NV	5	KDXA
	Lakewood	NJ	5	WOBM
	Mechanicville	NY	5	WMVI
	Trumansburg	NY	1	WPIE
	Red Springs	NC	5	WYRU

Frequency [kHz]	Station Site	State	Power [kW]	Call Sign
1 160	Tryon	NC	10	WTYN
(cont'd)	Homer City	PA	10	WCCS
	Lehighton	PA	4.4	WYNS
	Donelson	TN	50	WAMB
	San Antonio	TX	10	KFHM
	Salt Lake City	UT	50	KSL
	Oakland	NJ	10	WVNJ
	Fieldale	VA	5	WCBX
1 170	Montgomery	AL	10	WACV
	North Pole	AK	50	KJNP
	San Diego	CA	50	KCBQ
	San Jose	CA	50	KLOK
	Davie	FL	5	WAVS
	Laurel	DE	5	WMPP
	Cumming	GA	5	WHNE
	Mattoon	IL	5	WLBH
	Davenport	IA	1	KSTT
	Lakewood	NJ	5	WOBM
	Claremont	NC	7.7	WCXN
	Clinton	NC	5	WCLN
	Tulsa	OK	5	KVOO
	Lexington	SC	10	WLGO
	Bellingham	WA	10	KPUG
	Wheeling	WV	50	WWVA
1 180	Williams	AZ	10	KTRN
	Placerville	CA	25	KTLL
	Wasco	CA	50	KERI
	Trion	GA	5	WSAF
	Pearl	MS	10	WJNT
	Kalispell	MT	50	KOFI
	Bellevue	NE	5	KKAR
	Rochester	NY	50	WHAM
	Humble	TX	10	KGOL
	Lakewood	WA	2.4	KLAY
	Carolina Beach	NC	10	WMYT
	Timmonsville	SC	10	WLRG
	Knoxville	TN	10	WHJM
	Marathon Key	FL	50	VoA/R Marti
1 190	Tolleson	AZ	5	KRDS
	Anaheim	CA	10	KORG
	Kensett	AR	10	KMOA
	Boulder	CO	5	KBCO
	Pine Castle	FL	5	WAJL
	Royal Palm Beach	FL	1	WOOO

Frequency [kHz]	Station Site	State	Power [kW]	Call Sign
1 190	Atlanta	GA	10	WGKA
(cont'd)	Fort Wayne	IN	50	WOWO
	Annapolis	MD	10	WANN
	Jackson	MN	5	KKOJ
	Bay St Louis	MS	5	WBSL
	De Soto	MO	5	KHAD
	Kansas City	MO	5	KJLA
	New York	NY	10	WLIB
	Portland	OR	50	KEX
	Albuquerque	NM	10	KXKS
	Dunlap	TN	5	WSDQ
	Dallas	TX	50	KLIF
	Bluefield	VA	10	WBDY
1 200	Ozard	AL	10	WFSF
	Cathedral City	CA	5	KCPC
	Eureka	CA	10	KTCD
	Pismo Beach	CA	5	KRDE
	Soquel	CA	25	KOQI
	Pine Island Center	FL	10	WDCQ
	Thonotosassa	FL	10	WFLZ
	Chicago	IL	10	WOPA
	Radcliff	KY	5	WANG
	Brewer	ME	10	WKIT
	Framingham	MA	10	WKOX
	Taylor	MI	50	WCHB
	Virginia City	NV	10	KDXA
	Newburgh	NY	10	WGNY
	Atlantic Beach	NC	5	WBYY
	Graham	NC	10	WSML
	West Fargo	ND	10	KFNW
	New Castle	PA	5	WBZY
	James Island	SC	10	WWRJ
	Lebanon	TN	10	WQDQ
	Mt Carmel	TN	10	WRVX
	San Antonio	TX	50	WOAI
	Leesburg	VA	5	WAGE
1 210	Sahuarita	AZ	10	KQTL
	Fowler	CA	10	KRGO
	Rocklin	CA	5	KEBR
	San Marcos	CA	20	KPRZ
	Miami Springs	FL	25	WCMQ
	Dahlonega	GA	10	WDGR
	Denham Springs	LA	10	WBIU
	Saginaw	MI	10	WKNX
	Guymon	OK	10	KGYN

Frequency [kHz]	Station Site	State	Power [kW]	Call Sign
1 210	Philadelphia	PA	50	WOGL
(cont'd)	Arlington	TN	10	WGSF
	San Juan	TX	50	KUBR
	Washington	UT	10	KONY
	Auburn	WA	10	KBSG
	Sunnyside	WA	10	KREW
	Afton	WY	5	KRSV
	Laramie	WY	10	KLDI
	Huron	SD	10	KOKK
1 220	Palo Alto	CA	5	KDFC
	Jacksonville	FL	5	WJAX
	Salem	IN	5	WSLM
	Stillwater	MN	5	WTCN
	Newburgh	NY	5	WGNY
	Whiteville	NC	5	WENC
	Cleveland	OH	50	WKNR
	Falls Church	VA	5	WFAX
1 250	Fort Payne	AL	5	WZOB
	Wetumpka	AL	5	WAPZ
	Willcox	AZ	5	KHIL
	Little Rock	AZ	2	KZOU
	Santa Barbara	CA	2.5	KTMS
	Willits	CA	5	KLLK
	Fraser	CO	5	KGRJ
	Tampa	FL	5	WDAE
	Fort Wayne	IN	1	WGL
	Lawrence	KS	5	KFKU
	Topeka	KS	5	WREN
	Ware	MA	5	WARE
	Fergus Falls	MN	5	KBRF
	McComb	MS	5	WHNY
	Forsyth	MT	5	KIKC
	Manchester	NH	5	WKBR
	Morristown	NJ	5	WMTR
	Farmville	NC	5	WGHB
	Pittsburgh	PA	5	WTAE
	Charleston	SC	5	WTMA
	Port Arthur	TX	5	KALO
	San Antonio	TX	1	KXEP
	Roosevelt	UT	5	KNEU
	Danville	VA	5	WDVA
	Pullman	WA	5	KWSU
	Warrenton	VA	5	WPRZ
	Seattle	WA	5	KKFX
	Rupert	WV	5	WYKM

Frequency [kHz]	Station Site	State	Power [kW]	Call Sign
1 250	Milwaukee	WI	5	WEMP
(cont'd)	Bangor	ME	5	WARP
	Marion	NC	5	WBRM
1 260	Birmingham	AL	5	WCRT
	San Fernando	CA	5	KGIL
	San Francisco	CA	5	KOIT
	Aspen	CO	5	KSNO
	Washington	DC	5	WWDC
	Miami	FL	5	WSUA
	Baxley	GA	5	WUFE
	East Point	GA	5	WTJH
	Idaho Falls	ID	5	KTEE
	Belleville	IL	5	WIBV
	Indianapolis	IN	5	WNDE
	Boone	IA	5	KFGQ
	Boston	MA	5	WEZE
	Zeeland	MI	5	WWJQ
	Springfield	MO	5	KTTS
	Trenton	NJ	5	WBUD
	Santa Fe	NM	5	KVSF
	Syracuse	NY	5	WNDR
	Asheboro	NC	5	WKXR
	Cleveland	OH	5	WRDZ
	Portsmouth	OH	5	WNXT
	Wewoka	OK	1	KWSH
	McMinnville	OR	1	KLCY
	Erie	PA	5	WRIE
	Philipsburg	PA	5	WPHB
	Greenville	SC	5	WMUU
	Winner	SD	5	KWYR
	Chattanooga	TN	5	WNOO
	Dickson	TN	5	WQZQ
	Charlottesville	VA	5	WCHV
	Amery	WI	5	WXCE
	Powell	WY	5	KPOW
1 270	Prichard	AL	5	WKSJ
	Holbrook	AZ	5	KDJI
	Pine Bluff	AR	5	KPBA
	Tulare	CA	5	KJUG
	Naples	FL	5	WNOG
	Eatonville	FL	5	WBZS
	Tallahassee	FL	5	WYYN
	Columbus	GA	5	WHYD
	Commerce	GA	5	WJJC
	Twin Falls	ID	5	KTFI

Frequency [kHz]	Station Site	State	Power [kW]	Call Sign
1 270	Thousand Palms	CA	5	KNWZ
(cont'd)	Rock Island	IL	5	WKBF
	Elkhart	IN	5	WCMR
	Gary	IN	2.5	WWCA
	Cumberland	MD	5	WCBC
	Springfield	MA	5	WSPR
	Charlevoix	MI	5	WMKT
	Detroit	MI	5	WXYT
	Baxter	MN	5	WJJY
	Rochester	MN	5	KWEB
	Louisville	MS	5	WLSM
	Sparks	NV	5	KPLY
	Dover	NH	5	WTSN
	Niagara Falls	NY	5	WHLD
	Walton	NY	5	WDLA
	Belmont	NC	5	WCGC
	Smithfield	NC	5	WMPM
	Grants Pass	OR	5	KAJO
	Lebanon	PA	5	WLBR
	Surfside Beach	SC	5	WYAK
	Sioux Falls	SD	2.5	KNWC
	Newport	TN	5	WLIK
	Bay City	TX	1	KIOX
	Fort Worth	TX	5	KESS
	Newport News	VA	1	WTJZ
	Stuart	VA	5	WHEO
	Longview	WA	5	KBAM
	Gillette	WY	5	KIML
1 280	Tuscaloosa	AL	5	WNPT
	Arroyo Grande	CA	5	KKAL
	Long Beach	CA	1	KFRN
	Stockton	CA	1	KJAX
	Denver	CO	5	KXKL
	DeFuniak Springs	FL	5	WGTX
	Jacksonville	FL	5	WSVE
	Macon	GA	5	WIBB
	Aurora	IL	1	WYSY
	Evansville	IN	5	WWOK
	New Orleans	LA	5	WQUE
	Gardiner	ME	5	WABK
	Fitchburg	MA	5	WEIM
	Minneapolis	MN	5	WWTC
	Moorehead	MN	5	KVOX
	Henderson	NV	5	KREL
	Farmington	NM	5	KRZE

Frequency [kHz]	Station Site	State	Power [kW]	Call Sign
1 280	New York	NY	5	WADO
(cont'd)	Rochester	NY	5	WPXY
	Salisbury	NC	1	WSAT
	Scotland Neck	NC	5	WYAL
	Eugene	OR	5	KDUK
	Hanover	PA	5	WHVR
	New Castle	PA	5	WKST
	Anderson	SC	5	WANS
	Mullins	SC	5	WJAY
	Columbia	TN	5	WMCP
	Salt Lake City	UT	5	KDYL
	Spokane	WA	5	KUDY
	Yakima	WA	5	KIT
	Neenah	WI	5	WNAM
1 290	Opp	AL	2.5	WOPP
	Tucson	AZ	5	KCUB
	El Dorado	AR	5	KDMS
	Siloam Springs	AR	5	KUOA
	Chico	CA	5	KHSL
	San Jose	CA	5	KAZA
	San Bernadino	CA	5	KMEN
	Ocala	FL	5	WTMC
	West Palm Beach	FL	5	WPBG
	Canton	GA	5	WCHK
	Savannah	GA	5	WCHY
	Peoria	IL	5	WIRL
	Pratt	KS	5	KWLS
	Benton	KY	5	WCBL
	Manchester	KY	5	WKLB
	Houghton Lake	MI	5	WHGR
	Missoula	MT	5	KGVO
	Omaha	NE	5	KOIL
	Keene	NH	5	WKNE
	Binghamton	NY	5	WNBF
	Hickory	NC	5	WHKY
	Dayton	OH	5	WHIO
	Pendleton	OR	5	KUMA
	Lake Oswego	OR	5	KMJK
	Altoona	PA	5	WFBG
	Providence	RI	5	WCRP
	Sumter	SC	1	WQMC
	Lynchburg	TN	5	WTNX
	Oak Ridge	TN	5	WATO
	Weslaco	TX	5	KRGE
	Wichita Falls	TX	5	KLLF
	Kanab	UT	5	KKZN

Frequency [kHz]	Station Site	State	Power [kW]	Call Sign
1 290	Petersburg	VA	5	WPVA
(cont'd)	Colonial Heights	VA	5	WSTK
	Logan	WV	5	WVOW
	Milwaukee	WI	5	WMVP
	Sparta	WI	5	WCOW
	Laramie	WY	5	KOWB
1 300	Winfield	AL	5	WKXM
	Searcy	AR	5	KWCK
	Fresno	CA	5	KYNO
	Mendocino	CA	5	KPMO
	Pasadena	CA	5	KAZM
	Colorado Springs	CO	5	KVOR
	New Haven	CT	1	WAVZ
	Cocoa	FL	5	WXXU
	Marathon	FL	2.5	WFFG
	Tampa	FL	5	WQBN
	Moultrie	GA	5	WMTM
	Orofino	ID	5	KLER
	La Grange	IL	5	WTAQ
	Mason City	IA	5	KGLO
	Lexington	KY	2.5	WLXG
	Baton Rouge	LA	5	WIBR
	Shreveport	LA	5	KFLO
	Baltimore	MD	5	WLIF
	Grand Rapids	MI	5	WOOD
	Jackson	MS	5	WKXI
	McCook	NE	5	KBRL
	Carson City	NV	5	KPTL
	Plymouth	NH	5	WPNH
	Trenton	NJ	3.2	WIMG
	Lancaster	NY	2.5	WXRL
	Rensselaer	NY	5	WQBK
	Mount Airey	NC	5	WSYD
	Cleveland	OH	5	WERE
	Tulsa	OK	5	KAKC
	Phoenix	OR	5	KDOV
	West Hazelton	PA	5	WXPX
	Mobridge	SD	5	KOLY
	Morristown	TN	5	WMTN
	Nashville	TN	5	WNQM
	Austin	TX	5	KVET
	Harrisonburg	VA	5	WKCY
	Seattle	WA	5	KMPS
1 310	Marion	AL	5	WAJO
	Mesa	AZ	5	KXAM

Frequency [kHz]	Station Site	State	Power [kW]	Call Sign
1 310	Barstow	CA	5	KIQQ
(cont'd)	Oakland	CO	5	KDIA
	Greeley	CO	5	KFKA
	Norwich	CT	5	WICH
	DeLand	FL	5	WYND
	Wauchula	FL	5	WAUC
	Twin Falls	ID	5	KLIX
	Indianapolis	IN	5	WTUX
	Madisonville	KY	2.5	WTTL
	Prestonburg	KY	5	WDOC
	West Monroe	LA	5	KMBS
	Portland	ME	5	WLOB
	Worcester	MA	5	WORC
	Dearborn	MI	5	WMTG
	Traverse City	MI	5	WCCW
	Hattiesburg	MS	5	WHLV
	Joplin	MO	5	KFSB
	Great Falls	MT	5	KEIN
	Asbury Park	NJ	2.5	WJLK
	Corrales	NM	5	KZRQ
	Mount Kisco	NY	5	WVIP
	Utica	NY	5	WTLB
	Canandaigua	NY	2.5	WCGR
	Asheville	NC	5	WISE
	Charlotte	NC	1	WGSP
	Durham	NC	5	WTIK
	Grand Forks	ND	5	KNOX
	Newport	OR	5	KNPT
	Bedford	PA	5	WBFD
	Ephrata	PA	5	WGSA
	Warren	PA	5	WNAE
	Kingstree	SC	5	WDKD
	Chattanooga	TN	5	WDOD
	Jackson	TN	5	WDXI
	Dallas	TX	5	KAAM
	San Antonio	TX	5	KXTN
	Fairfax	VA	5	WDCT
	Newport News	VA	5	WRAP
	Prosser	WA	5	KARY
	White Sulphur Springs	WV	5	WSLW
	Madison	WI	5	WIBA
1 320	Birmingham	AL	5	WAGG
	Dothan	AL	1	WAGF
	Fort Smith	AR	5	KWHN
	Sacramento	CA	5	KCTC
	Farmerville	CA	5	KQIQ

Frequency [kHz]	Station Site	State	Power [kW]	Call Sign
1 320	Waterbury	CT	5	WATR
(cont'd)	Hollywood	FL	5	WLQY
	Jacksonville	FL	5	WQIK
	Venice	FL	5	WAMR
	Griffin	GA	5	WHIE
	Vivian	LA	5	KNCB
	Attleboro	MA	5	WARA
	Lansing	MI	5	WILS
	Marquette	MI	5	WDMJ
	Grand Rapids	MN	5	KOZY
	Picayune	MS	5	WRJW
	St Louis	MO	5	KSIV
	Scottsbluff	NE	5	KOLT
	Derry	NH	5	WDER
	Hornell	NY	5	WHHO
	Greensboro	NC	5	WGLD
	Murphy	NC	5	WKRK
	Oberlin	OH	1	WOBL
	Allentown	PA	5	WKAP
	Pittsburgh	PA	5	WJAS
	Columbia	SC	5	WOMG
	Sioux Falls	SD	5	KELO
	Kingsport	TN	5	WKIN
	Manchester	TN	5	WMSR
	Houston	TX	5	KXYZ
	Salt Lake City	UT	5	KUTR
	Richmond	VA	5	WLEE
	Aberdeen	WA	5	KXRO
	Wisconsin Rapids	WI	5	WFHR
1 330	Butler	AL	5	WPRN
	Scottsboro	AL	5	WZCT
	Tucson	AZ	2	KHYT
	Los Angelese	CA	5	KWKW
	Redding	CA	5	KRDG
	Los Banos	CA	5	KLBS
	Fort Pierce	FL	5	WDKC
	Milton	FL	5	WEBY
	Tallahassee	FL	5	WCVC
	Dublin	GA	3.4	WMLT
	Hailey	ID	5	KSKI
	Evanston	IL	5	WSSY
	Evansville	IN	5	WVHI
	Waterloo	IO	5	KWLO
	Wichita	KS	5	KFH
	Corbin	KY	5	WKDP
	Lafayette	LA	5	KVOL

Frequency [kHz]	Station Site	State	Power [kW]	Call Sign
1 330	Havre de Grace	MD	5	WASA
(cont'd)	Waltham	MA	5	WRCA
	Flint	MI	5	WDLZ
	St Paul	MN	5	KNOW
	Fulton	MS	5	WFTO
	Gallup	NM	5	KGAK
	New York	NY	5	WWRV
	Owego	NY	5	WEBO
	Springville	NY	1	WSPQ
	Wishek	ND	5	KDRQ
	Portland	OR	5	KUPL
	Erie	PA	5	WEYZ
	Somerset	PA	5	WADJ
	Conway	SC	5	WBIG
	Greenville	SC	5	WFBC
	Monahans	TX	5	KLBO
	Danville	VA	5	WBTM
	Marion	VA	5	WOLD
	Onley	VA	5	WESR
	Spokane	WA	5	KMBI
	Sheboygan	WI	5	WHBL
	Lander	WY	5	KOVE
1 350	Gadsden	AL	5	WGAD
	San Bernardino	CA	5	KCKC
	Santa Rosa	CA	5	KSRO
	Pueblo	CO	5	KGHF
	Norwalk	CT	1	WNLK
	Cocoa	FL	1	WLRQ
	Putnam	CT	5	WINY
	Blackshear	GA	5	WGIA
	Warner Robins	GA	5	WCOP
	Lewiston	ID	5	KRLC
	Peoria	IL	1	WXCL
	Kokom	IN	5	WIOU
	Des Moines	IA	5	KRNT
	Louisville	KY	5	WLOU
	New Orleans	LA	5	WSMB
	Laconia	NH	5	WLNH
	Princeton	NJ	5	WHWH
	Albuquerque	NM	5	KABQ
	Akron	OH	5	WSLR
	York	PA	5	WOYK
	Jasper	TX	5	KXTJ
	San Antonio	TX	5	KCOR
	Norton	VA	5	WNVA
	Norfolk	VA	5	WBSK

Frequency [kHz]	Station Site	State	Power [kW]	Call Sign
1 360	Mobile	AL	5	WMOB
	Wasilla	AK	5	KOBG
	Glendale	AZ	5	KLFF
	Helena	AR	1	KFFA
	Modesto	CA	5	KASH
	San Diego	CA	5	KPOP
	Hartford	CT	5	WDRC
	Cypress Gardens	FL	5	WYXY
	Jacksonville	FL	5	WCGL
	Miami Beach	FL	5	WKAT
	Bainbridge	GA	5	WYSE
	Sioux City	IA	5	KSCJ
	Baltimore	MD	5	WEBB
	Caro	MI	1	WKYO
	Kalamazoo	MI	5	WKMI
	Bemidji	MN	5	KKBJ
	Vineland	NJ	1	WWBZ
	Ruidoso	NM	5	KBUY
	Binghamton	NY	5	WRSG
	Chapel Hill	NC	5	WCHL
	Williston	ND	5	KEYZ
	Cincinnati	OH	5	WSAI
	Hermiston	OR	1	KOHU
	Hillsboro	OR	1	KUIK
	McKeesport	PA	5	WIXZ
	Pottsville	PA	5	WPPA
	Milan	TN	1	WWHY
	Baytown	TX	1	KWWJ
	Corpus Christi	TX	1	KRYS
	Fort Worth	TX	5	KNRB
	Galax	VA	5	WBOB
	Harrisonburg	VA	5	WHBG
	Tacoma	WA	5	KKMO
	Green Bay	WI	5	WGEE
	Rock Springs	WY	5	KRKK
1 370	Corona	CA	5	KWRM
	Quincy	CA	5	KPCO
	San Jose	CA	5	KEEN
	Deer Trail	CO	5	KTMG
	Ocala	FL	5	WOCA
	Pensacola	FL	5	WCOA
	Jessup	GA	5	WLOP
	Bloomington	IN	5	WGCL
	Gary	IN	1	WLTH
	Dubuque	IA	5	KDTH
	Dodge City	KS	5	KGNO

Frequency [kHz]	Station Site	State	Power [kW]	Call Sign
1 370	Grayson	KY	5	WGOH
(cont'd)	Ellsworth	ME	5	WDEA
	Leonardtown	MD	1	WKIK
	Cadillac	MI	5	WKJF
	Fairmont	MN	1	KSUM
	Butte	MT	5	KXTL
	Manchester	NY	5	WFEA
	Ellenville	NU	5	WELV
	Rochester	NY	5	WXXI
	Gastonia	NC	5	WLTC
	Lillington	NC	5	WLLN
	Tabor City	NC	5	WTAB
	Toledo	OH	5	WSPD
	Astoria	OR	1	KAST
	Corry	PA	1	WWCB
	Roaring Spring	PA	5	WKMC
	Santee	SC	5	WMNY
	Chattanooga	TN	5	WDEF
	Longview	TX	1	KFRO
	Salt Lake City	UT	5	KSOP
	Martinsville	VA	5	WHEE
	South Hill	VA	5	WJWS
	Frost	WV	5	WVMR
	Moundsville	WV	5	WEIF
	Neillsville	WI	5	WCCN
1 380	Vernon	AL	5	WVSA
	North Little Rock	AR	1	KPAL
	Sacramento	CA	5	KSMJ
	Salinas	CA	5	KTOM
	Waterbury	CT	5	WFNW
	Wilmington	DE	5	WAMS
	Ormond Beach	FL	5	WELE
	St Petersburg	FL	5	WRBQ
	Atlanta	GA	5	WAOK
	Ocilla	GA	5	WSIZ
	South Beloit	IL	5	WBEL
	Fort Wayne	IN	5	WQHK
	Carroll	IA	1	KCIM
	Fairway	KS	5	KCNW
	Baton Rouge	LA	5	WYNK
	Greenville	MI	1	WPLB
	Port Huron	MI	5	WPHM
	Brainerd	MN	5	KLIZ
	St Louis	MO	5	KGLD
	Portsmouth	NH	1	WCQL
	New York	NY	5	WKDM

Frequency [kHz]	Station Site	State	Power [kW]	Call Sign
1 380 *(cont'd)*	Asheville	NC	5	WTOO
	New Bern	NC	5	WSFL
	Winston-Salem	NC	5	WTOB
	Lawton	OK	1	KSWO
	Ontario	OR	5	KSRV
	Augusta	SC	5	WGUS
	Rapid City	SD	5	KOTA
	Franklin	TN	5	WIZO
	Millington	TN	2.5	WMPS
	Brownwood	TX	1	KBWD
	El Paso	TX	5	KTSM
	Rutland	VT	5	WSYB
	Richmond	VA	5	WTVR
	Everett	WA	5	KRKO
	Cliftonville	WI	3.9	WFCL
1 390	Anniston	AL	5	WHMA
	Fields Landing	CA	5	KKDV
	Long Beach	CA	5	KGER
	Turlock	CA	5	KMIX
	Denver	CO	5	KJME
	Gainesville	FL	5	WAJD
	Americus	GA	5	WISK
	Chicago	IL	5	WGCI
	Des Moines	IA	1	KJJY
	Hazard	KY	5	WKIC
	Presque Isle	ME	5	WTMS
	Plymouth	MA	5	WPLM
	Charlotte	MI	5	WNLF
	Waite Park	MN	2.5	KXSS
	Gulfport	MS	5	WROA
	Meridian	MS	5	WMER
	Waynesville	MO	5	KJPW
	Farmington	NM	5	KENN
	Hobbs	NM	5	KHOB
	Poughkeepsie	NY	5	WEOK
	Syracuse	NY	5	WFBL
	Rocky Mount	NC	5	WEED
	Minot	ND	5	KRRZ
	Middleport	OH	5	WMPO
	Youngstown	OH	5	WHOT
	Enid	OK	1	KCRC
	Salem	OR	5	KSLM
	Lancaster	PA	5	WLAN
	State College	PA	2	WRSC
	Charleston	SC	5	WCSE
	Jackson	TN	5	WTJS

Frequency [kHz]	Station Site	State	Power [kW]	Call Sign
1 390	Logan	UT	5	KLGN
(cont'd)	Burlington	VT	5	WDOT
	Arlington	VA	5	WMZQ
	Lynchburg	VA	5	WWOD
	Yakima	WA	5	KBBO
	Schofield	WI	5	WRIG
1 410	Mobile	AL	5	WMML
	Prattville	AL	5	WRNB
	Bakersfield	CA	1	KERN
	Carmel	CA	5	KRML
	Marysville	CA	5	KMYC
	Redlands	CA	5	KCAL
	Fort Collins	C0	5	KCOL
	Hartford	CT	5	WPOP
	Dover	DE	5	WDOV
	Fort Myers	FL	5	WMYR
	Leesburg	FL	5	WQBQ
	Tallahassee	FL	5	WBGM
	Rome	GA	1	WLAQ
	Leavenworth	KS	5	KKLO
	Wichita	KS	5	KQAM
	Bowling Green	KY	5	WLBJ
	Harlan	KY	5	WHLN
	Roseau	MN	5	KRWB
	Boyle	MS	5	WRDC
	Cuba	MO	5	KGNN
	North Platte	NE	5	KOOQ
	Las Vegas	NV	5	KFMS
	Elmira	NY	2.5	WELM
	Watertown	NY	5	WNCQ
	Durham	NC	5	WSRC
	Dayton	OH	5	WING
	Portland	OR	5	KBNP
	Lansford	PA	5	WLSH
	Pittsburgh	PA	5	KQV
	Cleveland	TX	1	KLEV
	Odessa	TX	1	KRIL
	Roanoke	VA	5	WRIS
	South Charleston	WV	5	WSCW
	LaCrosse	WI	5	WIZM
	Sheridan	WY	5	KWYO
1 420	Tuscaloosa	AL	5	WACT
	Bethel	AK	1	KSKM
	Hot Springs	AR	5	KXOW
	Stockton	CA	5	KSTN

Frequency [kHz]	Station Site	State	Power [kW]	Call Sign
1 420	Old Saybrook	CT	5	WLIS
(cont'd)	Delray Beach	FL	5	WDBF
	Palmetto	FL	2.5	WBRD
	Columbus	GA	5	WRCG
	Toccoa	GA	5	WLET
	Michigan City	IN	5	WIMS
	Davenport	IA	5	WOC
	Owensboro	KY	5	WVJS
	New Bedford	MA	5	WBSM
	Pittsfield	MA	1	WBEC
	Flint	MI	1	WFLT
	Mankato	MN	5	KTOE
	Wiggins	MS	5	WIGG
	Wolfeboro	NH	5	WASR
	Newark	NY	5	WACK
	Bernalillo	NM	5	KKTT
	Peekskill	NY	5	WLNA
	Cleveland	OH	5	WHK
	Coatesville	PA	5	WCOJ
	DuBois	PA	5	WCED
	Erwin	TN	5	WEMB
	Pulaski	TN	1	WKSR
	Lufkin	TX	5	KBLZ
	Warrenton	VA	5	WKCW
	Centralia	WA	5	KITI
	Walla Walla	WA	5	KUJ
	Kenova	WV	5	WTCR
1 430	Pell City	AL	5	WFHK
	Fresno	CA	5	KFIG
	San Gabriel	CA	5	KALI
	Santa Clara	CA	1	KNTA
	Aurora	CO	5	KEZW
	Grand Junction	CO	5	KMIY
	Homestead	FL	5	WOIR
	Lakeland	FL	5	WLKF
	Panama City	FL	5	WLTG
	Covington	GA	5	WGFS
	Tifton	GA	5	WWGS
	Highland Park	IL	1	WEEF
	Indianapolis	IN	5	WXTZ
	Mayfield	KY	1	WYMC
	Annapolis	MD	5	WNAV
	Amherst	MA	5	WTTT
	Everett	MA	5	WXKS
	Ionia	MI	5	WION
	Laurel	MS	5	WLAU

Frequency [kHz]	Station Site	State	Power [kW]	Call Sign
1 430	St Louis	MO	5	WIL
(cont'd)	Grand Island	NE	5	KRGI
	Newark	NJ	5	WNJR
	Roswell	NM	5	KCRX
	Endicott	NY	5	WENE
	Monroe	NC	2.5	WDEX
	Moranton	NC	5	WMNC
	Minot	ND	5	KTYN
	Fostoria	OH	1	WFOB
	Tulsa	OK	5	KSKS
	Keizer	OR	5	KYKN
	Altoona	PA	5	WVAM
	Batesburg	SC	5	WBLR
	Germantown	TN	2.5	WNWZ
	Knoxville	TN	5	WEMG
	Madison	TN	5	WHNK
	Gladewater	TX	5	KEES
	Houston	TX	5	KCOH
	Ogden	UT	5	KLO
	Ashland	VA	5	WPES
	Blacksburg	VA	5	WKEX
	Clintwood	VA	5	WDIC
	Mount Vernon	WA	5	KBRC
	Asotin	WA	5	KCLK
	Weirton	WV	1	WEIR
	Beaver Dam	WI	1	WBEV
1 440	Montgomery	AL	5	WHHY
	Scottsdale	AZ	5	KOPA
	Little Rock	AR	5	KITA
	Napa	CA	5	KVON
	Riverside	CA	1	KDIF
	Santa Maria	CA	5	KUHL
	Wray	CO	5	KRDZ
	Lehigh Acres	FL	5	WWCL
	Winter Park	FL	5	WPRD
	Brunswick	GA	5	WGIG
	Quincy	IL	5	WGEM
	Rockford	IL	5	WROK
	Topeka	KS	5	KEWI
	Monroe	LA	5	KJLO
	Glasgow	KY	5	WCDS
	Portland	ME	5	WWGT
	Worcester	MA	5	WFTQ
	Bay City	MI	5	WBCM
	Inkster	MI	1	WMKM
	Minneapolis	MN	5	KQRS

Frequency [kHz]	Station Site	State	Power [kW]	Call Sign
1 440	Lucedale	MS	5	WRBE
(cont'd)	Elizabethtown	NC	5	WBLA
	Lexington	NC	5	WLXN
	Warren	OH	5	WRRO
	Medford	OR	5	KMED
	The Dalles	OR	5	KODL
	Carbondale	PA	5	WCDL
	Greenville	SC	5	WSSL
	Cowan	TN	5	WZYX
	McKenzie	TN	5	WHDM
	Amarillo	TX	5	KPUR
	Corpus Christi	TX	1	KEYS
	Denton	TX	5	KDNT
	Livingston	TX	5	KETX
	Blackstone	VA	5	WBBC
	Bluefield	WV	5	WHIS
	Morgantown	WV	5	WAJR
	Green Bay	WI	5	WNFL
	Puyallup	WA	5	KJUN
1 460	Cullman	AL	5	WFMH
	Phoenix City	AL	5	WIQN
	Inglewood	CA	5	KTYM
	Salinas	CA	5	KDON
	Colorado Springs	CO	5	KWES
	DeFuniak Springs	FL	5	WZEP
	Jacksonville	FL	5	WFYV
	Buford	GA	5	WLKQ
	Des Moines	IA	5	KGGO
	Elkhorn City	KY	5	WBPA
	Baton Rouge	LA	5	WXOK
	Brockton	MA	5	WBET
	Big Rapids	MI	5	WBRN
	Montevideo	MN	1	KDMA
	St Charles	MO	5	KIRL
	Kearney	NE	5	KKPR
	Las Vegas	NV	5	KENO
	Mount Holly	NJ	5	WRLB
	Albany	NY	5	WGNA
	Rochester	NY	5	WWWG
	Fuquay-Varina	NC	5	WNBR
	Laurinburg	NC	5	WMXF
	Dickinson	ND	5	KLTC
	Columbus	OH	1	WBNS
	Harrisburg	PA	5	WCMB
	Tunkhannok	PA	5	WEMR
	Union	SC	1	WBCU

Frequency [kHz]	Station Site	State	Power [kW]	Call Sign
1 460	Waco	TX	1	WACO
(cont'd)	Manassas	VA	5	WPRW
	Radford	VA	5	WRAD
	Kirkland	WA	5	KARR
	Yakima	WA	5	KMWX
	Buckhannon	WV	5	WBUC
1 470	Palmdale	CA	5	KUTY
	Sacramento	CA	5	KXOA
	Meriden	CT	2.5	WMMW
	Clearwater	FL	5	WLVU
	Fort Lauderdale	FL	5	WRBD
	Rome	GA	5	WRGA
	Chicago Heights	IL	1	WCFJ
	Peoria	IL	5	WMBD
	Sioux City	IA	5	KWSL
	Atchison	KS	1	KERE
	Harlan	KY	5	WFSR
	Lake Charles	LA	5	KLCL
	Lewiston	ME	5	WLAM
	Salisbury	MD	5	WJDY
	Westminster	MD	1	WTTR
	Marlboro	MA	5	WSRO
	Flint	MI	5	WKMF
	Kalamazoo	MI	5	WQSN
	Brooklyn Park	MN	5	KANO
	Ithaca	NY	5	WTKO
	Greenboro	NC	5	WBIG
	Plymouth	NC	5	WPNC
	Spruce Pine	NC	5	WTOE
	Yadkinville	NC	5	WDIX
	Toledo	OH	1	WWWM
	Reedsport	OR	5	KDUN
	Allentown	PA	5	WXKW
	Columbia	SC	5	WQXL
	Berry Hill	TN	5	WVOL
	Abilene	TX	5	KNTS
	Henderson	TX	5	KWRD
	Tremonton	UT	5	KZZK
	Broadway	VA	5	WBTX
	Tazewell	VA	5	WTZE
	Chehalis	WA	5	KELA
	Moses Lake	WA	5	KBSN
	Huntington	WV	5	WHRD
	West Bend	WI	2.5	WBKV
1 480	Irondale	AL	5	WLPH
	Mobile	AL	5	WABB

Frequency [kHz]	Station Site	State	Power [kW]	Call Sign
1 480	Phoenix	AZ	5	KPHX
(cont'd)	Berryville	AR	5	KTHS
	Concord	CA	5	KWUN
	Eureka	CA	5	KRED
	Merced	CA	5	KYOS
	Santa Ana	CA	5	KWIZ
	Marco Island	FL	1	WMIB
	Atlanta	GA	5	WYZE
	Augusta	GA	5	WRDW
	Terre Haute	IN	5	WTHI
	Wichita	KS	5	KZSN
	Neon	KY	5	WNKY
	Fall River	MA	5	WSAR
	Grand Rapids	MI	5	WMAX
	Kentwood	MI	5	WMAX
	Ypsilanti	MI	3.8	WSDS
	Austin	MN	1	KAUS
	Fosston	MN	5	KKCQ
	Sidney	MT	5	KGCX
	Lincoln	NE	5	KLMS
	Hobbs	NM	5	KKEL
	New York	NY	5	WZRC
	Remsen	NY	5	WADR
	Charlotte	NC	5	WCNT
	Franklin	NC	5	WAJA
	Canton	OH	5	WHBC
	Cincinnati	OH	5	WCIN
	Philadelphia	PA	5	WDAS
	Shamokin	PA	1	WISL
	Memphis	TN	5	WMQM
	Dallas	TX	5	KDBN
	Springfield	VT	5	WCFR
	Richmond	VA	5	WBBL
	Salem	VA	5	WTOY
	Vancouver	WA	1	KBMS
	Madison	WI	5	WTDY
1 500	Burbank	CA	50	KRCK
	San Jose	CA	50	KSJX
	Milford	CT	5	WFIF
	Washington	DC	50	WTOP
	Clarkesville	GA	5	WCHM
	Indianapolis	IN	5	WBRI
	Detroit	MI	50	WLQV
	St Paul	MN	50	KSTP

Frequency [kHz]	Station Site	State	Power [kW]	Call Sign
1 500	Winston-Salem	NC	10	WSMX
(cont'd)	Pawhuska	OK	5	KXVQ
1 510	Mesa	AZ	10	KFNN
	Fresno	CA	10	KIRV
	Ontario	CA	10	KNSE
	Littleton	CO	10	KDKO
	New London	CT	10	WNLC
	Boston	MA	50	WKKU
	Jackson	MI	5	WJCO
	Independence	MO	10	KIDZ
	Dover	NJ	10	WMHQ
	Annville	PA	5	WAHT
	Milbank	SD	5	KMSD
	Nashville	TN	50	WLAC
	Nederland	TX	10	KQXY
	West Jordan	UT	10	KLLB
	Spokane	WA	50	KGA
	Waukesha	WI	10	WAUK
1 520	Opelika	AL	5	WZMG
	Hollister	CA	5	KMPG
	Oxnard	CA	10	KTRO
	Orlando	FL	5	WTLN
	Seminole	FL	1	WTIN
	Wilton Manors	FL	3.5	WEXY
	Clinton	IL	5	WHOW
	Greenup	KY	5	WLGC
	Lafayette	LA	10	KACY
	Greenfield	MA	10	WGAM
	Brunswick	MD	9.3	WTRI
	Muskegon	MI	10	WQWQ
	St Louis	MI	1	WMLM
	Rochester	MN	10	KOLM
	Sikeston	MO	5	KMPL
	Buffalo	NY	50	WWKB
	Mocksville	NC	5	WDSL
	Warrenton	NC	5	WARR
	Toledo	OH	1	WVOI
	Oklahoma City	OK	50	KOMA
	Portland	OR	50	KFXX
	Myrtle Beach	SC	5	WKZQ
	Dayton	TN	5	WREA
	Sequim	WA	20	KSJM
1 530	Sacramento	CA	50	KFBK
	Moreno Valley	CA	50	KHPY

Frequency [kHz]	Station Site	State	Power [kW]	Call Sign
1 530	Bridgeport	CT	10	WDJZ
(cont'd)	Jacksonville	FL	50	WJGC
	Dalton	GA	10	WTTI
	Lapeer	MI	5	WDEY
	Shakopee	MN	8	KKCM
	Poplarville	MS	10	WRPM
	Lincoln	NE	5	KHAT
	Durham	NC	10	WRTP
	Cincinnati	OH	50	WCKY
	Harlingen	TX	50	KGBT
	Wagoner	OK	5	KXTD
	Ralls	TX	5	KCLR
	Fox Farm	WY	10	KSHY
1 540	Phoenix	AZ	10	KASA
	Aptos	CA	10	KLAU
	Los Angeles	CA	50	KSKQ
	Waterloo	IA	50	KXEL
	Wheaton	MD	5	WMDO
	Exeter	NH	5	WMYF
	Albany	NY	50	WPTR
	Charlotte	NC	10	WOGR
	Philadelphia	PA	50	WPGR
	Punxsutawney	PA	5	WECZ
	Pickens	SC	10	WTBI
	Fort Worth	TX	50	KSGB
	San Antonio	TX	5	KEDA
	Richmond	VA	10	WRBN
	Bellevue	WA	5	KLSY
1 550	Huntsville	AL	50	WAAJ
	Tucson	AZ	50	KUAT
	Fresno	CA	5	KXEX
	San Francisco	CA	10	KKHI
	Arvada	CO	10	KQXI
	Bloomfield	CT	5	WLVX
	Miami	FL	10	WRHC
	Tampa	FL	10	WAMA
	Augusta	GA	5	WNTA
	Smyrna	GA	50	WYNX
	Port Allen	LA	5	WLUX
	Shreveport	LA	10	KVKI
	Newton	MA	10	WNTN
	Jackson	MS	50	WOKJ
	Springfield	MO	5	KLFJ
	Cape Girardeau	MO	5	KAPE
	St Joseph	MO	5	KSFT

Frequency [kHz]	Station Site	State	Power [kW]	Call Sign
1 550	Santa Fe	NM	50	KSWV
(cont'd)	Seaside Park	NJ	10	WNJO
	Fargo	ND	10	KQWB
	Pittston	PA	5	WARD
	Bennettsville	SC	5	WBSC
	Bristol	TN	5	WBCV
	Clarksville	TN	2.5	WCTZ
	West Valley City	UT	10	KZQQ
	Vinton	VA	10	WKBA
	Virginia Beach	VA	5	WVAB
	Ferndale	WA	10	KNTR
	Vancouver	WA	10	KJMK
	Spokane	WA	10	KSVY
	Charles Town	WV	5	WXVA
	Madison	WI	5	WHIT
1 560	Daleville	AL	5	WRDJ
	Bakersfield	CA	10	KNZR
	Inverness	FL	5	WINV
	Miami	FL	10	WRHC
	Melbourne	FL	5	WTAI
	Iowa City	IA	1	KCJJ
	Paducah	KY	10	WPAD
	Slidell	LA	1	WSLA
	Portage	MI	5	WHEZ
	Joplin	MO	10	KQYX
	New York	NY	50	WQXR
	Webster	NY	10	WMJO
	Warsaw	NC	10	WTRQ
	Fairfield	OH	5	WCNW
	Toledo	OH	5	WTOD
	Chickasha	OK	1	KWCO
	Lancaster	SC	50	WAGL
	Aberdeen	SD	10	KKAA
	Nashville	TN	10	WWGM
	West Lake Hills	TX	2.5	KTXZ
1 570	Selma	AL	5	WTQX
	Lodi	CA	5	KCVR
	Riverside	CA	5	KPRO
	Salinas	CA	5	KTGE
	Auburndale	FL	5	WTWB
	Fernandina Beach	FL	5	WQAI
	Pensacola Beach	FL	5	WBND
	Morrow	GA	5	WSSA
	Freeport	IL	5	WFRL
	New Albany	IN	2	WOBS

Frequency [kHz]	Station Site	State	Power [kW]	Call Sign
1 570	Baltimore	MD	5	WFEL
(cont'd)	Golden Valley	MN	2.5	KYCR
	Bay Springs	MS	5	WIZK
	Penn Yan	NY	5	WFLR
	Doylestown	PA	5	WBUX
	Centerville	TN	5	WHLP
	Cleveland	TN	5	WCLE
	Minocqua	WI	5	WMYM
1 580	Tempe	AZ	50	KCWW
	Santa Monica	CA	50	KDAY
	Colorado Springs	CO	10	KWYD
	Chattahoochee	FL	5	WTCL
	Fort Lauderdale	FL	10	WSRF
	Mount Dora	FL	5	WBGD
	Columbus	GA	2.3	WEAM
	Georgetown	KY	10	WAXU
	Lake Charles	LA	1	KXZZ
	Morningside	MD	50	WPGC
	Amory	MS	5	WAMY
	West Greenville	MS	1	WESY
	Pascagoula	MS	5	WKNN
	Albuquerque	NM	10	KZKL
	Icard Township	NC	5	WUIV
	Camp LeJeune	NC	10	WWOF
	Travelers Rest	SC	5	WBBR
	Knoxville	TN	5	WMRE
	Pulaski	VA	5	WPUV
1 590	Atmore	AL	5	WGYJ
	Tuscumbia	AL	5	WVNA
	St Johns	AZ	5	KSSU
	Pine Bluff	AR	5	KYDE
	San Jose	CA	5	KLIV
	Ventura	CA	5	KOGO
	Waterbury	CT	5	WQQW
	Port St Lucie	FL	5	WPSL
	St Petersburg Beach	FL	5	WRXB
	Albany	GA	5	WALG
	La Fayette	GA	5	WQCH
	Evanston	IL	1	WONX
	Galesburg	IL	5	WAIK
	Beach Grove	IN	5	WNTS
	Great Bend	KS	5	KVGB
	Glen Burnie	MD	1	WJRO
	Coldwater	MI	5	WTVB
	East Grand Forks	MN	5	KCNN

Frequency [kHz]	Station Site	State	Power [kW]	Call Sign
1 590	Jackson	MS	5	WZRX
(cont'd)	Sun Valley	NV	5	KHIT
	Nashua	NH	5	WSMN
	Auburn	NY	0.5	WAUB
	Brockport	NY	1	WASB
	Salamanca	NY	5	WGGO
	Clayton	NC	5	WHPY
	Akron	OH	5	WAKR
	Tillamook	OR	5	KTIL
	Chambersburg	PA	5	WCBG
	Chester	PA	1	WCZN
	Warwick	RI	5	WARV
	Jonesboro	TN	5	WKTP
	El Paso	TX	5	KELP
	Houston	TX	5	KYOK
	Lubbock	TX	1	KLLL
	Manti	UT	5	WMTI
	Richmond	VA	5	WFTH
	Seattle	WA	5	KZOK
	New Richmond	WI	5	WIXK
1 600	Huntsville	AL	5	WEUP
	Montgomery	AL	5	WXVI
	South Tucson	AZ	2.5	KXEW
	Bellefonte	AR	5	KNWA
	Fresno	CA	5	KGST
	Pomona	CA	5	KMNY
	Yuba City	CA	5	KUBA
	Lakewood	CO	5	KRXY
	Dover	DE	5	WKEN
	Atlantic Beach	FL	5	WQRB
	West Palm Beach	FL	5	WPOM
	Orlando	FL	5	WOKB
	Austell	GA	5	WAOS
	Algona	IA	5	KGLA
	Cedar Rapids	IA	5	KCRG
	Brewer	ME	5	WTKS
	Rockville	MD	1	WTKZ
	Boston	MA	5	WUNR
	East Longmeadow	MA	5	WIXY
	Ann Arbor	MI	5	WAAM
	Muskegon	MI	5	WSNX
	Watertown	MN	5	KWOM
	St Louis	MI	5	KATZ
	New York	NY	5	WWRL
	Charlotte	NC	2.5	WGIV
	Hendersonville	NC	5	WTZQ

Frequency [kHz]	Station Site	State	Power [kW]	Call Sign
1 600	Reidsville	NC	1	WRNC
(cont'd)	Eugene	OR	5	KEED
	Bedford	PA	5	WAYC
	Harriman	TN	5	WWBR
	Borger	TX	5	KBBB
	Brownsville	TX	1	KBOR
	Plano	TX	5	KSSA
	Orange	TX	5	KOGT
	Centerville	UT	5	KBBX
	Bountiful	UT	5	KBBX
	Chesapeake	VA	5	WJQI
	Saltville	VA	5	WXMY
	Dungeness	WA	5	KCDV
	Milton	WV	5	WNST
	Wheeling	WV	5	WBBD
	Ripon	WI	5	WCWC

Section 11

INTERNATIONAL RADIO BROADCASTS IN ENGLISH

This chapter details the main international service broadcasts in English beamed throughout the world.

Time		Station	Frequencies [kHz]
0000–2400		R Luxembourg	15 350
0000–0015		R Prague Intl	7 345, 9 540, 11 990
0000–0015		Vo People of Cambodia	1 360, 9 695, 11 938
0000–0025		R Finland	252, 558, 963, 9 645, 11 755
0000–0030		Kol Israel	7 465, 9 435, 11 605
0000–0030		R Luxembourg	1 440, 6 090
0000–0100		R Kiev	7 400, 9 750, 15 180, 17 690, 17 720
0000–0100		WYFR	5 985, 13 695, 15 170
0000–0100		R Pyongyang	13 760, 15 115
0000–0100		R Korea	15 575
0000–0100		R Sofia	9 700, 11 68
0000–0100		R Beijing	9 770, 11 715
0000–0130	M-F	R Canada Intl	5 960, 9 755
0000–0200		R Exterior de Espana	9 630, 11 880
0000–0200		Christian Science Mon	7 395, 17 555
0000–0200	•	R Havana Cuba	11 820
0000–0230		FEBC Manila	15 490
0000–0400		WRNO	7 355
0000–1100		WHRI	7 355
0030–0100		BRT Brussels	9 925
0030–0125		R Netherlands	6 020, 6 165, 11 740
0030–0230		Sri Lanka BC	6 005, 9 720, 15 425
0030–0700		HCJB	9 745, 15 155
0050–0115		Vatican R	6 150 9 605
0100–0120		RAI Rome	9 575, 11 800
0100–0125		Kol Israel	7 465, 9 435, 11 605
0100–0130		R Sweden	1 179, 9 770
0100–0130		R Prague Intl	5 930, 7 345, 9 540
0100–0130	Su-Mo	R Norway Intl	11 925, 15 360
0100–0145		R Yugoslavia	6 005, 11 735
0100–0150		Deutsche Welle	6 040, 6 085, 6 115, 6 145, 9 565, 9 735, 11 865, 11 890, 13 610, 13 770, 15 440
0100–0200		WYFR	9 505, 15 170
0100–0200		R Japan	17 810, 17 845

Time		Station	Frequencies [kHz]
0100–0200		Vo Indonesia	11 752, 11 785
0100–0545		R New Zealand Intl	17 675
0130–0140	Mo-Sa	Vo Greece	9 395, 9 420, 11 645
0130–0200		R Austria Intl	9 875, 13 730
0130–0200	Sun	R Canada Intl	5 960, 9 755
0130–0200	Mon	R Alma Ata	5 035, 5 915
0200–0225		Kol Israel	7 465, 9 435, 11 605
0200–0230		Swiss R Intl	6 095, 6 135, 9 650, 9 885, 12 035, 17 730
0200–0230		R Sweden	9 695, 11 705
0200–0230		R Budapest	6 025, 9 520, 9 585, 9 835, 11 910, 12 000
0200–0230	Su-Mo	R Norway	15 360
0200–0250		Deutsche Welle	1 548, 6 035, 7 285, 9 615, 9 690, 11 945, 11 965
0200–0300		R Cairo	9 475, 9 675
0200–0300		R Romania Intl	5 990, 9 510, 9 570, 11 830, 11 940, 15 380
0200–0300		Vo Free China	5 950, 9 680, 9 765, 11 860
0200–0300		AWR Guam	13 720
0200–0400		R Havana Cuba	11 820, 9 505
0200–0600		WWCR	7 520
0200–0800		Christian Science Mon	9 455
0230–0245		R Pakistan	9 545, 15 115, 17 640, 17 725, 21 730
0230–0300	M-F	RDP Lisbon	9 680, 9 705
0230–0300		R Tirana	9 760, 11 825
0230–0430		Sri Lanka BC	9 720, 15 425
0230–0430		R Baghdad	11 810, 11 830
0300–0330		R Japan	9 465, 17 825, 21 610
0300–0330		R Budapest	6 025, 9 520, 9 585, 9 8356, 11 910, 12 000
0300–0330		R Prague Intl	5 930, 7 345, 9 540
0300–0350		Deutsche Welle	6 040, 6 085, 6 120, 9 545, 9 605, 11 890, 13 610, 13 770, 15 440
0300–0400		TIFC Costa Rica	5 055
0300–0400		Vo Free China	5 950, 9 680, 9 765, 11 745
0300–0400		WYFR	9 505
0300–0400		R Beijing	9 690, 9 770, 11 715
0300–0400		R Japan	5 960, 11 870, 17 810
0310–0330		Vatican R	9 635
0330–0430		TWR Bonaire	800, 9 535, 11 930
0330–0400		UAE R Dubai	11 945, 13 675, 15 400, 15 435

Time		Station	Frequencies [kHz]
0330–0400		R Tirana	9 760, 11 825
0330–0400		Yerevan R	7 400, 9 750, 15 180, 17 690, 17 720
0330–0400		R Sweden	9 695, 11 705
0330–0425		R Netherlands	9 590, 11 720
0340–0350	M-Sa	Vo Greece	9 395, 9 420, 11 645
0400–0415		R Prague Intl	5 930, 7 345, 9 540
0400–0430		R Romania Intl	5 990, 9 510, 9 570, 11 830, 11 940, 15 380
0400–0430		Swiss R Intl	6 135, 9 650, 9 885, 12 035
0400–0430	Su-Mo	R Norway Intl	11 865
0400–0450		R Havana Cuba	9 505, 9 750, 11 760, 11 820
0400–0500		R Beijing	11 695
0400–0500		R Sofia	9 700, 11 680
0400–0500		Vo Turkey	9 445, 17 880
0400–0500		R Pyongyang	15 180, 15 230, 17 765
0400–0600		TIQ Costa Rica	5 955
0400–0600		WRNO	6 185
0400–0700		WMLK	9 465
0450–0600		R Havana Cuba	9 750, 11 760, 11 820
0500–0515		Kol Israel	7 410, 7 465, 9 435, 11 605, 17 575
0500–0550		Deutsche Welle	5 960, 6 120, 9 670, 9 700, 11 890, 13 610, 13 770, 15 440
0500–0600		WYFR	5 950, 9 680, 11 580, 15 556, 17 640
0500–0600		R Exterior de Espana	9 630
0500–0600		R Beijing	11 840
0500–0600		R Japan	11 870, 17 810, 17 825, 17 890
0500–0600		R Thailand	927, 9 655, 11 905
0530–0600		R Austria Intl	6 015, 6 155, 13 730
0530–0600		UAE R, Dubai	15 435, 17 830, 21 700
0545–0610		R New Zealand Intl	9 855, 17 675
0555–0825		Vo Malayasia	6 175, 9 750, 15 295
0600–0620		Vatican R	526, 1 530, 6 185, 6 245
0600–0800		WYFR	6 065
0600–0800		R Havana Cuba	11 835
0600–1000		WCSN	9 840
0600–0700		R Pyongyang	15 180, 15 230
0600–0800	Sa-Su	R Thailand	927, 9655, 11 905
0600–0800		Christian Science Mon	17 555, 17 780
0610–0700		R New Zealand Intl	9 855, 17 675
0615–0630		R Canada Intl	6 050, 6 150, 7 155, 9 740, 9 760, 11 840

Time		Station	Frequencies [kHz]
0630–0700		R Polonia	7 270, 9 675
0630–0700		R Tirana	7 205, 9500
0645–0715		R Romania Intl	11 810, 11 940, 15 250, 15 365, 17 720, 17 805, 21 665
0650–0715	M-F	R Finland	15 400, 21 550
0700–0730	M-Sa	R New Zealand Intl	9 855
0700–0730	Su	R Riga Intl	5 935
0700–0800		WYFR	7 355, 13 760
0700–0800		R Japan	15 325, 17 810, 17 890, 21 690
0700–0800		Vo Free China	5 950
0700–0800		R Pyongyang	15 340, 17 765
0700–0830		HCJB	6 205, 9 615, 11 835, 25 950
0730–0755		BRT	6 035, 11 695, 13 675
0730–0800		R Finland	6 120, 9 560, 9 825, 11 755
0730–0800		R Sofia	11 765, 15 160, 17 825
0730–0800		Swiss R Intl	3 985, 6 165, 9 535
0730–0800		R Prague Intl	17 840, 21 705
0730–0825		R Netherlands	9 630, 15 560
0730–0900		R New Zealand Intl	9 855
0730–1100		HCJB	9 745, 11 925
0740–0800		TWR, Monaco	9 480
0800–0830		R Tirana	9 500, 11 835
0800–0900		R Korea	7 550, 13 670
0800–0900		R Pyongyang	15 180, 15 230
0800–1000		Christian Science Mon	9 530, 13 760, 15 610
0800–1000		KTWR Guam	11 805
0830–0855	Mo-Sa	R Netherlands	15 190
0830–0925		R Netherlands	17 575, 21 485
0830–0900		R Austria Intl	6 155, 13 730, 15 450, 21 490
0830–0900		Swiss R Intl	9 560, 13 685, 17 670, 21 695
0830–0925		R Netherlands	17 575, 21 485
0840–0850		Vo Greece	15 625, 17 535
0900–0925		R Finland	17 800, 21 550
0900–0950		Deutsch Welle	6 160, 11 740, 17 780, 17820, 21 465, 21 540, 21 650, 21 680
0900–1000		R Japan	15 270, 17 890, 21 610
0900–1000		R New Zealand Intl	9 695
0900–1100		FEBC Manila	9 800, 11 845
0900–1100		R Beijing	11 755, 15 440, 17 710
0910–0940		R Ulan Bator	11 850, 12 015
0930–0955		R Finland	15 245, 17 800
0930–1030		R Afghanistan	4 940, 9 635, 17 655, 21 600

Time	Station	Frequencies [kHz]
1000–1025	BRT	6 035, 13 675
1000–1030	Vo Vietnam	9 840, 15 010
1000–1100	WYFR	5 950, 11 830
1000–1100	All India R	15 050, 15 335, 17 387, 17 865, 21 735
1000–1200	WCSN	11 705
1000–1200	R Pyongyang	9 977, 11 735
1000–1400	Christian Science Mon	9 495
1030–1100	UAE R Dubai	15 320, 15 435, 21 605, 21 675
1030–1100	R Korea	11 715
1030–1100	R Budapest	9 835, 11 910, 15 160, 15 220, 17 710
1030–1125	R Netherlands	6 020, 11 890
1030–1130	Sri Lanka BC	11 835, 15 120, 17 850
1100–1120	R Pakistan	17 565, 21 520
1100–1130	Kol Israel	11 585, 17 575, 17 590, 21 790
1100–1130	Swiss R Intl	13 635, 15 570, 17 830, 21 770
1100–1130	Voice of Vietnam	7 430, 9 730
1100–1200	R Japan	6 120, 11 815
1100–1200	WYFR	5 950, 11 580, 11 830
1100–1200	TIQ, Costa Rica	5 955
1100–1200	Vo Asia	585, 7 445
1100–1300	TWR Bonaire	800, 11 815, 15 345
1100–1315	R Jordan	13 655
1100–1500	WHRI	9 465
1115–1145	R Nepal	5 005, 7 165
1130–1200	R Austria Intl	6 155, 13 730, 21 490
1130–1200	AWR Europe	7 230
1130–1200	R Tirana	9 480, 11 835
1130–1225	R Netherlands	5 955, 9 715, 17 575, 21 480, 21 520
1130–1230	VoIRI	9 575, 9 705, 11 715, 11 790
1130–1230	R Thailand	927, 9 655, 11 905
1130–1500	HCJB	11 740
1150–1220	R Bucharest	9 585, 9 835, 11 910, 15 160, 17 710
1200–1215	Vo People of Cambodia	1 360, 9 695, 11 938
1200–1225	R Polonia	6 095, 11 815
1200–1230	R Tashkent	5 945, 9 540, 9 600, 11 860, 15 470
1200–1230	R Ulan Bator	11 850, 12 015
1200–1230	R Romania Intl	15 380, 17 720
1200–1230 Sa-Su	R Norway	17 820, 21 695
1200–1300	R Beijing	9 665, 11 600, 15 450

Time		Station	Frequencies [kHz]
1200–1300		WYFR	5 950, 6 015, 11 580, 17 612.5
1200–1300		R Bras	11 745
1200–1400		Christian Science Mon	9 895, 13 625, 21 780
1200–1400		R Beijing	1 341, 9 670, 11 660
1200–1600		HCJB	15 115, 17 890
1215–1315		R Korea	9 750
1215–1330		R Cairo	17 675
1230–1300		R France Intl	9 805, 11 670, 15 155, 15 195, 17 605, 21 635
1230–1300		R Sweden	11 715, 17 740, 21 570
1230–1300		R Bangladesh	15 195, 17 815
1230–1730		Sri Lanka BC	6 075, 9 720
1235–1250		Vo Greece	15 625, 15 650, 17 535
1300–1325		R Finland	15 400, 21 550
1300–1330		Swiss R Intl	6 165, 9 535, 12 030
1300–1330		R Canada Intl	11 955, 15 210
1300–1330		R Peace and Progress	7 150, 15 490, 17 870
1300–1330		R Yugoslavia	17 725, 21 635, 21 715
1300–1330	Sa-Su	R Norway Intl	9 590, 11 860
1300–1400		TWR Bonaire	800, 11 815, 15 345
1300–1400		R Pyongyang	9 325, 9 345, 9 640, 13 650, 15 230
1300–1400		R Romania Intl	17 720, 21 665
1300–1400	M-F	R Canada Intl	9 635, 11 855, 17 820
1300–1400		WYFR	5 950, 6 015, 11 580, 11 830, 13 695, 17 612.5
1300–1400		R Beijing	11 600
1300–1500		WWCR	15 690
1300–1500		WYFR	15 055
1320–1600		R Jordan	9 560
1330–1400		UAE R Dubai	15 320, 15 435, 21 605, 21 675
1330–1400		TWR Bonaire	800, 11 815, 15 345
1330–1400		Swiss R Intl	11 695, 13 635, 15 570, 17 830, 21 695
1330–1500		All India R	9 565, 11 760
1400–1425	M-F	R Finland	15 400, 21 550
1400–1425	M-Sa	BRT Brussels	21 810
1400–1430		R Tirana	9 500, 11 985
1400–1430		R Sweden	9 765, 17 740, 21 570
1400–1500		R Japan	9 505, 11 815
1400–1500		WYFR	5 950, 11 580, 13 695
1400–1500		R Korea	9 570
1400–1500		R France Intl	7 125, 21 770
1400–1500		King of Hope Lebanon	6 280

Time	Station	Frequencies [kHz]
1400–1600	R Beijing	11 815, 15 165
1400–1600	Christian Science Mon	9 530, 13 625, 13 760, 15 610, 21 780
1400–1700 Sun	R Canada Intl	11 955
1430–1500	R Polonia	6 135, 9 540, 11 815
1430–1500	R Austria Intl	6 155, 11 780, 13 730, 21 490
1430–1525	R Netherlands	5 955, 13 770, 15 150, 17 575, 17 605
1445–1500	Vatican R	526, 1 530, 6 245, 9 645, 11 740
1445–1515	R Ulan Bator	9 575, 13 780
1500–1515	WYFR	11 550
1500–0200	WWCR	15 690
1500–1530	R Finland	6 120, 9 640, 11 755
1500–1530	R Romania Intl	11 775, 11 940, 15 250, 15 335, 17 720, 17 745
1500–1530 Sa-Su	R Norway Intl	15 305, 17 790
1500–1600	R Japan	9 505, 21 700
1500–1600	FEBA Seychelles	9 590, 11 865, 15 330
1500–1600	KNLS	7 355
1500–1600	R Pyongyang	9 325, 11 760
1500–1600	WYFR	11 580, 11 830, 13 695
1500–1700	WHRI	21 840
1515–1530	R Canada Intl	9 555, 11 915, 11 935, 13 650, 15 315, 15 325, 17 820, 21 545
1530–1550	Vo Greece	11 645, 15 625, 17 535
1530–1600	R Sweden	17 875, 21 500
1530–1600 Mo-Sa	R Budapest	9 835, 11 910, 15 160, 15 220
1545–1700	KTWR Guam	11 910
1600–1630	R Polonia	6 135, 9 540
1600–1630 Mo-Fr	RDP Lisbon	11 870, 21 530
1600–1630 Sa-Su	R Norway Intl	21 705
1600–1640	UAE R Dubai	11 795, 15 320, 15 435, 21 605
1600–1650	Deutsche Welle	1 548, 6 170, 7 225, 9 615, 11 785, 15 105, 15 240, 15 595, 17 825
1600–1700	R France Intl	6 175
1600–1700	WYFR	15 440, 17 612.5, 21 615
1600–1700	AWR Guam	11 980
1600–1800	Christian Science Mon	13 625, 15 610, 17 555
1600–2000	WINB	15 295
1600–2000	WYFR	11 580, 13 695, 15 170
1600–2100	BSKSA Riyadh	9 705, 9 720
1600–2400	WRNO	15 420

Time		Station	Frequencies [kHz]
1630–1700		R Peace and Progress	6 005, 7 130, 9 715, 15 480
1645–1745	Mo-Fr	R New Zealand Intl	15 485
1700–1730	Sa-Su	R Norway Intl	9 655
1700–1800		R Pyongyang	9 325, 11 760
1700–1800		R Japan	9 505, 11 815
1700–1900		WYFR	17 750
1700–2400		WHRI	13 760
1715–1730		R Canada Intl	5 995, 7 325, 13 650, 15 325, 17 820, 21 545
1715–1800		R Pakistan	11 570, 15 605
1730–1745		R Surinam Intl	17 755
1730–1800		R Austria Intl	5 945, 6 155
1745–2105		R New Zealand Intl	15 485
1800–1830		R Prague Intl	5 930, 6 055, 7 345, 9 605
1800–1830		R Sweden	1 179, 6 065, 9 655, 11 900
1800–1830		Vo Vietnam	9 840, 15 010
1800–1830	Sa-Su	R Norway	17 755
1800–1900		R Bras	15 265
1800–1900		R Korea	15 575
1800–1900		KNLS	7 355
1800–2000		KHBI	11 650
1800–2000		Christian Science Mon	11 650, 21 780
1800–2200		Christian Science Mon	13 625
1815–1830		Kol Israel	11 585, 11 655
1815–1900		R Bangladesh	12 030, 15 255
1830–1900		R Afghanistan	7 310, 9 635
1830–1900		R Tirana	7 120, 9 480
1830–1900		R Polonia	1 503, 5 995, 6 135, 7 285
1830–1900		BRT Brussels	5 910
1830–1900	Sa	R Riga Intl	5 935
1830–2000		Sri Lanka BC Corp	9 720, 15 120
1845–1945		All India R	7 412, 9 730, 9 950, 11 620, 11 860
1900–1930		Vo Vietnam	9 840, 15 010
1900–1930		R Japan	9 505, 11 850, 15 270
1900–1930	Sa-Su	R Norway	15 175, 17 730
1900–2000		R Exterior de Espana	9 875, 11 790
1900–2000		R Algiers	9 640, 15 215
1900–2000		RAE Buenos Aires	15 345
1900–2000		HCJB	15 270, 17 790, 21 480
1900–2000		WYFR	15 566, 21 615
1915–2000		DLF	1 269
1920–1950	M-Sa	Vo Greece	9 395, 11 645

Time		Station	Frequencies [kHz]
1930–1945		R Prague Intl	6 055, 9 605
1930–2000		R Austria Intl	5 945, 6 155
1930–2000		R Budapest	6 110, 7 220, 9 520, 9 585, 9 835, 11 910
1930–2000		R Finland	6 120, 9 550, 11 755
1930–2000	M-F	R Canada Intl	5 995, 7 235, 11 945, 15 325, 17 875
1930–2000		R Sofia	6 070, 7 155, 9 700
1930–2000		R Sweden	6 065, 7 265
1930–2000		R Yugoslavia	6 165, 7 165
1930–2030		R Romania Intl	5 955, 9 690, 9 750, 11 810
1930–2000		VoIRI	6 035, 9 022
1935–1955		RAI Rome	7 275, 9 710, 11 800
1940–2010		R Ulan Bator	11 850, 12 015
1945–2000		R Prague Intl	6 055, 9 605
2000–2030	M-F	RDP Lisbon	11 740
2000–2030		Kol Israel	7 465, 9 435, 11 605, 17 630
2000–2030		Swiss R Intl	3 985, 6 165, 9 535
2000–2030	Sa-Su	R Norway Intl	15 165
2000–2100		R Pyongyang	9 325, 11 760
2000–2100		KNLS	11 700
2000–2100		Vo Indonesia	7 125, 9 675, 11 752, 11 785
2000–2200		Christian Science Mon	13 770, 15 610
2000–2200		WYFR	11 580, 13 695, 15 170, 15 566, 21 525
2000–2200		R Beijing	9 920, 11 500
2000–2200		King of Hope, Lebanon	6 280
2000–2245		WINB	15 185
2005–2105		R Damascus	12 085, 15 095
2015–2145		R Cairo	9 670
2030–2100		Vo Vietnam	9 840, 15 010
2030–2100		R Romania Intl	756
2030–2130		R Korea	6 480, 15 575
2045–2230		All India R	7 412, 9 730, 9 910, 11 620, 11 715, 15 265
2050–2110		Vatican R	526, 1 530, 6 245, 7 250
2100–2130		R Budapest	6 110, 7 220, 9 520, 9 585, 9 835, 11 910
2100–2130		R Prague Intl	5 930, 6 055, 7 345, 9 645
2100–2130		R Romania Intl	9 690, 9 750, 11 810, 11 940
2100–2130		R Beijing	3 985
2100–2150		Deutsche Welle	9 670, 9 765, 11 785, 13 780, 15 350
2100–2200		Vo Turkey	9 795

Time		Station	Frequencies [kHz]
2100–2200		R Kiev	6 185
2100–2200		R Japan	15 230, 15 270, 17 810, 17 890
2100–2300		R Baghdad	13 660
2105–2300		R New Zealand Intl	17 675
2110–2210		R Damascus	12 085, 15 095
2130–2200		R Sofia	6 070, 7 155, 9 700
2130–2200		R Riga	5 935
2130–2200	Mon	R Tallin	5 925
2130–2200		HCJB	15 270, 17 790, 21 480
2200–2215		R Prague Intl	5 930, 6 055, 7 345, 9 645
2200–2225		RAI Rome	5 990, 9 710, 11 800
2200–2230		R Finland	6 120, 11 755
2200–2230		R Sweden	1 179, 6 065
2200–2230		BRT Brussels	5 910, 9 925
2200–2230		R Canada Intl	11 705
2200–2230	Sa-Su	R Norway Intl	21 705
2200–2245		R Yugoslavia	5 955, 6 100
2200–2300		R Peace and Progress	1 386, 4 795, 6 145, 7 205, 7 360, 9 775
2200–2300		R Canada Intl	9 760, 11 945
2200–2300		R Havana Cuba	7 215
2200–2300		Vo Free China	9 852, 11 805
2200–2400		Christian Science Mon	15 275, 15 405
2205–2230		Vatican R	7 125, 9 615, 11 830
2230–2300		Vo Vietnam	9 840, 15 010
2230–2300		R Tirana	7 215, 9 480
2230–2300		R Polonia	1 503, 5 995, 6 135, 7 270
2230–2300		R Vilnius	666, 6 100, 9 710
2230–2300		Kol Israel	7 465, 9 435, 11 605, 11 655
2230–2300		Swiss R Intl	6 190
2245–2335		TWR Monaco	1 467
2300–2330		R Vilnius	11 770, 11 860, 15 180, 17 690, 17 720
2300–2400		R Japan	11 735, 15 230, 17 810
2300–2400		Vo Turkey	9 445, 9 685, 17 880
2300–2400		WYFR	5 950, 5 985, 11 580, 15 170
2300–2400		R Pyongyang	11 700, 13 650
2300–0100		AWR Guam	15 225
2300–0100	Mo-Sa	R New Zealand Intl	17 675
2300–0430		R Thailand	927, 9 655, 11 905
2305–2355		R Polonia	738, 1 206, 1 503, 5 995, 6 135, 7 270

Time	Station	Frequencies [kHz]
2315–0115	All India R	9 535, 9 910, 11 715, 11 745, 15 110
2330–2400	Vo Vietnam	9 840, 15 010
2330–2400	R Sweden	1 179
2330–2400	R Tirana	6 120, 9 760, 11 825

BBC World Service

The whole schedule for BBC World Service in English is listed, although some frequencies may not be audible in all parts of the regions shown since they are directed to more specific areas.

Frequency [kHz]	Time
Europe	
17 705	0900–1615
17 695	1615–1745
17 640	0800–1830
15 590	0400–0730
15 070	0400–2300
12 095	0200–2300
11 850	1900–2300
9 760	0700–1515
9 750	0900–1615
9 660	0800–1430
9 410	0200–0915, 1500–2300
7 325	0700–0915, 1800–2300
7 230	0400–0730
6 195	0200–0730, 1515–2300
6 180	0300–1515, 1700–2200
6 045	0900–1515
3 955	0400–0630, 1800–2300
Africa and the Middle East	
21 660	0700–1745
21 490	1500–1530
21 470	0430–1745
17 885	0330–0430, 0500–1400
17 880	1400–2100
17 860	1515–1745
17 790	0900–1515
17 705	0900–1615
17 695	1615–1745
17 640	1030–1830
15 590	0300–0330, 0400–0915
15 575	0915–1515
15 420	0300–0315, 0330–1215, 1245–1400, 1500–1530, 1615–1745
15 400	0430–1130, 1500–2300
15 105	0730–0815, 1300–1345
15 070	0400–2300
12 095	0300–0430, 0500–0915
11 940	0600–1700
11 860	0730–0915, 1500–1530
11 850	1900–2300
11 760	0300–0815, 0900–1300

Frequency [kHz]	Time
9 670	0200–0330
9 630	1615–1745, 1830–2030
9 600	0300–0815
9 410	0500–0730, 2000–2300
7 160	1700–1830, 1900–2030
6 190	0300–2030
6 005	0300–0545, 1700–1745, 1830–2300
3 255	0300–0600, 1700–2200
Near East	
17 640	0900–1615
15 590	0400–0945
15 575	0945–1515
15 310	0300–0815, 0900–1615
15 070	1300–2030
11 955	0230–0430
9 670	0230–0330
9 600	1800–2030
9 580	0030–0230
7 160	1700–1800, 1900–2030
7 135	0030–0330
5 975	1600–1830
5 965	0030–0200
Asia and the Pacific	
21 715	0100–1030
17 830	0600–1000, 2300–0030
17 790	0600–0815, 0900–0945
15 380	0145–0230, 0300–0330
15 360	0000–0330, 0600–0915
15 340	2000–2300
15 310	0300–0815, 0900–1830
15 280	0900–0915
15 140	1900–2000
11 955	2200–0430, 0600–0915
11 945	2300–0030
11 820	1300–1500
11 750	0900–1615, 1800–2300
9 740	0900–1830
9 640	0600–0815
9 580	0000–0230
9 570	2200–2400
7 180	1300–1615
7 150	0600–0815
7 145	2300–0030

Frequency [kHz]	Time
6 195	0900–1615, 2100–0030
5 975	1600–1830
5 965	0000–0200
3 975	1515–1745, 2200–2300
The Americas	
15 260	1500–1745, 2000–0330
15 220	1100–1400
15 190	0900–1100
15 070	2100–0030
13 660	2130–2200
12 095	2200–0330
11 775	1500–1745
11 750	2200–0330
9 915	2200–0430
9 640	0500–0630
9 590	2100–0230
7 325	0000–0330
6 195	1100–1400
6 175	2300–0330
6 005	0000–0330
5 975	2000–0630
5 965	1100–1200

Radio Australia

Radio Australia broadcasts principally to Asia and the Pacific, but is audible throughout the rest of the world at various times of the day. The English service has been listed in frequency order, with times of the operation of each channel shown alongside, and it is suggested that listeners try all frequencies to find the strongest signal.

Frequency [kHz]	Time
21 825	0900–1000, 1100–1230
21 775	0100–1430
21 740	0030–0330, 2200–2400
21 525	0100–0900
17 855	0030–0800, 2230–2400
17 795	2030–0800
17 750	0000–0600, 0800–1000
17 715	0830–1400, 2300–2400
17 630	0100–0400, 0500–1000, 1430–1800
15 530	0100–0630
15 465	2030–0100
15 320	0400–0800, 2030–2200
15 240	2230–0100
15 160	0130–0600, 0800–0900, 1100–1330, 2000–2400
13 745	1530–1800
13 705	0630–0930
13 605	2200–0100
12 000	1800–2100
11 930	0700–0800, 1100–2100
11 880	1700–2000, 2100–0800
11 800	1430–1830
9 770	1230–1330, 1430–1530
9 760	1000–1200
9 710	1100–1230, 1330–1430
9 580	0830–2000
7 240	1100–2100
6 080	1000–2100
6 060	1500–1930
5 995	1600–2000

Voice of America

The English service of the Voice of America operates for most of the day, but is not directed to all parts of the world at all times. We have included the service in to three principal regions and list frequencies and times of operation to those parts of the world.

Time	Frequency [kHz]
To Europe, North Africa and the Middle East	
0100–0300	21 550, 17 740, 15 160, 7 205
0400–0500	5 995
0400–0600	9 715, 7 200
0400–0700	7 170, 6 140
0500–0600	9 670, 9 700
0500–0700	15 205, 11 750, 6 060, 5 995
0600–0700	11 805, 7 325, 6 095
400–1700	15 205
1500–2100	9 700
1700–2200	15 205, 9 760, 6 040
1900–2200	11 710
2100–2200	11 960, 9 700
To Africa	
0300–0430	11 835, 6 145
0300–0700	17 715, 15 350, 9 575, 6 035
0600–0700	9 530, 6 125
1600–2000	11 920, 9 575
1600–2200	21 625, 17 800, 15 580, 15 410
2000–2100	9 570
2000–2200	21 485
To Asia	
0000–0100	17 820, 17 735, 15 290, 15 185, 11 760, 9 770, 7 120
0100–0300	21 550, 21 545, 17 740, 17 735, 15 250, 15 160, 11 705, 7 205, 7 115
1000–1200	11 720, 5 985
1000–1500	15 425
1100–1400	15 155
1100–1700	9 760
1200–1300	11 715
1300–1800	6 110
1400–1500	15 160
1400–1800	15 395, 9 645, 7 125
1900–2000	15 180, 11 870, 9 525
2100–2200	11 870
2100–2400	17 735, 15 185
2200–2400	17 820, 15 305, 15 290, 11 760, 9 770, 7 120

Radio Moscow World Service

This is not the complete schedule for Radio Moscow's English services. The frequency usage of the station is extremely complex, with up to forty frequencies on the air at any one time carrying Radio Moscow World Service. Some transmitters switch at the half-hour to foreign language broadcasts, or to carry Soviet domestic services.

At the beginning of 1991, Radio Moscow dropped all its regional English services which had until then run in parallel with a separate World Service stream. Only the West Coast of North America service between 0400 and 0800 gmt remains.

Time	**Frequency [kHz]**
0000–0300	21 790, 21 690, 17 890, 17 825, 17 700, 17 665, 17 655, 17 570, 15 425, 12 050, 12 045, 11 980, 11 755, 9 715, 9 685, 7 150, 6 060, 4 895
0300–0800	21 790, 21 690, 21 635, 17 890, 17 825, 17 700, 17 675, 17 655, 17 590, 15 420, 15 295, 15 140, 7 310
0800–1300	21 725, 21 680, 21 635, 21 450, 17 810, 17 790, 17 710, 17 665, 17 655, 17 625, 17 605, 17 570, 15 550, 15 520, 15 465, 15 345, 15 280, 13 705, 11 920, 11 705
1300–1600	17 810, 17 790, 17 780, 17 670, 17 665, 15 345, 13 705, 11 705, 9 705
1600–1900	9 830, 9 795, 7 315, 7 235, 7 170
1900–2000	15 475, 15 470, 11 775, 11 630, 9 875, 9 830, 9 765, 9 685, 7 170, 7 130, 7 105, 6 065, 6 030
2000–2100	15 470, 12 060, 12 020, 11 685, 9 895, 9 860, 9 830, 9 820, 9 795, 9 780, 9 765, 9 720, 9 685, 9 620, 7 170, 7 105, 6 175, 6 030, 5 950
2100–2400	12 050, 9 870, 9 790, 9 765, 9 685, 7 150

Section 12

PROGRAMMES FOR DXERS AND SHORT WAVE LISTENERS

Many international radio broadcasters produce regular programmes for short wave listeners and DXers. A number of the programmes also include news about computers, and devlopments in all forms of electronic communications (including space).

We have included a selection of the more popular programmes in this section, but it is by no means exhaustive. Frequencies for the programmes can be found in the Broadcasts in English section of the book.

Radio Australia: COMMUNICATOR

Transmitted on Sunday at 1430, Monday at 0730 and Friday at 0430 and 1000, this half-hour programme includes media news and listening tips concentrated, mainly on the Pacific region, but of interest to a world-wide audience.

BBC World Service: WAVEGUIDE

News about developments in BBC World Service, advice for better listening, satellite information and regular reviews of new equipment for the short wave broadcast listener. Produced by Gary Stevens and Tom Walters, and heard on Saturday at 0905, Monday at 0530, Tuesday at 1115 and Thursday at 0130.

Radio Canada International: SHORT WAVE LISTENERS' DIGEST

Hosted by Ian McFarland, this weekly programme is heard on Sundays in the European service of Radio Canada International at 2235, and at 0035, 1835 and 2335 in other services. There are regular equipment reviews by Larry Magne, and listening tips, with a North American orientation, from Glenn Hauser.

HCJB Quito Ecuador: DX PARTY LINE

Heard at 0730, 1030 and 2130 on Saturday and 0030, 0230 and 0500 on Sunday, the DX Party Line often concentrates on one subject each week, including reviews of individual stations, equipment news or listening tips.

Radio Kiev

Sunday at 2145 and Monday at 0045.

Radio Moscow

Heard on Thursday at 2000.

Radio Netherlands: MEDIA NETWORK

A weekly magazine of world-wide communications and media news, with regular reviews of new equipment, reports on major short wave events around the world, and listening tips each week concentrating on a different part of the world. Produced and presented by Jonathan Marks, the programme is heard on Thursdays at 0751, 0851, 1051, 1151, 1451, 1651, 1851, 2051 and Fridays 0051, 0351.

Radio New Zealand International: MAILBOX

DX tips from Arthur Cushen are heard on the 1st and 3rd Monday of the month in the Mailbox programme at 0430, with a repeat on the 1st and 3rd Friday at 1905.

Radio Exterior de Espana: DX PROGRAMME

Frequency news and listening tips, produced by REE's DX Editor Ambrosio Wang An-Po. Heard on Saturdays at 1938 and 2138, and on Sundays at 0037, 0137 and 0533.

Radio Sweden: SWEDEN CALLING DXers

The world's oldest short wave news programme, produced by George Wood, and heard on the 1st and 3rd Tuesday of the month in each English programme from 1230 through to 0330 on Wednesday. The programme includes listening tips from throughout the world, together with satellite, computer and media news.

Swiss Radio International: SWISS SW MERRY-GO-ROUND

Presented by Bob Thomann and Bob Zanotti (known as the "two Bobs") and heard each Saturday around 15 minutes into each transmission. The programme features answers to listeners' technical queries and problems, as well as news about international radio.

Voice of America: COMMUNICATIONS WORLD

Produced and presented by Gene Reich, the programme features news about the electronic media in North America, together with technical features and news from the international broadcasting world. Heard at 1210, 1710 and 2110 on Saturday, and at 0110 on Sunday.

WRNO: WORLD OF RADIO

With Glenn Hauser and his listening tips. Heard on Thursday 0130 and 1630, Friday 0000 and 0130, Saturday 0400, Sunday 0030 and 2130. The programme will be heard one hour earlier during the summer months in North America.

Radio Vilnius

Mondays at 2250 and 2320.

Section 13

UK FM RADIO STATIONS

Frequency [MHz]	Station	Site
National Networks		
89.1–90.2	BBC Radio Two	Multiple Locations
90.3–9.26	BBC Radio Three	Multiple Locations
91.1	BBC Radio Two	Les Platons, CI
92.5–94.6	BBC Radio Four	Multiple Locations
92.5–94.6	BBC Radio Cymru	Multiple Locations
92.5–94.7	BBC Radio Scotland	Multiple Locations
92.6	BBC Radio Three	Pendle Forest
94.8	BBC Radio Three	Les Platons, CI
94.9	BBC Radio Four	Forfar; Londonderry
95.3	BBC Radio Four	Meldrum; Kirkconnel
95.8	BBC Radio Four	Black Hill
95.9	BBC Radio Four	Haverfordwest
96.8	BBC Radio Cymru	Wenvoe
97.1	BBC Radio Four	Les Platons, CI
97.7–99.7	BBC Radio One	Multiple Locations
103.6	BBC Radio Four	Anglesey; Rosemarkie
103.8	BBC Radio Four	Rosneath
103.9	BBC Radio Four	Ashkirk
104.0	BBC Radio Four	Blaenplwyf
104.3	BBC Radio Four	Darvel
104.9	BBC R Scotland	Port Ellen
Regional and Local Stations		
88.6	BBC R Sheffield	Sheffield City Centre
88.8	BBC R Jersey	Les Platons, CI
89.0	Manx Radio	Snaefell, IoM
92.4	BBC R Leeds	Holme Moss
92.5	BBC R Highland; Nan Gaidheal	Ballachulish; Mallaig
92.6	BBC R Highland	Knock More
92.7	BBC R Aberdeen; Orkney; Shetland	Bressay
92.8	BBC R Tweed	Peebles
92.9	BBC R Highland; Nan Gaidheal	Skriaig, Skye
93.0	BBC R Ulster	Rostrevor Forest
93.1	BBC R Aberdeen	Meldrum
	BBC R Solway	Cambret Hill
	BBC R Ulster/Foyle	Londonderry
93.2	BBC R Guernsey	Les Touillets
93.3	BBC R Highland; Nan Gaidheal	Oban

Frequency [MHz]	Station	Site
93.5	BBC R Highland; Nan Gaidheal	Melvaig
	BBC R Tweed	Ashkirk
	BBC R Ulster	Larne
	BBC R Highland	Kingussie
93.7	BBC R Highland; Nan Gaidheal	Fort William
93.8	BBC R Ulster	Brougher Mountain; Kirkeel
	BBC R Aberdeen	Durris
93.9	BBC R Nan Gaidheal	Glengorm
	BBC R Ulster	Newry South
	BBC R Tweed	Innerleithen
	BBC R Highland; Nan Gaidheal	Penifiler
94.0	BBC R Highland	Rosemarkie
94.1	BBC R Solway	Stranraer
	BBC R Highland; Nan Gaidheal	Kinlochleven
94.2	BBC R Nan Gaidheal	Eitshal
	BBC R Derby	Derby City Centre
94.5	BBC R Ulster	Divis
	BBC R Aberdeen	Tullich
94.6	BBC R Highland	Grantown-on-Spey
	*BBC R Berkshire	Henley-on-Thames
94.7	BBC R Solway	Sandale
	BBC Hereford & Worcester	Ridge Hill
	BBC R Sheffield	Chesterfield
94.8	BBC CWR	Meriden
	BBC R Devon	Huntshaw Cross
94.9	BBC R Lincolnshire	Belmont
	BBC GLR	Crystal Palace
	BBC R Bristol	Ilchester Crescent
95.0	BBC R Cleveland	Billsdale West Moor
	BBC R Gwent	Ebbw Vale
	BBC R Shropshire	Ludlow
	BBC R Gloucestershire	Stroud
	BBC R Sussex	Newhaven
95.1	BBC R Wales/Gwent	Blaenavon
	BBC R Leicester	Anstey Lane
	BBC GMR	Holme Moss
	BBC R Norfolk	Tacolneston
	BBC R Ulster	Ballycastle
	BBC R Sussex	Horsham
95.2	BBC R Cornwall	Caradon Hill
	BBC R Furness/Cumbria	Kendal
	BBC R Oxford	Oxford
	BBC R Wales/Gwent	Abervagenny
95.3	BBC R Derby	Stanton Moor
	BBC R Essex	South Benfleet
	BBC R Leeds	Wharfedale
	BBC R Sussex	Brighton

Frequency [MHz]	Station	Site
95.4	BBC R Newcastle	Pontop Pike
	BBC R Ulster	Limavady
	*BBC R Berkshire	Windsor
95.5	BBC R Bedfordshire	Sandy Heath
	BBC R Bristol	Mendip
	BBC R Nottingham	Mansfield
	BBC R Lancashire	Blackburn
	BBC R York	Scarborough
95.6	BBC R Cumbria	Sandale
	BBC R WM	Birmingham
95.7	BBC R Cambridgeshire	Peterborough
95.8	BBC R Cleveland	Whitby
	BBC R Devon	Exeter
	BBC R Merseyside	Allerton Park
	Capital FM	London
95.9	BBC R Wales/Gwent	Christchurch
	BBC R Humberside	Hull
	Invicta FM	Thanet
96.0	BBC R Cambridgeshire	Madingley
	BBC R Cornwall	Scilly Isles
	BBC R Devon	Okehampton
	BBC R Newcastle	Chatton
	BBC R Shropshire	The Wrekin
96.1	BBC R Furness/Cumbria	Morecambe Bay
	BBC R Solent	Rowridge
	Hallam R	Rotherham
	Invicta FM	Ashford
96.2	Trent FM	Nottingham
96.3	R Aire	Morley, Leeds
	Essex R	Southend-on-Sea
	GWR	Bristol
96.4	BRMB Sutton	Coldfield
	County Sound/Premier	Guildford
	Devonair	Torbay
	Downtown R	Limavady
	Saxon R	Bury St Edmunds
	Swansea Sound	Swansea
	R Tay	Perth
	Signal Radio	Sutton Common, Cheshire
96.5	Orchard FM	Staple Hill, Somerset
	GWR	Marlborough
96.6	Chiltern R/Northants 96	Northampton
	Plymouth Sound	Tavistock
	R Tees	Teesside
	Downtown R	Brougher Mountain

Frequency [MHz]	Station	Site
96.7	BBC R Kent	Wrotham
	BBC R Norfolk	Norwich
	R City FM	Liverpool
	West Sound	Ayr
	Ocean Sound	Winchester
	Belfast Community R	Belfast
	CentreSound	Stirling
96.8	R Borders	Selkirk
96.9	Chiltern R	Bedford
	North Sound	Aberdeen
	Viking R	Humberside
	Choice FM	Croydon
	Southern Sound	West Brighton
	Signal R	Stafford
97.0	Mercia Sound	Coventry
	Devonair	Exeter
	Invicta R	Dover
	Plymouth Sound	Plymouth
	210 FM	Reading
97.1	Metro FM	Newcastle-on-Tyne
	R Orwell	Ipswich
	Orchard FM	Chedington, Somerset
	County Sound [Delta R]	Haslemere
	Marcher Sound [MFM]	Moel-y-Parc
97.2	*Beacon R	Wolverhampton
	*GWR	Swindon
	Manx R	Carnane, IoM
	South West Sound	Dumfries
	Galaxy	Pur Down, Bristol
97.3	R Forth	Edinburgh
	LBC NewsTalk	London
97.4	Downtown R [Cool FM]	Belfast
	Moray Firth R	Inverness
	R Hallam	Sheffield
	Red Dragon R	Newport
	Red Rose R	Winter Hill, Lancashire
	Fox FM	Banbury
97.5	Ocean Sound	East Portsmouth
	Pennine R	Bradford
	R Mercury	Horsham
	West Sound	Girvan
	Southern Sound	Hastings
	R Borders	Berwick-on-Tweed
97.6	Chiltern R	Luton
	R Wyvern	Hereford
	R Forth	Black Hill

Frequency [MHz]	Station	Site
100.0	Kiss FM	London
102	Sunset R	Manchester
102.2	Jazz FM	London
	GWR West	Wiltshire
102.3	2CR	Bournemouth
102.4	Saxon/R Broadland	Norwich/Great Yarmouth
	Downtown R	Londonderry
	Severn Sound	Gloucester
	Southern Sound	East Heathfield
	Buzz FM	Birmingham
102.5	R Clyde	Glasgow
	Pennine FM	Huddersfield
102.6	Essex R	Chelmsford
	Signal R	Stoke-on-Trent
	Fox FM	Oxford
	Orchard FM	Mendip
	R Harmony	Coventry
102.7	Hereward R	Peterborough
	R Mercury	Reigate
102.8	Invicta FM	Canterbury
	R Tay	Dundee
	R Trent	Derby
	R Wyvern	Worcester
102.9	210 FM	Hannington
	Hallam FM	Barnsley
	Mercia Sound	Leamington Spa
103.0	GWR	Bath
	Piccadilly Key 103	Manchester
	Devonair R [South West 103]	Stockland Hill, E Devon
	CN-FM 103	Madingley
	Severn Sound	Stroud
	Metro FM	Newcastle-on-Tyne
103.1	Beacon R	Shrewsbury
	Invicta FM	Maidstone
	R Borders	Peebles
103.2	Leicester Sound [Sound FM]	Leicester
	Ocean Sound	Southampton
	Bradford City R	Bradford
	Red Dragon R	Cardiff
103.3	Horizon R	Milton Keynes
	London Greek R/WNK	London N
103.4	BBC R Devon	North Hessary Tor
	Marcher Sound	Wrexham
	Hallam FM	Doncaster
	R Borders	Eyemouth
	Wear FM	Sunderland

Frequency [MHz]	Station	Site
103.5	BBC R Essex	Great Braxted
	BBC Wiltshire Sound	Salisbury
	Southern Sound	West Brighton
	East End R	Glasgow
103.6	BBC R Northampton	Geddington
	BBC R Wiltshire	Blunsdon
103.7	Manx R	Jurby
	BBC R York	Acklam Wold
	BBC CWR	Lark Stoke
103.8	BBC R Bedfordshire	Luton
	BBC R Nottingham	Colwick Park
	*BBC R Dorset	Dorchester
	RTM R	London SE
103.9	BBC R Cornwall	Redruth
	BBC R Lancashire	Winter Hill
	BBC R Suffolk	Manningtree
	BBC R Leeds	Beecroft Hill
104.0	BBC R Sussex	Reigate
	BBC Hereford & Worcester	Great Malvern
104.1	BBC R Berkshire	Hannington
	BBC R Sheffield Holme	Moss
104.2	BBC R Furness/Cumbria	Windermere
	BBC R Kent	Dover
	BBC R Northampton	Northampton
104.3	BBC R York	Woolmoor
	BBC Wiltshire Sound	Naish Hill
104.4	BBC R Newcastle	Fenham
	BBC R Norfolk	Massingham
	BBC R Berkshire	Reading
104.5	BBC R Derby Sutton	Coldfield
	BBC R Lancashire	Lancaster
	BBC R Sussex	Heathfield
	BBC R Bedfordshire	Bow Brickhill
104.6	BBC R Bristol	Bath
	BBC R Hereford & Worcester	Kidderminster
	BBC R Suffolk	Great Barton
	BBC R Surrey	Guildford
104.7	BBC R Gloucestershire	Churchdown Hill
	BBC R Leeds	Keighley
104.8	BBC R Sussex	Burton Down
104.9	BBC R Leicestershire	Copt Oak
	Melody R	Croydon
	KFM	Stockport

*N.B. * indicates a projected station.*

Section 14

TIME DIFFERENCES FROM GMT

North America

Newfoundland	−3½
Atlantic zone	−4
Eastern zone	−5
Central zone	−6
Mountain zone	−7
Pacific zone	−8

Central and South America

Mexico	−6
Argentina	−3
Bahamas	−5
Barbados	−4
Belize	−6
Bermuda	−4
Bolivia	−4
Brazil [east]	−3
Brazil [west]	−4
Chile	−4
Colombia	−5
Costa Rica	−6
Cuba	−5
Ecuador	−5
Falkland Islands	−4
Guatemala	−6
Guyana	−3
Honduras	−6
Jamaica	−5
Nicaragua	−6
Panama	−5
Paraguay	−4
Peru	−5
Trinidad	−4
Uruguay	−3
Venezuela	−4

Europe

Albania	+1
Austria	+1
Belgium	+1
Bulgaria	+2

Europe (cont'd)

Czechoslovakia	+1
Denmark	+1
Finland	+2
France	+1
Germany	+1
Gibraltar	+1
Greece	+2
Hungary	+1
Italy	+1
Luxembourg	+1
Malta	+1
Netherlands	+1
Norway	+1
Poland	+1
Portugal	gmt
Romania	+2
Spain	+1
Sweden	+1
Switzerland	+1
USSR [Moscow]	+3
Yugoslavia	+1

Africa and Middle East

Angola	+1
Botswana	+2
Cameroon	+1
Chad	+1
Congo	+1
Cyprus	+2
Djibouti	+3
Egypt	+2
Ethiopia	+3
Iran	+3½
Iraq	+3
Israel	+2
Jordan	+2
Kenya	+3
Kuwait	+3
Lebanon	+2
Lesotho	+2

Africa and Middle East (cont'd)

Libya	+1
Madagascar	+3
Malawi	+2
Mauritius	+4
Mozambique	+2
Nigeria	+1
Saudi Arabia	+4
Seychelles	+4
Somalia	+3
South Africa	+2
Sudan	+2
Syria	+2
Tanzania	+3
Tunisia	+1
Turkey	+2
Uganda	+3
Zaire	+1
Zambia	+2
Zimbabwe	+2

Near and Far East

Afghanistan	+4½
Bangladesh	+6
Brunei	+8
Burma	+6½
China	+8
Hong Kong	+8

Near and Far East (cont'd)

India	+5½
Indonesia	+7
Japan	+9
Kampuchea	+7
Korea	+9
Lao	+7
Malaysia	+8
Nepal	+5¾
Pakistan	+5
Philippines	+8
Singapore	+8
Sri Lanka	+5½
Taiwan	+8
Thailand	+7
Vietnam	+7

Pacific

Australia [Canberra, New Sth Wales, Queensland, Victoria]	+10
[South Australia, Northern Territory]	+9½
[Western Australia]	+8
[Lord Howe Island]	+10½
[Tasmania]	+10
Fiji	+12
New Zealand	+12

Daylight saving time has not been taken into account in this table.

Section 15

WAVELENGTH/FREQUENCY CONVERSION

$$\text{Wavelength in Metres} = \frac{300{,}000}{\text{Frequency in kHz}} \qquad \text{(a)}$$

$$\text{Wavelength in Metres} = \frac{300}{\text{Frequency in MHz}} \qquad \text{(b)}$$

$$\text{Frequency in kHz} = \frac{300{,}000}{\text{Wavelength in Metres}} \qquad \text{(c)}$$

$$\text{Frequency in MHz} = \frac{300}{\text{Wavelength in Metres}} \qquad \text{(d)}$$

Examples:

No.1 Convert 180kHz to Wavelength in Metres.
Using formula–(a)

$$\text{Wavelength} = \frac{300{,}000}{180} = 1667 \text{ metres}$$

No.2 Convert 91MHz to Wavelength in Metres.
Using formula–(b)

$$\text{Wavelength} = \frac{300}{91} = 3.3 \text{ metres}$$

No.3 Convert a wavelength of 1500 Metres to Frequency.
Using formula–(c)

$$\text{Frequency} = \frac{300{,}000}{1500} = 200 \text{ kHz}$$

No.4 Convert a wavelength of 4 Metres to Frequency.
Using formula–(d)

$$\text{Frequency} = \frac{300}{4} = 75 \text{ MHz}$$

PLEASE NOTE

Babani books should be available from all good Booksellers, Radio Component Dealers and Mail Order Companies.

However, should you experience difficulty in obtaining any title in your area, then please write directly to the publisher enclosing payment to cover the cost of the book plus adequate postage.

If you would like a complete catalogue of our entire range of Radio, Electronics and Computer Books then please send a Stamped Addressed Envelope to:

BERNARD BABANI (publishing) LTD
THE GRAMPIANS
SHEPHERDS BUSH ROAD
LONDON W6 7NF
ENGLAND